THE EURO-DOLLAR MARKET

THE
EURO-DOLLAR
MARKET

BY

E. WAYNE CLENDENNING

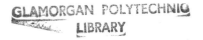

CLARENDON PRESS · OXFORD

1970

Oxford University Press, Ely House, London W.1

GLASGOW NEW YORK TORONTO MELBOURNE WELLINGTON
CAPE TOWN SALISBURY IBADAN NAIROBI LUSAKA ADDIS ABABA
BOMBAY CALCUTTA MADRAS KARACHI LAHORE DACCA
KUALA LUMPUR SINGAPORE HONG KONG TOKYO

0198281b5X

PRINTED IN REPUBLIC OF IRELAND
BY HELY THOM LIMITED DUBLIN

PREFACE

THE development of the Euro-currency markets has been one of the most important innovations in international financial activity during the past decade. These markets, in which commercial banks accept interest-bearing deposits denominated in a currency other than the currency of the country in which they operate and then re-lend these funds either in that same currency, in the currency of the country in which they operate, or in the currency of a third country, have no national boundaries and therefore have been able to operate outside many of the existing exchange control regulations and rigidities in national banking practices. This has allowed participants to take advantage of the international and national interest rate differentials caused by these impediments to the free international movement of capital. As a result, the Euro-currency markets have been able to channel internationally mobile short-term capital into the most remunerative employment in accordance with pure supply and demand considerations on a world-wide scale.

Because of the dominant position of the U.S. dollar in international finance since World War II one of these markets —the Euro-dollar market—has been dominant. It was the first to develop and is now larger than all the other Euro-currency markets combined. As a result, it has reached a higher stage of development and is more suitable for the application of economic analysis. Consequently, in this study, I limit my discussion and analysis to the Euro-dollar market. It must be emphasized, however, that since the other Euro-currency markets are basically similar and have developed for similar reasons, the analysis used and the conclusions reached could, to a large extent, just as readily be applied to them.

The existing literature on the Euro-dollar market is sparse and mainly concerned with the institutional and operational side of the market. A number of writers have defined the market, discussed how it operates, attempted to measure its size, and outlined the major participating institutions and countries; but very few have done more than hint at its theoretical implications. As a result, an aura of mystery seems to surround the market and its national and international economic impact. The present study hopes to dispel this mystery by means of a rigorous theoretical analysis.

My main concern has been to establish the theoretical underpinnings of the market and, from this, to determine its national and international significance. Standard generally accepted economic theory and methods of analysis have been used to determine and examine the mechanism through which the Euro-dollar market has an impact on national economies and on the international financial system. No attempt has been made to develop new theoretical models in the areas of theory upon which I touch. Instead I have introduced the Euro-dollar market into relatively simple models, which by consensus of opinion can be considered as generally acceptable, and attempted to determine its impact on the various aspects of the national and international economic systems. From this analysis I then draw conclusions as to the significance of the market at the present time.

The main difficulty encountered was the problem of obtaining statistical data with which to test my theoretical conclusions. This was especially so in attempting to measure the total volume of Euro-dollars and the volume of capital flows between the Euro-dollar market and other financial markets. Because of the international nature of the Euro-dollar market very little comprehensive data are available for the market as a whole. In addition, the available national data are not complete, so that it is often difficult to segregate Euro-dollar flows from other short-term capital flows and to determine the eventual destination of Euro-dollar funds. The solution to this problem, however, is beyond the scope of an individual researcher and requires the resources of a large institution, along with the co-operation of the central and commercial banks involved. Much has been done in this regard by the Bank for International Settlements, but the task is far from complete. I hope that the present study will provide a theoretical framework within which an empirical investigation could be conducted.

The research for this study was conducted during the years 1965–8 when I was a graduate student at St. John's College, Oxford. In April 1968 the initial results were submitted as a doctoral dissertation to the University of Oxford, and it was from this thesis that the present study evolved. In addition, Chapter 10 is a revised and up-dated version of an article previously published in the April 1968 issue of *The Banker*. Portions of this article are reproduced in this volume by kind permission of that journal.

During my period of research at Oxford, I benefited from the knowledge and experience of many individuals. Most importantly, I wish to express my gratitude to my supervisor, Mr. R. G. Opie, for his guidance and assistance during the preparation of my thesis. Throughout my studies at Oxford his suggestions and criticisms were invaluable. In addition, I would like to thank Mr. P. M. Oppenheimer for his interest in reading and commenting upon the final draft of my dissertation, and to acknowledge the comments and suggestions given by my examiners, Sir Roy Harrod and Mr. C. W. McMahon.

While conducting my doctoral research, I also received assistance from individuals at a number of central and commercial banks. In this regard, I particularly wish to acknowledge my debt to Mr. G. W. Lucas of the Economic Intelligence Department of the Bank of England and to Mr. Michael Dealtry and Dr. H. Mayer of the Bank for International Settlements, all of whom gave of their time and knowledge in assisting me with the preparation of this study. Without their expert advice my task would have been much more difficult. Finally, I would like to express my appreciation to three Canadian economists, Dr. D. W. Slater of Queen's University, Dr. T. L. Powrie of the University of Alberta, and Mr. G. F. MacDowell of Brandon University, for their advice and suggestions during the preparation of the present manuscript. Needless to say, all errors and omissions must remain the sole responsibility of the author.

In conclusion, I wish to express my gratitude for the financial support which made my research possible. This included a doctoral fellowship from the Canada Council and a travel grant from the Houblon-Norman Fund of the Bank of England. Lastly, I wish to acknowledge the support and assistance given by my present employers, Richardson Securities of Canada, throughout the preparation of this manuscript.

Winnipeg, Canada,   E.W.C.
July, 1969

CONTENTS

APPENDICES

1

INTRODUCTION

THROUGHOUT the past decade there has been a distinct
tendency towards the freer international movement of capital
and a greater interdependence between national capital
markets. The substantial movement of short-term funds
between the major financial markets of the world which has
been an important feature of this process has been encouraged
by the development and growth of a new channel through
which short-term capital can flow internationally. This new
aspect of the international financial system involves a series of
markets dealing in foreign currency deposits, in which national
commercial banks accept interest-bearing deposits denominated
in currencies other than their own domestic currency and re-
lend these balances either in that same currency, in their own
domestic currency, or in the currency of a third country. These
markets, because they have no national boundaries, are able to
mobilize short-term capital on a world-wide scale and satisfy
the needs of investors and borrowers around the world. As a
result, transactions in them have had a substantial impact on
the direction and magnitude of international short-term capital
movements.

This series of markets has become known as the Euro-
currency system and includes markets dealing in Euro-dollars,
Euro-sterling, Euro-francs, Euro-Swiss francs, Euro-Deutsche
marks, Euro-lire, Euro-guilders, and so on. In reality, the term
'Euro-currency' is something of a misnomer. It implies that all
transactions in these markets have something to do with
Europe—which, in practice, may or may not be true. It is true,
however, that the original development of these markets was
centred in Europe and that European banks still play the
dominant role in them. This seems to have been the reason for

adopting the term 'Euro-currency'. In addition, the prefix 'Euro' does not mean that the currencies involved in these markets are in any way different from the corresponding currencies when used domestically. It merely describes a particular type of operation in which these currencies are involved from time to time. In fact, the feature of a Euro-currency transaction that distinguishes it from other transactions involving the same currency is that it is conducted by a bank (or series of banks) operating outside the country whose currency is being used. The nationality of the original-owner or of the final-borrower is of no consequence in this distinction—with both, in some cases, being residents of the country whose currency is being used.

The Euro-currency markets have been referred to in the literature as international money markets operating in much the same way as national money markets. This comparison is not entirely valid. The Euro-currency markets can be divided into two parts: (1) a market dealing in the placement of short-term funds by the original-owners with commercial banks and the re-lending of these funds by the banks to final-users; and (2) a market involving inter-bank transactions in which commercial banks borrow and lend Euro-currency deposits among themselves. The first part involves operations very similar to the retail operations of domestic financial intermediaries in which savings are passed along to investors by means of accepting and re-lending deposits. These operations are not normally considered to be part of a national money market, which is primarily a wholesale market concerned with providing liquidity for the domestic banking system. The second part, on the other hand, does operate in a manner similar to that of a national money market—with commercial banks adjusting their positions vis-à-vis each other by lending or borrowing short-term funds in large amounts to or from each other. A Euro-currency market then is something more than a pure money market and combines these two aspects of a national credit system in one market. The distinction between the two aspects, however, becomes somewhat blurred in the Euro-currency markets by the fact that both types of operations are conducted in large wholesale amounts.

Essentially the Euro-currency system has developed because

of the forms of official exchange control still in existence between countries and the rigidities in national banking practices (resulting from either regulatory controls or cartel arrangements) that inhibit the free movement of short-term funds through normal channels in response to ordinary considerations of supply and demand. These factors, which vary in intensity from country to country, have tended to create interest rate differentials both between countries and within particular countries. Efforts to circumvent these impediments and take advantage of the interest differentials have resulted in the development of new types of international financial activity—the most important of which has been the development of the Euro-currency markets. The basic function of these markets then has been to channel internationally mobile short-term funds into the most remunerative employment according to pure supply and demand considerations.

In this study we limit the discussion and analysis to one particular Euro-currency market—the Euro-dollar market. This market, because of the dominant role played by the U.S. dollar in international finance since World War II, was the first to develop and is now by far the largest individual market. In fact it is larger than all the other markets added together. As a result, it has reached a higher stage of development and sophistication than the other markets and is, therefore, more suitable for the application of economic analysis. However, since the other Euro-currency markets are basically similar and have developed for similar reasons, the same analysis could just as readily be applied to them. So, to a large extent, could the conclusions reached from the analysis of the Euro-dollar market.

The existing literature on the Euro-dollar market has been mainly concerned with the institutional and operational side of the market. There have been a number of publications which have defined the market, discussed its operations and techniques, attempted to measure its size, and outlined the main participating groups and countries. These publications, however, have generally only hinted at the theoretical implications of the market and have often drawn conclusions regarding its international and national impact without going through a rigorous theoretical analysis. In many cases dangers and weaknesses of the market have been stressed without giving any proof of their existence or measure of their relative importance. As a result, an aura of mystery seems to have developed around the market and its impact on the international financial system. It is this mystery that the present study hopes to dispel.

The main emphasis in this study then will be to establish the theoretical underpinnings of the market. We shall use standard generally accepted economic theory and methods of analysis to determine and examine the mechanism through which the Euro-dollar market has an impact on the international financial system and on national economies. From this analysis we shall draw conclusions as to the significance and consequences of the market at the present time. No attempt will be made, however, to predict its growth and importance in the future. Even though the market is likely to undergo many changes in techniques and organization, its major theoretical impact should remain relatively unchanged. As a result, our analysis should still be generally valid even if substantial changes do occur in the methods and development of the market.

The study will be divided into three basic sections. First there will be a descriptive institutional section devoted to a re-interpretation and up-dating of the existing literature. This will occupy us throughout the next three chapters. The main body of the study, involving chapters five to nine inclusive, will be theoretical in nature and will attempt to outline the theoretical impact of the Euro-dollar market on national interest rates, the forward exchange mechanism, domestic credit creation and monetary policy, foreign exchange rates, the balance of payments, and international liquidity. The final two chapters will attempt to determine the significance of the Euro-dollar market in the world today. In particular the desirability of bringing this international market under some form of international control and the problems involved in doing so will be discussed at length. The available statistics will be interwoven throughout the three sections wherever appropriate.

2

THE NATURE OF THE MARKET

短期资金优算

THE Euro-dollar market is an international market dealing in short-term funds denominated in U.S. dollars. It is part of the international short-term credit system made up of the large national money markets—notably those of New York and London—and the markets for foreign currency deposits. The rise of this market to prominence in recent years has had a profound influence on the international movement of short-term capital. In order to appreciate its impact fully, however, we must first examine the Euro-dollar market and the way in which it operates. In this chapter we will look at the institutional and geographical framework within which the market operates and the organization and methods of the market. In addition, the important role of the commercial banks will be discussed and the types of transactions that take place in the market will be outlined.

The Institutional and Geographical Framework

The institutional framework within which the Euro-dollar market operates is basically the same as that of any national money market—with the main participating institutions being commercial banks, central banks, corporations and private individuals. A major difference, of course, results from the fact that the Euro-dollar market moves short-term funds internationally both between original-owners and final-users and between the commercial banks themselves; whereas a national money market is primarily concerned with the inter-bank movement of short-term funds within a national economy. As a result, the Euro-dollar market usually involves institutions of two or more countries while a national money market is

2

normally dominated by domestic institutions. As we have seen, a more significant distinction arising from this is that the Euro-dollar market has combined both inter-bank money market activities and financial intermediary activities in one market; while in the national case the activities of financial inter-mediaries are not part of the money market as such.

In addition, there are important differences between the roles played by the various institutions in the Euro-dollar market and in a national money market. In a national money market, although the main participants are the commercial banks, the central bank of the country involved plays an important role. It stands behind the market as a lender of last resort and, as a result, can influence the domestic money market rates whenever these rates are not in line with other economic conditions. In addition, it can also actively influence money market rates by means of open market purchases or sales of money market instruments. In the Euro-dollar market, however, although the main participants are again the commercial banks, the central banks participate to a much lesser extent and without their direct powers of control. This situation arises from the fact that there is no international central institution to which the market can turn and from the inability of any one central bank to control such an international market.

The central bank of any one country, of course, could act as a lender of last resort for the commercial banks of that country with regard to their Euro-dollar operations by selling or swapping U.S. dollars to their commercial banks. The amount of support that could be given, however, would be limited by the size of the country's foreign exchange reserves and the extent to which it could borrow reserves internationally. In addition, the U.S. Federal Reserve System, because it has the power to create U.S. dollars, could act as the ultimate lender of last resort. However, there is no single institution in the Euro-dollar market that can be called upon to perform this role automatically. Although the individual central banks of the countries involved in the market, and especially the Federal Reserve System, could exert a limited influence on the trend of Euro-dollar rates, the only way to obtain a significant degree of control over these rates seems to be through some means of co-operative action on the part of the central banks of the major participating countries. More will be said about this in Chapter 10.

The Euro-dollar market then has been developed and organized by commercial banks operating outside the United States. These banks act mainly as intermediaries—borrowing dollar deposits from central banks, corporations, and individuals and lending them to other banks, corporations, governments, and individuals. The central banks have participated only to the extent of placing dollar deposits and making dollar swaps from time to time with commercial banks operating outside the U.S. (although, of course, they also supply dollars indirectly through the foreign exchange market in maintaining their exchange rates). As a result, the Euro-dollar market is basically a free and uncontrolled market in which interest rates reflect supply and demand conditions in the market with only a limited influence being exerted by national or international policy-makers. It is this fact that is of fundamental importance in analyzing and understanding the effects of the Euro-dollar system.

Due to the international nature of the Euro-dollar market, the institutions of many countries participate in it; and, as a result, the market is not geographically located in any one particular country or financial centre. However, the market has tended to develop around a relatively small number of financial centres in Western Europe and Canada—with London emerging as the most important of these centres. This latter, in turn, has resulted mainly from the fact that London already possessed highly developed money and foreign exchange markets and could apply the wide experience and contacts gained in these markets to the development of this new market.

A number of other financial centres—notably Paris, Frankfurt/Main, Amsterdam, Zürich, Basle, Geneva, Milan, Vienna, Toronto, and Montreal—also do a substantial amount of Euro-dollar business; but the volume in any one of these centres still does not equal the volume of transactions conducted through London. In addition, London is still the only market where it is possible to deal in large amounts at any time both ways in the market. This is partly due to the fact that London has specialized to a great extent in the inter-bank sector of the Euro-dollar market and, therefore, acts mainly as an intermediary centre for borrowing and lending dollar deposits between banks. Many of the other centres are more concerned with the commercial banking aspect of the market—either specializing in accepting deposits from original-owners or in placing deposits with final-borrowers. As a result, the markets in these centres have tended to be one-sided. This contrast, however, is not so great now and a considerable volume of two-way business is also being conducted through the other centres.

Although London has developed into the leading Euro-dollar centre, no attempts have been made to organize any form of physical market in London. All Euro-dollar business within London and between London and other financial centres is conducted by means of telephone and telex facilities. The Euro-dollar market, therefore, can be pictured as a series of telephone and telex links between the major commercial banks operating outside the United States and especially between those of Western Europe and Canada. In addition, there is no international central authority for the control or regulation of the market and the central bank of any individual country, if it takes part at all, is likely to have only a limited influence on the market.

The Mechanics of the Market

In this study, because of the dominance of London in the Euro-dollar system, the discussion of the mechanics of the Euro-dollar market will be mainly restricted to the organization and methods of the London market. In general, however, this description would be applicable to the other Euro-dollar centres as well.

The transactions involved in the placing and taking of Euro-dollar deposits are essentially loan transactions—with the owner lending (placing) the deposit and the accepting institution borrowing (taking) the deposit. As Einzig states: 'Basically . . . the transaction involves not the exchange of one currency against another but a loan in terms of a foreign currency, repayable in the same currency.'[1] From the time that it enters

---

[1] Paul Einzig, *The Euro-Dollar System* (London: Macmillan and Co. Ltd., 1964), p. 11.

the Euro-dollar system until the time it is used by a final borrower, a dollar deposit may follow a chain of these loan transactions between banks in the same country and between banks of different countries. Along the way these loan transactions may be accompanied by one or more foreign exchange transactions. These foreign exchange transactions, however, are incidental to the operation of the Euro-dollar market and are not a necessary part of any particular transaction or chain of transactions.

Because of its fundamental concern with the lending and borrowing of short-term funds, the Euro-dollar system has created a market, dealing in unsecured non-transferable[1] credits, which is parallel with the local money market and partly a rival to it. The London Euro-dollar market is mainly confined to inter-bank dealings and is, therefore, really a bankers' money market—with the merchant banks, the British overseas banks, and the branches of foreign banks in London playing the dominant roles. However, a considerable volume of business in accepting deposits from original-owners and making loans to final-users is also undertaken. Business in both aspects of the market is transacted in large amounts with the usual minimum unit being $1 million. Since it is limited to dealings in these large units, the Euro-dollar market could best be described as an international wholesale market in short-term unsecured dollar credits.

The standard maturities involved in the Euro-dollar market are similar to those of the money market and forward exchange market—with the most usual being deposits at call, for seven days, for one month, for three months, and for six months. Recently, there has been a tendency in the London Euro-dollar market towards longer maturities of one year and greater. These longer maturities, however, are usually a matter of individual negotiations and are relatively rare when compared to the volume of business conducted in the shorter maturities. For the purposes of this study the three month maturity will be taken as the standard maturity for Euro-dollar deposits and

[1] Recently, a market in negotiable Euro-dollar certificates of deposit has developed in London. This, in effect, has made a portion of the Euro-dollar deposits transferable. However, since this development will not greatly affect our analysis it will not be considered further in this study.

will be used throughout the analytical sections of the study.[1]

In London, the Bank of England plays no active part in the Euro-dollar market. Its attitude, as Einzig points out, is one of 'benevolent neutrality'[2] and, as Einzig continues, 'The organization of this market has been left to private initiative and it has no direct access to the central institution. Euro-dollar rates find their level without any official intervention, except in an indirect sense.'[3] The London Euro-dollar market, therefore, is a market organized by and for the commercial banks, in which supply and demand conditions are not greatly influenced by official intervention.

Although the Euro-dollar market is essentially an international market for borrowing and lending short-term dollar funds, the London banks (and European banks in general) prefer to conduct their Euro-dollar activities through their foreign exchange departments rather than through their credit departments. This has resulted from the fact that Euro-dollar transactions were at first primarily international lending and borrowing operations between banks, which were often linked with or took the place of foreign exchange transactions. Since they were of a low risk nature and foreign exchange dealers already had the necessary facilities and contacts for carrying them out, these operations were readily added to the duties of the foreign exchange departments at very little additional cost. It was only with the expansion of direct industrial lending that more expert credit knowledge was required. However, because of the established role of the foreign exchange departments in Euro-dollar operations, the international nature of many of the transactions, and the pre-occupation of the credit departments with domestic financing, even this need was generally met by adding specialized staff to the foreign exchange departments rather than by transferring the Euro-dollar operations to the credit departments.

In the case of the continental European countries the

[1] This choice was made partly because the three-month maturity is one of the most common maturities used in Euro-dollar operations and partly because of the ready availability and comparability of the data for this maturity—not only in the Euro-dollar market but also in domestic money markets and the forward exchange market.

[2] Einzig, op. cit., p. 17.

[3] Ibid., p. 17.

integration of Euro-dollar activities into the foreign exchange departments of commercial banks also emphasizes the close connection between money management and foreign exchange management in these countries. This interdependence, arising from the lack of broad domestic money markets, forces the authorities of these countries to use foreign exchange operations (of which Euro-dollar transactions are an important part) as part of their monetary controls.

Foreign exchange brokers also play a significant part in the Euro-dollar market by acting as intermediaries between banks and between banks and non-banks. They are particularly useful in helping banks to find outlets for U.S. dollars deposits in the market and are often employed by the banks as a convenience in arranging their transactions. In the continental centres—especially Paris—nearly all Euro-dollar activities are conducted through foreign exchange brokers.

Once a bank has accepted a Euro-dollar deposit it may do one of three things: (1) it may lend this deposit directly to its own customers who want to borrow Euro-dollars, (2) it may use it to meet its own liquidity requirements (notably for year-end 'window-dressing' purposes), or (3) as more often happens, it may seek an outlet for this deposit through the market. If it must enter the market, the bank contacts another bank in a foreign centre or locally either through the intermediary of a foreign exchange broker or directly through its own foreign exchange department. The deal is usually made verbally via telephone and confirmed later in writing. All dealings in Euro-dollars are treated as spot transactions and the lender must deliver the amount of the deposit on the second full business day after the completion of the deal (although business can also be transacted on a same day or following day basis).

Due to the fact that Euro-dollar transactions involve unsecured credits, the lending bank always requires the broker to disclose the identity of the borrower before the deal is concluded. This is also the reason why many banks prefer to deal directly with the borrower wherever possible. As a result, the banks involved in the market place great emphasis on the names of borrowers, and set fairly rigid limits on the amount they will lend to any one bank and to the banks of any one country. The enforcement of these limits for the banks as a whole, however, is a very difficult task due to the international nature of the market and the lack of communication between the participants. The risks involved in lending in the Euro-dollar market, therefore, are as yet an unknown factor and could, in many cases, be quite substantial.

Since the risks involved in the market must be assumed by the lender in each link of the chain of transactions, the commercial banks have tended to specialize according to the degree of risk they wish to assume—with some dealing only with prime names and others dealing with higher risk proposi-tions. They also specialize as to maturities—with some banks borrowing and immediately re-lending deposits of the same maturity and others borrowing short and lending long. This tendency towards specialization has reduced the risks of operating in the market considerably and has enabled each bank to enter into the type of transactions for which its knowledge and experience best suit it.

The Role of Commercial Banks

The commercial banks outside the United States have been instrumental in the formation and development of the Euro-dollar market. At one end of a Euro-dollar operation is a bank that borrows dollar deposits from the original-owners and at the other end is a bank which lends these dollar deposits to the final-borrowers. In addition, during the process of moving funds from someone who wants to lend to someone who wants to borrow, there can be any number of commercial banks acting as intermediaries by transferring dollar deposits from one bank to another at small interest margins. The Euro-dollar market then is essentially a short-term financial market organized by and for the commercial banks who operate outside the United States (including the foreign branches of the U.S. banks).

By operating in the Euro-dollar market commercial banks have three motives in mind—profit, liquidity, and expansion. In order to achieve these ends they can enter the market in a number of ways: (1) by acting as intermediaries, (2) by seeking funds for the expansion of their own commercial operations,

(3) by lending and borrowing funds in order to adjust their liquidity positions, and (4) by entering into arbitrage and speculative operations. Generally, the large commercial banks involved in the market, because they are influenced to some extent by all three motives, do not restrict themselves to any one of these types of operations and usually undertake a diversified range of business.

In acting as intermediaries the commercial banks deal only with other banks and, therefore, operate with a minimum of risk. As a result, they must be content to operate on relatively narrow margins. In many cases the banks prefer to deal only with prime names and attempt to diversify their risks as far as possible by limiting the amount of deposits placed with any one bank, in any one market, and at any one maturity. In addition, they often take into account the probable way in which the dollar funds will be used by the recipient bank. The main function of the banks acting as intermediaries, therefore, is to reduce materially the risks of operating in the Euro-dollar market by spreading the risks among many banks according to the degree of risk that each bank is willing and able to assume.

By seeking funds in the Euro-dollar market for their own commercial operations the banks are attempting to expand or maintain their volume of domestic and international lending activities. After obtaining Euro-dollar deposits for this purpose a bank may use them for three basic purposes: (1) to finance international trade for either residents or non-residents, (2) to finance domestic activity in other countries, or (3) to finance domestic activity in its own country. The motive behind its participation in foreign trade financing and domestic financing in other countries is primarily the desire to expand its international borrowing and lending activities. In many cases the Euro-dollar market has been the quickest and cheapest means by which a bank can enter into or expand its international activities without restricting its domestic operations. On the other hand, its motive in using Euro-dollars to finance domestic activity in its own country is to expand or maintain its level of domestic lending in a situation where it cannot obtain enough domestic resources to meet the needs of its domestic customers. This latter possibility becomes especially attractive if the domestic monetary authorities are attempting to impose some degree of monetary restraint; and, in some circumstances, may offer a convenient method of avoiding the control of the central bank.

Commercial banks may also use Euro-dollars in adjusting their own liquidity positions—especially in countries that do not have highly developed domestic money markets. In these countries one of the main functions of the Euro-dollar market has been to provide the banks with additional and more suitable instruments in which to place their liquidity. By providing a very flexible and convenient high-yield outlet for these liquid funds, the Euro-dollar market has essentially taken over the role of a domestic money market—with banks placing funds in the market during periods of excess liquidity and withdrawing funds when they have a shortage of liquidity. In this sense then Euro-dollars are a very useful money market instrument for the banks of many countries.

In addition, commercial banks (even those in countries with highly developed money markets) may also borrow funds in the Euro-dollar market for short periods of time—especially at year-ends when they need additional liquidity for 'window-dressing' purposes. These operations are attractive (even though the cost may be relatively high) in that they allow the banks to alter their liquidity positions for a very short period without disrupting their other investments and loans. It is doubtful, however, whether banks would use borrowed Euro-dollars as a source of liquidity over any extended period of time because of the relatively high cost of borrowing in the Euro-dollar market.

Finally, the commercial banks employ relatively large amounts of Euro-dollars in arbitrage operations—involving interest, space and time arbitrage. The most important of these operations involve interest arbitrage between Euro-dollar deposits and domestic short term claims and between Euro-dollar deposits and other Euro-currency deposits. The incentive, for these transactions depends on the constellation of forward exchange rates and interest rates, with the commercial banks moving funds in response to any significant differentials that develop. From time to time there have been considerable amounts of Euro-dollars invested in domestic money market securities—notably in local authority loans in the U.K. In addition, there is an almost constant movement of funds between Euro-dollars and the other Euro-currencies—with the commercial banks willing to take advantage of any covered differentials that develop between these various markets. Undoubtedly, a number of banks have also employed Euro-dollar deposits in taking speculative positions in various currencies. It is apparent then that the Euro-dollar market has created new possibilities for arbitrage and speculation. These possibilities will be discussed more fully in Chapter 6.

Although many banks in the Euro-dollar market are willing to take part in nearly all of these types of operations more or less simultaneously, there has been a tendency for various banks to specialize in certain types of operations—with some preferring to act mainly as intermediaries, others willing to swap Euro-dollars into domestic currency for investment locally, others preferring to finance foreign trade, others desiring only to act as arbitragers, and still others willing to use Euro-dollars for speculative purposes. Many banks have also specialized as to the maturities that they are willing to handle, with some handling only short-term Euro-dollar deposits and others willing to borrow short and lend long. As a result, the participants in the Euro-dollar market have become highly specialized and it is difficult to find any one bank that is willing to deal in all maturities and types of operations.

The commercial banks outside the United States have played the dominant role in the formation and development of the Euro-dollar market. They recognized the desire of foreign dollar holders for a higher return on their deposits than they could earn in the United States and the economic need for more and cheaper dollar financing in many parts of the world. They capitalized on this situation by being able and willing to operate on smaller interest margins than those acceptable to the U.S. banks. In order to do this their borrowing and lending rates had to fall within the range bounded on the bottom by the rate paid on dollar deposits in the U.S. and on the top by the effective U.S. lending rate for loans of equivalent risk. Because this range was relatively wide during the late 1950s and early 1960s the commercial banks outside the U.S. were able to meet this requirement and still make a worthwhile profit on their Euro-dollar operations. Consequently, since there were virtually no restrictions imposed upon the market by the monetary authorities of the countries involved, the commercial banks were able to develop and organize the Euro-dollar market in the manner that best suited their own needs and the needs of their customers.

The Types of Transactions

In much of the literature there has been some uncertainty as to which U.S. dollar transactions conducted by banks outside the U.S. are Euro-dollar operations and which are not. Obviously some U.S. dollar operations cannot be considered as Euro-dollar transactions. Let us begin then by defining a Euro-dollar transaction as any transaction in U.S. dollars undertaken by a commercial bank operating outside the U.S. (including the foreign branches of U.S. banks) at Euro-dollar rates. Although this definition is somewhat circular, it does use the most distinctive feature of the Euro-dollar market—namely the creation of an international interest rate structure that is distinct from national interest rates[1]—to differentiate between Euro-dollar and ordinary U.S. dollar operations conducted by banks outside the U.S. In fact, this seems to be the only satisfactory basis for making the distinction between these types of transactions. This definition immediately eliminates from the Euro-dollar system such items as drawings on lines of credit from U.S. banks and holdings of dollar deposits (such as compensating or working balances) with U.S. correspondent banks because they would have been conducted at interest rates prevailing in the U.S.[2] We will now examine, in accordance with our definition, the types of transactions that can be considered as Euro-dollar operations.

In a typical Euro-dollar transaction there are three basic groups involved—the original-owners of the dollar deposits, one or more banks acting as intermediaries, and the final-borrowers of Euro-dollars. The original-owners may be individuals, corporations, commercial banks, central banks, or

---

[1] This relationship between Euro-dollar and national interest rates will be explored more fully in Chapter 5 below.

[2] An exception to this would occur if a bank outside the U.S. borrowed on its line of credit from a U.S. bank (at U.S. interest rates) and used these funds in its Euro-dollar operations. These transactions, however, because of their high cost, are likely to be relatively small in size and of short duration; and, hence, of limited significance.

governments and may be residents or non-residents of the United States. The final-borrowers are usually commercial banks, corporations, individuals, or governments but are very seldom central banks. Similarly, the final-borrowers may also be either residents or non-residents of the United States. In the market the original-owners determine the supply structure and the final-borrowers the demand structure.

On the supply side the original-owners may create Euro-dollars in one of two ways: (1) they may transfer their demand or time dollar deposits from a commercial bank resident in the United States to a commercial bank outside the United States or (2) they may convert funds denominated in other currencies into U.S. dollars and place these dollars on deposit with commercial banks outside the United States. Similarly, Euro-dollars may be destroyed by the reverse of these transactions. In the literature there is some dispute as to whether or not dollar deposits transferred by a U.S. resident to a non-U.S. bank should be considered as Euro-dollars if they are immediately re-invested in the U.S. banking system or money market. It is argued that this type of transaction is merely an additional step in the process of investing U.S.-owned dollar deposits in the U.S. banking system or money market and is not a true Euro-dollar operation. On the basis of our definition, however, these transactions would be Euro-dollar operations if they were conducted at Euro-dollar rates.

The ownership transfer of foreign or U.S.-owned dollar deposits from a U.S. bank to a foreign bank is the usual type of transaction on the supply side. This type of transaction does not involve a foreign exchange transaction and, therefore, the owners respond only to the differentials that develop between U.S. and Euro-dollar deposit rates (ignoring, of course, any non-economic incentives for transferring dollar deposits from the U.S.). On the other hand, the conversion of foreign currency deposits into U.S. dollar deposits does involve a foreign exchange transaction which may or may not be covered in the forward exchange market depending upon the intentions of the owner. If a transaction takes place with forward cover, it is a covered arbitrage operation between the foreign currency deposits involved and Euro-dollar deposits; and the incentive to undertake this type of transaction, therefore, involves the behaviour of both forward exchange rates and interest rates. If the transaction is undertaken on an uncovered basis, it involves an exchange risk and possibly a speculative motive on the part of the original-owner.

On the demand side of the market Euro-dollars may be used by the final-borrowers in four basic ways:

(1) they may be used in the form of U.S. dollars to finance foreign trade.
(2) they may be converted into other currencies to finance either foreign trade or domestic activity; or by way of speculation against the U.S. dollar.
(3) they may be used to finance economic activity in the United States.
(4) they may be used for liquidity (window-dressing) purposes by commercial banks in either the U.S. or other countries.

In the financing of foreign trade Euro-dollars may be used in the form of U.S. dollars to pay for imports from either the United States or another country. If the Euro-dollars are used to pay for imports from the United States, the dollar deposit returns to U.S. ownership; while if they are used to pay for imports from another country the ownership merely changes from one foreign holder to another. On the other hand, if the Euro-dollars are borrowed and then converted into any one of a number of other currencies for the purposes of financing foreign trade, domestic activity, or speculation against the dollar, it is impossible to trace their eventual destination because they lose their identity and become part of the huge pool of U.S. dollars that exists in the foreign exchange market. They could end up either being owned by private individuals and corporations (which could be either residents or non-residents of the U.S.) or in the foreign exchange reserves of a central bank.

The transactions involving the conversion of Euro-dollars into some other currency can be conducted on either a covered or an uncovered basis—with a covered transaction being an arbitrage operation and an uncovered transaction being essentially speculative in nature. If the conversion is made by a commercial bank, which then makes loans denominated in the foreign currency, it is almost always done on a covered basis. In many cases, however, the conversion is made by a final non-bank borrower who often leaves the foreign exchange transaction uncovered. Therefore, Euro-dollars will often be converted into foreign currencies even though there is no incentive for such a transaction on a covered basis.

Euro-dollars may be used to finance economic activity in the United States by means of non-U.S. banks and the foreign branches of U.S. banks making dollar advances to banks in the United States. In actual fact, however, these advances do not increase the volume of deposits in the U.S. banking system as a whole. Since all dollar deposits are automatically part of the United States banking system, the transfer of a dollar deposit from a resident or a non-resident of the United States to a bank outside the U.S. only changes the ownership of the deposit and does not create an additional deposit. As a result, the transfer of a deposit back to a bank resident in the U.S. merely returns it to U.S. ownership and serves to reallocate deposits among the individual U.S. banks; thereby increasing the capacity of some U.S. banks (while decreasing that of others) to finance economic activity in the United States. These transactions, however, could result in an increase in U.S. economic activity if the banks receiving the additional liquidity had outlets for it and if the banks losing the deposits were in positions of excess liquidity (or a decrease if the positions of the U.S. banks were reversed).

Finally, Euro-dollars may be used as a money market instrument by commercial banks in adjusting their liquidity positions —especially at specific times of the year when they need additional funds for 'window-dressing' purposes. Although Euro-dollars have been used in this manner by both U.S. and non-U.S. banks, the additional source of liquidity which they provide has been particularly important to banks operating in countries with poorly developed domestic money markets. In many of these countries the Euro-dollar market is the most readily accessible source of short-term funds. Euro-dollars used in this way are usually borrowed by the banks for very short periods of time with the transactions being quickly reversed after the 'window-dressing' date. As a result of these transactions then dollar deposits often circulate endlessly among the commercial banks—thereby creating a true international money market.

In all of these cases the chain of Euro-dollar transactions through which the deposit has passed in moving from the original-owner to the final-borrower comes to an end when the final-borrower uses the Euro-dollars. The ownership of the original dollar deposit which has passed from the original-owner through any number of intermediary banks to the final-borrower now passes on to someone other than a commercial bank operating outside the U.S. Once this occurs the deposit loses its Euro-dollar identity and becomes merely another foreign or U.S.-owned dollar deposit held at a U.S. bank. It would return to the Euro-dollar market only if the new owner deposited it with a bank outside the U.S.—thereby starting another chain of transactions.

However, it must be pointed out that, even though the original deposit is no longer part of the Euro-dollar market after it has been used by the final borrower, the chain of short-term U.S. dollar assets and liabilities created by the market in passing the deposit from the original-owner to the final-borrower still remains. It is only when the final-borrower repays his Euro-dollar loan that this chain begins to disappear. As a result, the data measuring the volume of Euro-dollar assets and liabilities will include the claim of the original-owner and the liability of the final-user (but not all the intermediary transactions resulting from the redepositing of funds from bank to bank—which would be merely double-counting) until the final-borrower repays his Euro-dollar loan and the initial bank meets its deposit liability to the original-owner.

It is apparent then that the transactions involving Euro-dollars can take many forms and that the sources and uses of Euro-dollars can be many and varied. The exact sources and uses of Euro-dollars and the effects of these various transactions on the international and national economic systems will be analyzed in more detail throughout the remainder of this study. Meanwhile, in the next chapter we will turn to a detailed examination of the origins and development of the market in order to set the stage for our later discussion.

3

THE ORIGINS AND DEVELOPMENT
OF THE MARKET

ALTHOUGH U.S. dollar deposits have been placed in banks outside the United States for many years, it was not until 1957 that the Euro-dollar market, as we now know it, began to develop. Until then U.S. dollar deposits held in foreign banks had been re-invested mainly in U.S. money market securities; and, therefore, the market in these deposits was little more than an appendage to the U.S. money market. In 1957, however, a major change occurred and a broad active market for U.S. dollar deposits began to develop in Europe in which the U.S. dollars were not re-invested in the United States but were instead re-lent to other European banks, corporations and individuals. It was this development that signalled the start of the Euro-dollar market.

This chapter will attempt to account for the major factors leading to the development of the Euro-dollar market and to trace this development up to the present time. In addition, the size of the Euro-dollar market and the difficulties involved in measuring the size of the market will be discussed in some detail.

The Origins of the Market

The practice of commercial banks accepting deposits denominated in a currency other than that of the country in which they operate goes far back through the history of international finance. As Einzig[1] points out it may have gone back as far as the medieval fairs in Europe and it certainly existed in the years before and after World War I. After World War II the practice revived, with Canadian and Swiss banks particularly

[1] Einzig, op. cit., p. 3.

active in accepting U.S. dollar deposits which they placed in the U.S. money market through their New York agencies. In the mid-1950s the practice of accepting U.S. dollar deposits became more widespread among European banks—with the U.K. banks playing a major role. However, instead of returning the funds to the U.S. money market, these banks began to lend them to other European banks and to their own customers in Europe for the purpose of financing either foreign trade or domestic economic activity.

The innovation involved in the development of the Euro-dollar market was not, therefore, the acceptance of U.S. dollar deposits by foreign banks but instead their placement outside the U.S. money market and banking system. This change in the functions performed by the U.S. dollar deposits is what distinguishes the Euro-dollar market from the previous foreign market for U.S. dollar deposits. The main factors leading to the development of the market were the readily available supplies of U.S. dollars in Europe looking for profitable outlets and the existence of international and national interest rate differentials caused partly by rigidities in the U.S. banking system. These rigidities kept U.S. deposit rates considerably lower than interest rates in Europe and maintained a wide spread between deposit and lending rates in the U.S. As a result, European banks were able to attract U.S. dollar deposits by offering higher deposit rates and to find profitable outlets for these funds by undercutting the U.S. lending rates.

Although it is difficult to determine precisely which factors created the initial pressure for the development of the market, it does seem clear that during the early stages of its development supply factors provided the main stimulant for expansion. Large supplies of foreign-owned dollar deposits had accumulated as a result of the increasing U.S. balance of payments deficit and there was an incentive to hold these funds in the form of U.S. dollars because of the dominant position of the U.S. dollar in international finance. More importantly, many of these holders were not satisfied with the low yields obtainable on these funds in the U.S. during this period and began to seek more profitable outlets for their U.S. dollar deposits by offering them to European banks. In addition, Eastern European countries preferred, for political reasons, to hold their U.S. funds in

European banks rather than in New York. As the volume of U.S. dollar deposits available to them became substantial, the European banks began to look for profitable outlets for these funds; and, because of the low yields available in the U.S., they were forced more and more to find these outlets in Europe among their own customers and other European banks.

Although there had previously been some borrowing by U.K. local authorities, the first major incentive from the demand side came with the sterling crisis of 1957 when the use of sterling to finance foreign trade was restricted. British banks attempted to overcome this restriction by using U.S. dollars in their foreign trade financing activities. This development, therefore, led to the first substantial demand for U.S. dollar deposits in Europe and caused a general awakening of European banking institutions to the advantages of mobilizing their U.S. dollar resources and also to the possibilities of acting as intermediaries by accepting U.S. dollar deposits and placing them with other banks. It was at this point that demand forces led to the active solicitation of U.S. dollar deposits by European commercial banks.

The success of the European banks in attracting U.S. dollar deposits resulted mainly from the limitations placed on the U.S. banking system by the regulatory controls imposed upon U.S. deposit rates by the Federal Reserve System under Regulation Q. In 1957–8, U.S. commercial banks, under the terms of Regulation Q, were prohibited from paying interest on demand deposits and were limited to paying 1 per cent on time deposits of less than ninety days.[1] These limitations, when combined with the willingness of European banks to operate on narrower interest margins, allowed the European banks to outbid the U.S. banks in the market for U.S. dollar deposits and to under-cut them in making U.S. dollar loans.

During 1958 additional impetus was given to the market when there was a return to external convertibility and a further relaxation of exchange controls throughout Western Europe. This increased the supply of privately held U.S. dollar deposits available in Europe by allowing Europeans to hold U.S. dollars rather than requiring them to sell their holdings immediately

---

[1] For complete details of Regulation Q and the amendments that have been made in its terms since 1957 see Appendix A.

to the foreign exchange authorities, and by allowing them to swap other currencies for U.S. dollars. It also increased the demand for U.S. dollar loans since the dollar proceeds could now be used domestically by swapping them into local currency. The return to more normal conditions in the foreign exchange market also led to the development of the other Euro-currency markets—namely the markets for Euro-sterling, Euro-francs, Euro-deutsche marks, Euro-lire, etc. These markets soon became instrumental in arbitrage operations and thereby increased the turn-over of Euro-dollar deposits.

Finally, the increase in the U.S. balance of payments deficit and the emergence of tight money policies throughout many parts of the world during the 1958–60 period gave further stimulus to the Euro-dollar market. The large U.S. balance of payments deficits (resulting partly from the tight money policies in Europe) increased the supply of U.S. dollar deposits held in Europe while the general tightening of credit led to increased demands for U.S. dollar financing. As a result, these two factors increased both the supply of and demand for Euro-dollars and thereby provided the impetus for further development of the market.

The major factors favouring the initial development and expansion of the Euro-dollar market, therefore, were the rigidities in the U.S. banking system that allowed international and national interest rate differentials to persist and the fact that European banks were able and willing to operate on relatively narrow interest margins. This situation, when combined with the great expansion of international trade and dollar financing needs, enabled the market to provide benefits to all three of the major groups involved—the owners of the U.S. dollar deposits, the European banks operating as intermediaries, and the final-borrowers. It was these benefits then that provided the main impetus for the development of the Euro-dollar market; and they are, in fact, the reason for its existence.

U.S. Rigidities and the Market

It has been argued that the main origin of the Euro-dollar market was the fact that commercial banks in the United States could not, under the terms of Regulation Q, pay rates of interest on time deposits that were competitive with those paid on dollar deposits in Europe. Two conclusions, as Altman points out, have been drawn from this proposition:

... first, that the Euro-dollar market is temporary, and exists only by reason of the limitations and interest rates imposed by Regulation Q; and second, that the United States should abolish Regulation Q, or at least raise ceiling rates substantially on all foreign time deposits, in order to limit or 'kill' the Euro-dollar market.[1]

If these conclusions are valid, any move by the United States to abolish or alter the ceiling rates imposed under Regulation Q could seriously threaten the development, and even the existence, of the Euro-dollar market. As a result, the effects of changes in the maximum rates allowed under Regulation Q on the Euro-dollar market must be analyzed in detail.

Undoubtedly, the limitations imposed upon the American banking system by Regulation Q caused the interest rate structure on dollar deposits in the U.S. to be rigid and unresponsive to changes in both U.S. and foreign monetary conditions. Consequently, because of the generally higher level of interest rates in Europe, deposit rate differentials between the U.S. and Europe were for several years substantial. These limitations by themselves, however, were not sufficient to account for the complete development of the Euro-dollar market. In order to find outlets for the U.S. dollar deposits placed with them, European banks had to be willing to undercut U.S. lending rates. This, of course, involved a willingness on the part of European banks to operate on much narrower margins than the U.S. banks were prepared to accept. It is apparent, therefore, that the unwillingness of U.S. commercial banks to accept lower operating margins was just as important as the limitations imposed by Regulation Q in the formation of the Euro-dollar market.

If the United States had abolished Regulation Q or substantially raised the ceiling rates early in the life of the Euro-dollar market, its growth and development would probably have been restricted. This would have reduced the incentive for foreign owners of U.S. dollar deposits to place

[1] Oscar L. Altman, 'Recent Developments in Foreign Markets for Dollars and Other Currencies', *International Monetary Fund Staff Papers*, X (1963), 78.

their deposits with European banks and thereby reduced the supply of dollar deposits available for use in the Euro-dollar market. Since the main stimulus for expansion during the early stages appeared to come from the supply side, this reduction in the supply of U.S. dollar deposits could have restricted the development of the market.

At the present stage of development, however, it is doubtful whether the abolition or substantial alteration of Regulation Q would be able to limit or 'kill' the Euro-dollar market. First of all, it is doubtful that U.S. commercial banks would substantially raise their deposit rates unless they were in a position to raise lending rates considerably—which would be impossible over any extended period of time because of the influence exerted on these rates by monetary policy. As a result, even if Regulation Q were abolished, any set-back suffered by the Euro-dollar market during a period of monetary restraint in the U.S. would likely be of a temporary nature—with the market again resuming its expansion after monetary conditions in the U.S. had eased.

It must be admitted, however, that during periods of monetary restraint in the U.S. (notably during 1966 and 1968) when U.S. lending rates were high and the U.S. banks were willing to operate on narrower interest margins, Regulation Q has been instrumental in preserving and expanding the Euro-dollar market. In this situation the U.S. banks are willing to compete among themselves by paying higher deposit rates than those allowed under Regulation Q—especially on large amounts obtained through the issuance of negotiable certificates of deposit—in order to maintain or expand their volume of domestic lending activities. Because of Regulation Q, however, they can only do this by competing for deposits in the Euro-dollar market. This competition then has had the impact of raising Euro-dollar deposit rates and thereby maintaining the incentive for placing deposits in the Euro-dollar market rather than in New York. On the other hand, without Regulation Q the U.S. banks would have competed with each other within the U.S. by raising deposit rates above those allowed under Regulation Q and funds would have moved into the U.S. directly without going through the intermediary of the Euro-dollar market.

Secondly, the major incentive for the continuation and growth of the Euro-dollar market now seems to be coming from the demand side. This has been particularly true since February 1965, when the U.S. instituted a voluntary programme for controlling short-term capital outflows. This programme has limited the volume of short-term lending by U.S. banks to a given percentage of the 31 December 1964 base figure—to 105 per cent in 1965, to 109 per cent in 1966 and 1967, and to 103 per cent in 1968.[1] Consequently, the ability of U.S. banks to provide dollar financing to foreigners has been severely restricted with the result that foreign borrowers have been forced to turn to the Euro-dollar market for their dollar financing needs. This has served to push Euro-dollar rates upwards—thereby off-setting any increases in U.S. deposit rates and maintaining the incentive for placing funds in the market.

It has also been suggested that rates should be raised on foreign-owned U.S. dollar deposits held in the U.S. but not on domestically-owned deposits. This could lead to a two-way interest arbitrage movement with foreign-owned deposits moving to U.S. banks and U.S. owned deposits moving to the Euro-dollar market; and could result in even more adverse effects on the U.S. banking system and balance of payments than the present situation. A move in this direction was actually taken in October 1962, when official foreign deposits were exempted from the terms of Regulation Q. Official institutions, however, are more concerned with factors such as convenience and liquidity and leave a large proportion of their U.S. dollar deposits in the U.S. regardless of the yield obtainable. As a result, this exemption has so far had only a minor effect on the Euro-dollar market.

A number of increases have been made in the maximum rates allowed under the terms of Regulation Q since the inception of the Euro-dollar market.[2] To date, these increases have not limited or hindered the growth of the Euro-dollar market to any great extent. Since the imposition of the Voluntary Restraint Programme by the U.S. the most important factor

---

[1] For details of the U.S. Voluntary Foreign Credit Restraint Programme see Appendix E.

[2] For the details of these increases see Appendix A.

for would-be borrowers is not the cost of Euro-dollars but instead their availability. On the other hand, if Regulation Q had been abolished altogether it is probable that during 1966 and 1968 when there was a period of severe monetary restraint in the U.S. the market would have suffered a set-back. Even so, it probably would have resumed its growth upon the return to easier monetary conditions in the U.S.

The Historical Development of the Market

As stated earlier the Euro-dollar market became firmly established in late 1957 and early 1958. Since that time the market has expanded rapidly with more and more owners of U.S. dollar deposits and borrowers of U.S. dollars turning to this market as a profitable outlet for their funds and as a relatively cheap source of dollar financing.

Unfortunately there is no overall statistical series available that can be used to trace the development of the whole Euro-dollar market during the period from 1957 to the present. However, since London has become the geographical focal point of the Euro-dollar system, it appears that a number of series prepared by the Bank of England could provide some evidence. These series, however, cannot be used as a measure of the size of the market at any point of time because their coverage is restricted to the London banks.

The first set of statistical series to be analyzed involves the overseas deposits and advances of the overseas banks and accepting houses in London. These statistics have been published by the Bank of England yearly from 1951 to 1959, half-yearly for 1959 and 1960, and quarterly thereafter. Even though the coverage, in some instances, is not complete and there are a number of discontinuities in the data, these series appear to be the best available to show the development of the Euro-dollar market since its inception in 1957. The two series from the beginning of 1957 to the end of 1968 are plotted in Chart 1.[1]

The danger in using these series to measure the growth of the Euro-dollar market is that the data cover non-resident deposits and advances denominated in both sterling and foreign

[1] For the detailed data of these statistical series see Appendix B.

currencies and do not reflect the growth of U.S. dollar deposits alone. As a result, part of the sharp increase that has occurred in non-resident deposits since 1957 is undoubtedly attributable to deposits made and denominated in sterling and other foreign currencies. However, because of the dominance of the U.S. dollar in international finance during this period, the Bank of

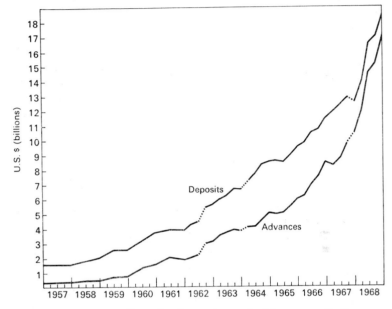

CHART 1 Overseas Deposit Accounts and Advances of Overseas Banks and Accepting Houses in London 1956–68

England has observed that 'most of the steep rise shown since 1958 has occurred in foreign currency deposits, predominantly in U.S. dollars or Euro-dollars.'[1] The two series involving overseas advances and deposits, therefore, should be able to provide at least a rough indication of the growth and development of the Euro-dollar market.

Both series must be used because neither the growth of deposits nor that of advances alone accurately reflects the growth of Euro-dollar activities. This arises from the fact that foreign currency deposits and advances are not necessarily equal

[1] Bank of England, 'The Overseas and Foreign Banks in London', *Quarterly Bulletin*, I (1961), 19.

due to conversions to and from sterling and to the inclusion of items in the data that are not connected with the acceptance and placement of foreign currency deposits.

Using the growth of overseas deposits and advances as a guide, it is apparent from Chart 1 that the Euro-dollar market has grown steadily since the beginning of 1958. Throughout 1958 and 1959, as owners of U.S. deposits and potential borrowers became more aware of the facilities offered by the Euro-dollar market, the market underwent substantial, although not spectacular, growth. During 1960 growth accelerated. This is particularly apparent from the series involving overseas deposits which rose sharply throughout 1960. On the other hand, there was a levelling off in 1961 with very little growth occurring in non-resident deposits after the first quarter of the year.

In 1962 a discontinuity appears in the data and two essentially new series start in September of that year. Even so, it can be seen that the Euro-dollar market expanded substantially from the beginning of 1962 until the third quarter of 1963, when it began to flatten out again. Although another discontinuity clouds the picture, the market grew steadily throughout 1964 and into the first quarter of 1965 and then more rapidly again from mid-1965 until the end of 1967. This was followed by a period of very rapid growth throughout 1968.

The other helpful statistical series which have been published quarterly by the Bank of England since December of 1962, involve the external liabilities and claims of U.K. banks in U.S. dollars. The U.K. banks covered by these series include the domestic banks, the accepting houses, and the London offices of British overseas and foreign banks. In addition to the liabilities to, and claims on, non-residents the series also include the U.K. banks' foreign currency balances with their correspondents abroad and the balances held by the banks on behalf of their U.K. customers. However, as the Bank of England concludes: '. . . the large growth in their external claims and liabilities in foreign currencies during recent years has come about as a result of their onlending abroad of currency funds which have been deposited with them by overseas residents.'[1]

---

[1] Bank of England, 'U.K. Banks' External Liabilities and Claims in Foreign Currencies,' *Quarterly Bulletin*, IV (1964), 101.

These series, because they deal exclusively with the external claims and liabilities of the U.K. banks in U.S. dollars, should be relatively accurate measures of the London Euro-dollar market and should aid in tracing the development of the Euro-dollar market as a whole. The problem with using these series, however, is that they cover a much shorter period of time than the series plotted in Chart 1. As a result, their main usefulness is in checking the accuracy of the conclusions drawn from the longer series in Chart 1 during the period from December 1962 to the end of 1968. These series are plotted in Chart 2.[1]

From Chart 2 it can be seen that the Euro-dollar market in London expanded rapidly from December 1962 until the fourth quarter of 1963. It grew at a lower rate until March of 1964 but again resumed its rapid growth until the first quarter of 1965. During the last half of 1965 and the last three quarters of 1966 both series indicate that the market grew at a rapid rate. This growth continued throughout most of 1967 and then accelerated sharply during 1968.

The conclusions drawn from Chart 2 regarding the growth of the Euro-dollar market correspond closely to those drawn from Chart 1 for the period during which the two sets of statistical series overlap. It seems safe to assume, therefore, that the statistical series in Chart 1 reflect fairly accurately the growth and development of the Euro-dollar market in London since 1957. Because of the dominance of London in the Euro-dollar system, they also probably provide a reasonably accurate picture of the overall development of the Euro-dollar system.

Recently, the Bank for International Settlements (B.I.S.) has published broader data covering non-resident short-term dollar liabilities and assets of the commercial banks operating in ten countries—Belgium, Canada, France, Germany, Italy, Japan, the Netherlands, Sweden, Switzerland, and the United Kingdom. They have collected these data in two series—with one series including and the other excluding the dollar positions of the banks vis-à-vis the United States. This was necessary because some dollar transactions vis-à-vis the U.S. are Euro-dollar operations while others are obviously not. As a result, the actual growth of the Euro-dollar market falls somewhere between these two series. In addition, these series involve a

[1] For the detailed data of these statistical series see Appendix C.

considerable amount of double-counting as deposits are transferred between the banks of the individual countries within the
ten country area. Despite these difficulties, however, these
series should provide us with a reasonably accurate measure of

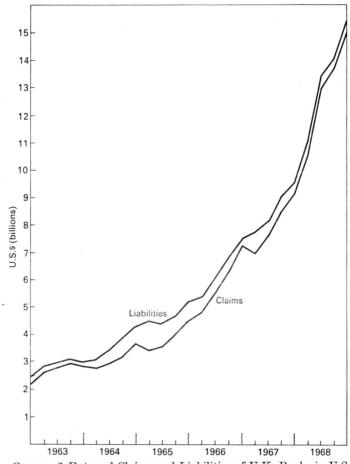

CHART 2 External Claims and Liabilities of U.K. Banks in U.S.
Dollars 1962–8

the net growth of the market during the period covered by the
data. The two sets of series are plotted in Charts 3 and 4.[1]

The value of these series is to determine whether or not our
conclusions regarding the growth and development of the

[1] For complete details of these statistical series see Appendix D.

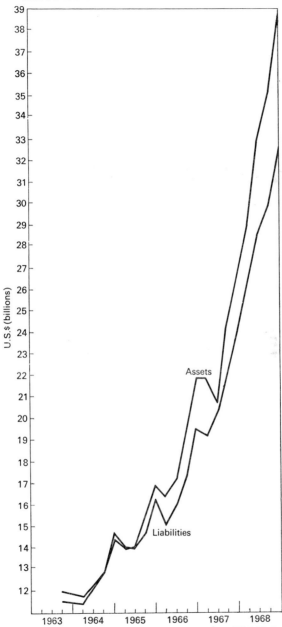

CHART 3 Non-Resident Short-term Dollar Liabilities
and Assets of Ten Countries' Commercial Banks
(including Positions vis-à-vis the U.S.) 1963–8

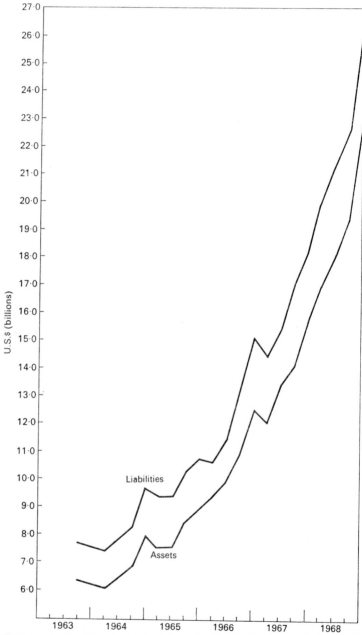

CHART 4 Non-Resident Short-term Dollar Liabilities and Assets of
Ten Countries' Commercial Banks (excluding Positions vis-à-vis the
U.S.) 1963–8

Euro-dollar market made on the basis of the previous series of London data can be applied to the market as a whole. As we can see from comparing Charts 3 and 4 with Charts 1 and 2 the growth patterns of the London and B.I.S. series are quite similar. This is true regardless of whether we look at the positions of the ten countries' banks including or excluding the positions vis-à-vis the U.S. As a result, our conclusions drawn from the London data, at least for the period from September 1963 to the end of 1968, seem to be valid for the market as a whole as well as for the London Euro-dollar market.

In summary then we can conclude that the Euro-dollar market has followed a consistent upward trend since the beginning of 1958 and has shown a surprising resistance to any substantial or prolonged set-back in its growth pattern. From the data it can be seen that there were a number of periods of rapid growth—notably during the whole of 1960, the whole of 1962, the first three quarters of 1963, the last three quarters of 1964, the last half of 1965, the last three quarters of 1966, the last three quarters of 1967, and the whole of 1968. In addition there have also been periods during which there has been almost negligible growth or even slight declines—in particular the last half of 1959, the whole of 1961, the first quarter of 1964, the first half of 1965, the first quarter of 1966, and the first quarter of 1967. However, the declines that took place during the early months of the years 1964–7, resulting mainly from the reversal of year-end 'window-dressing' operations, have been seasonal in nature, and therefore, of limited significance in the overall development of the market.

The Size of the Market

Since its inception, and particularly in recent years, there have been a number of attempts to measure the size of the Euro-dollar market. In 1960 Holmes and Klopstock estimated that the volume of dollar deposits placed in the market exceeded $1 billion.[1] Altman, on the other hand, estimated that at the end of 1960 the size of the Euro-dollar market in the U.K. was at least $1 billion and that the European dollar market as a

[1] Alan R. Holmes and Fred H. Klopstock, 'The Market for Dollar Deposits in Europe', *Federal Reserve Bank of New York Monthly Review* (November, 1960), 197.

whole could involve a minimum of $2 billion in deposits.[1] Both of these writers, however, have stressed the tenuous nature of their estimates, with Altman summing up their uncertainty by stating that '. . . the size of the Euro-dollar market can be nothing but a guess—perhaps a very wild guess'.[2] As a result of this uncertainty, therefore, there has been a great deal of variation between the estimates of the size of the Euro-dollar market and it has been impossible to obtain one precise measure of the amount of dollar deposits in the market.

The main difficulties standing in the way of obtaining a meaningful measure of the market are: (1) the problem of defining the market, and (2) the problem of obtaining comprehensive statistics. Since the market is international in character it is very difficult to define its boundaries precisely (i.e. to define which U.S. dollar deposits are Euro-dollars and which are not). In addition, because of its international nature, the market has no central authority or agency that has the power or the facilities to collect and prepare statistics covering all of the participants in the market. As a result, the only statistics that can be prepared must be obtained by adding together national figures many of which are incomplete and not fully homogeneous. This method also brings in the difficulty of double counting.

The most readily available statistics for measuring the size of the Euro-dollar market are the data (available in most countries) involving the non-resident U.S. dollar assets and liabilities of the commercial banks operating outside the U.S. It seems at first sight that if these data were added together for all of the countries participating in the market, a reasonably accurate picture of the size of the Euro-dollar market could be obtained. There are, however, a number of difficulties involved in using these figures.

In the first place, the banks may have dollar assets and liabilities that are not connected with their Euro-dollar activities. For example, in the case of liabilities the banks may draw on lines of credit with their U.S. correspondents for reasons unconnected with their Euro-dollar activities; and, in the case

---

[1] Oscar L. Altman, 'Foreign Markets for Dollars, Sterling and other Currencies', *International Monetary Fund Staff Papers*, VIII (1961), 328.

[2] Ibid., p. 328.

of assets, may place U.S. dollars in the U.S. money market for reasons independent of their Euro-dollar business. As a result, not all of the dollar liabilities of the non-U.S. banks, nor all of their dollar assets, can be regarded as Euro-dollars. It is difficult to eliminate these non-applicable balances from the data because it is impossible to tell whether or not they are connected with Euro-dollar activities.

Secondly, some of the dollar holdings of non-U.S. banks may have been acquired not through dollar deposits but through conversion of deposits denominated in other currencies into U.S. dollars. In addition, U.S. dollar funds may be invested not only in dollar loans but also in loans in other currencies obtained by swapping the U.S. dollars. Because of these types of transactions discrepancies arise between the dollar assets and the dollar liabilities of the banks. These discrepancies could be eliminated by considering all foreign currencies together, except in the case where conversion to and from domestic currencies is involved. As a result, it is apparent that Euro-dollars cannot be defined exclusively either as dollar liabilities of banks outside the U.S. or as dollar assets. In attempting to measure the size of the market we must use both sides of the balance sheet.

Thirdly, there is the problem of double counting. Euro-dollars may be redeposited many times from one bank to another between countries. As a result, a U.S. dollar deposit may be counted over and over again depending on how many times it is redeposited from the banks of one country to those of another. There is, therefore, a large but unknown amount of overlapping and duplication when the statistics of U.S. dollar assets and liabilities for a number of financial centres are added together.

Finally, the data for some financial centres are either not reported or are seriously inadequate; thereby making it difficult to obtain a meaningful total covering all the participants in the market. In addition these figures deal only with non-resident dollar assets and liabilities and, therefore, ignore Euro-dollar transactions with residents of the country in which the banks operate. Regardless of all these difficulties, however, it seems that the data available on U.S. dollar assets and liabilities of banks outside the U.S. must still be the starting

4

point for any attempts at measuring the size of the Euro-dollar market—simply because they are the only relevant statistics available.

The most comprehensive attempts at measuring the size of the Euro-dollar market have been those made by the Bank for International Settlements (B.I.S.). The B.I.S. made their first estimates as at the end of September 1963, and the end of March 1965. As the basis of these estimates the B.I.S. has employed two sets of data involving the U.S. dollar assets and liabilities of the commercial banks of nine countries—Belgium, France, Germany, Italy, Japan, the Netherlands, Sweden, Switzerland, and the United Kingdom.

The two series employed involve the short-term U.S. dollar assets and liabilities of the banks vis-à-vis non-residents—with one series including and the other excluding the positions vis-à-vis the United States. The figures excluding the banks' positions vis-à-vis the U.S. underestimate the size of the Euro-dollar market because some transactions vis-à-vis the U.S. should obviously be included in Euro-dollar operations; and the figures including the positions vis-à-vis the U.S. overestimate the size of the market because a sizable volume of the transactions vis-à-vis the U.S. cannot be considered as part of the Euro-dollar market. The actual size of the market, therefore, must fall somewhere between these two series. In addition, the figures are gross in the sense that they include interbank deposits between countries. On the other hand, they exclude for the lack of statistics the positions vis-à-vis residents. These two series are summarized in Table 1.

After making allowance for the element of double counting, as well as for placements in the U.S. money market, and inserting an estimate of the banks' Euro-dollar positions vis-à-vis residents, the B.I.S. concluded that the net volume of Euro-dollars was approximately $5 billion as at the end of September 1963, and had increased to somewhat more than $7 billion by the end of March 1965. Unfortunately the B.I.S. did not give any details of the adjustments that had to be made to the gross figures in Table 1 in order to arrive at their final estimates. As a result, it appears that, although they were the most comprehensive and accurate available, the B.I.S. estimates at these dates were not entirely satisfactory.

TABLE 1

Total Short-Term Dollar Positions of Nine Countries' Commercial Banks vis-à-vis Non-Residents, 1963–5

End of Period	Including Positions Vis-à-vis the U.S.		Excluding Positions Vis-à-vis the U.S.	
	Liabilities	Assets	Liabilities	Assets
	Millions of U.S. Dollars			
1963—September	9,210	9,330	6,840	5,580
1964—March	9,240	9,590	6,530	5,440
—September	10,350	10,290	7,370	5,990
—December	12,030	11,640	8,740	6,780
1965—March	11,620	11,360	8,270	6,490

Source: Bank for International Settlements, *Thirty-Fifth Annual Report* (Basle: Bank for International Settlements, 1965).

In their more recent attempts at estimating the size of the market, the B.I.S. has adopted a somewhat different, although basically similar, technique. They start with the data showing the dollar positions vis-à-vis non-residents (including positions vis-à-vis the U.S.) of the commercial banks operating in eight European countries—Belgium, France, Germany, Italy, the Netherlands, Sweden, Switzerland, and the United Kingdom. From these data they exclude the positions vis-à-vis the U.S. which are not involved in Euro-dollar activities. This, they point out, has been done on the basis of rough estimates. As a starting point, the B.I.S. estimated that, as at the end of 1964, only about half of the dollar liabilities and about two-thirds of the dollar assets vis-à-vis the U.S. should be included in the Euro-dollar market. Since 1964, they have assumed that the bulk of the expansion in dollar positions vis-à-vis the U.S. has been related to Euro-dollar activities and, therefore, should be included in their calculations.

Next, the B.I.S. has attempted to exclude the positions of the reporting banks vis-à-vis other banks within the eight country area. This eliminates the double-counting involved in deposits being placed over and over again with banks inside the area. Dollar positions vis-à-vis banks outside the eight country area, however, are included in their estimates. Finally, estimates of the reporting banks' assets and liabilities vis-à-vis residents of their own countries and the funds obtained (or used) by the banks themselves through conversions into (or out of) dollars (including the funds involved in special swap arrangements with official monetary institutions) are added to the banks' revised dollar positions vis-à-vis non-residents to give an overall estimate of market size. These estimates for the period 1963–8 are presented in Table 2.

In making these estimates the B.I.S. has also tried to determine the principal sources and uses of Euro-dollar funds. In their breakdown the sources and uses are divided into those which are inside and those which are outside the eight European countries. The outside component is further divided into four geographical regions: (1) the United States and Canada, (2) Japan, (3) Eastern Europe, and (4) other countries; while the inside component is divided into two categories: (1) dollars received from or used by persons or non-bank institutions located within the eight countries; and (2) dollars received from or used by banks located within the eight country region (including swaps with official monetary institutions). We will return to examine this breakdown of sources and uses more thoroughly in the next chapter.

As can be seen from Table 2 the B.I.S. estimated that the total net size of the Euro-dollar market was approximately $9 billion as at the end of 1964. This rose to $11·5 billion by the end of 1965, to $14·5 billion by the end of 1966, and to $17·5 billion by the end of 1967. During 1968, the market expanded by a further $7·5 billion to a total of $25 billion—an increase of $16 billion over the four year period. These estimates, although they are the best available, still do not give a precise or comprehensive measure of the market. In particular, they understate the size of the market by including only the Euro-dollar transactions that pass through at least one of the banks in the eight European countries. Transactions then that do not touch Europe (notably some transactions by Canadian and Japanese banks) are excluded from the B.I.S. estimates. On the other hand, the figures may include some duplication as a result of outside banks re-depositing funds that had previously been obtained from within the reporting area with banks in the eight European countries. A similar type of duplication also arises if non-banks borrow Euro-dollars from the reporting banks and re-deposit them with these banks.

TABLE 2

Estimated Net Size of the Euro-Dollar Market, 1963–8

	Sources					Uses			
	1964	1965	1966	1967	1968	1965	1966	1967	1968
	End of Year Figures in Billions of U.S. Dollars								
Outside Area									
U.S. and Canada	1·5	1·3	1·7	2·6	4·5	2·7	5·0	5·8	10·2
Japan	—	—	—	—	0·1	0·5	0·6	1·0	1·7
Eastern Europe	0·3	0·3	0·4	0·5	0·6	0·5	0·7	0·8	0·9
Other	2·8	3·3	4·0	4·8	6·6	1·5	1·9	3·0	4·2
Total	4·6	4·9	6·1	7·9	11·8	5·2	8·2	10·6	17·0
Inside Area									
Non-banks	1·8	2·2	2·8	3·9	5·2	3·3	3·7	4·1	4·7
Banks	2·6	4·4	5·6	5·7	8·0	3·0	2·6	2·8	3·3
Total	4·4	6·6	8·4	9·6	13·2	6·3	6·3	6·9	8·0
Total Net Size	9·0	11·5	14·5	17·5	25·0	11·5	14·5	17·5	25·0

Source: Bank for International Settlements, *Thirty-Ninth Annual Report* (Basle: Bank for International Settlements, 1969)

Finally, the information available on the positions of the reporting banks vis-à-vis non-bank residents within the area is incomplete and a number of gaps in the statistics have to be closed by means of estimates. These estimates probably tend to under-estimate the true positions in this category. These non-bank figures, however, despite their shortcomings, are of considerable importance since they are an attempt to broaden the data beyond the measurement of inter-bank transactions. These B.I.S. estimates, therefore, although they are not perfect, are the first real attempts at measuring the size of both the commercial banking and money market aspects of the Euro-dollar market.

Although these estimates are of importance in that they give us some idea of the quantities involved, the Euro-dollar market is continuously changing and developing to such an extent that the precise size of the market at any particular point of time is a relatively unimportant matter. As Altman sums up:

The significance of these or any other estimates of the foreign dollar market rests not on these numbers, which are meaningless after the market has attained a certain operating size, but on the fact that the market is large and diversified, that it consists of many elements which can and will operate on one side or the other, that large amounts can be loaned or borrowed without noticeably affecting the going rates, and that operations are competitive. These character-istics would not change even if the market were somewhat smaller or much larger than it now is.[1]

It is these characteristics and their significance that we will discuss in the following sections of this study.

[1] 'Foreign Markets . . .', p. 328–9.

4

THE SUPPLY AND DEMAND PATTERNS
IN THE MARKET

As pointed out earlier the Euro-dollar market is a free market in which supply and demand conditions are the all important factors. In order to lay the groundwork for our later analysis, therefore, we must first obtain a clear understanding of the supply and demand patterns existing in the market. In this chapter we will determine the types of institutions that constitute the major suppliers and the major users of Euro-dollars and the motivation behind the participation of each type of institution. If they are motivated by different factors, it is important to determine which institutions act as the major suppliers and which as the major users, so that we can analyze the reaction of supply and demand to any changes in the conditions underlying the market. On the basis of this analysis we will then outline the factors that affect the supply of and demand for Euro-dollars and attempt to determine the importance of each.

The Suppliers of Euro-dollars

Basically, there are three types of institutions that can act as suppliers of Euro-dollar deposits:

(1) Official institutions—including central banks, governments, and international organizations.
(2) Commercial banks.
(3) Non-banks—consisting of business corporations and individuals.

In the majority of countries all or some of these institutions are able to obtain and hold U.S. dollar deposits and are free to place these deposits in either of the two major markets for short-term U.S. funds—the U.S. money market or the Euro-dollar market.

Official institutions may supply U.S. dollar deposits to the Euro-dollar market in a number of ways—both directly and indirectly. Central banks and governments may supply Euro-dollars directly by depositing a portion of their U.S. dollar reserves with commercial banks outside the United States. Alternatively, they could place deposits with an international organization—especially the Bank for International Settlements (B.I.S.)—which in turn re-deposits the funds with a non-U.S. commercial bank. The major reason for these institutions to enter into this type of transaction is their desire to earn a higher yield on their official dollar reserves than that obtainable on similar investments in the United States. The yield obtainable in the Euro-dollar market, however, is not the only factor taken into consideration by central banks. In order to attract official dollar deposits from the United States to the Euro-dollar market, the primary investment considerations of liquidity, safety and adequacy of trading facilities also had to be provided, along with a higher yield. In some cases, political considerations also entered into governmental decisions (especially in the case of the Eastern European countries).

Official dollar deposits may also enter the Euro-dollar market indirectly by means of the central banks facilitating the holding of dollar deposits by their commercial banks through swap arrangements or direct deposits. Under the swap arrangements the central banks sell U.S. dollars to their commercial banks and agree to purchase these funds back at an agreed forward rate sometime in the future. The commercial banks, for their part, agree to use these U.S. funds to acquire foreign currency assets, to reduce foreign currency liabilities, or to finance foreign trade for domestic customers. In the case of direct deposits the central banks deposit U.S. dollars in their commercial banks without requiring the surrender of the local currency equivalent and the commercial banks are then free to invest these funds abroad or domestically.

The primary reasons for central banks entering into these types of operations are: (1) to carry out domestic monetary policy, or (2) to control short-term capital inflows as part of balance-of-payments or foreign exchange reserve policy. The swap arrangements, by requiring the surrender of local currency, absorb domestic liquidity; while the direct deposits add to the supply of liquidity in the domestic economy. The need to carry out monetary policy by means of these operations usually results from the fact that domestic money markets are not developed sufficiently to meet the needs of the monetary authorities. The investment of these U.S. funds abroad by the commercial banks also results in an induced capital outflow that can neutralize excessive short-term capital inflows.

The placement of U.S. dollar deposits at the disposal of the commercial banks, however, does not necessarily mean that an equivalent amount of deposits will enter the Euro-dollar market. The decision whether to place these funds in the U.S. money market, to use them domestically, or to place them in the Euro-dollar market rests with the commercial banks (except in cases where specific uses are stipulated by the central bank). Their main considerations in making this decision again involve the three factors of liquidity, safety and yield. In order to attract these funds, therefore, the Euro-dollar market must provide a similar degree of liquidity and safety as the U.S. money market and domestic outlets along with a higher yield.

There are two motivations involved, therefore, in the indirect placement of official dollar deposits in the Euro-dollar market. In placing the dollar deposits with the commercial banks, the central banks want to control domestic monetary conditions or short-term capital inflows. They are not concerned to any great extent with the yield obtainable on these deposits. The commercial banks, on the other hand, in deciding whether or not to place these funds in the Euro-dollar market are influenced by the yield obtainable in the market as compared to that obtainable in the U.S. money market or in domestic uses. In general they want to obtain the highest possible yield on the deposits.

Although commercial banks act primarily as intermediaries in Euro-dollar transactions, they may also contribute to the net supply of Euro-dollar deposits. Non-U.S. banks may do this by purchasing dollars in the foreign exchange market against local currency from, for example, resident exporters. They may then place these deposits with other non-U.S. banks or use them to finance foreign or domestic trade. U.S. banks may supply the market, if they are free to do so, by placing deposits with overseas banks (mainly their own foreign branches) or by granting credit to overseas correspondents. Due to their relatively high cost, it is unlikely that lines of credit constitute a major source of Euro-dollars but they could be used occasionally by non-U.S. banks to meet temporary liquidity shortages in their Euro-dollar operations.

In the investment of a portion of their own funds in the Euro-dollar market the commercial banks take into account the three basic factors of liquidity, safety and yield—with yield probably being somewhat more and liquidity and safety rather less important than for the central banks participating in the market. In most cases the investment of commercial bank funds involves an interest arbitrage transaction—either between Euro-dollars and domestic securities or between Euro-dollars and other Euro-currencies. In many countries the desire on the part of commercial banks to place their own funds in the market is increased by the absence of a sufficiently developed domestic money market and a consequent shortage of suitable money market instruments in which to invest their liquidity. In general though the major objective of the commercial banks is to obtain an improved yield over that obtainable on other available securities with the same degree of liquidity and safety.

Non-banks—both business corporations and individuals— have also been major suppliers of Euro-dollar deposits. Since the U.S. dollar is widely used in international trade it would be expected that non-U.S. firms involved in foreign trade and other international activities would hold substantial deposits in the form of U.S. dollars. In addition, the role of U.S. firms is also large and has increased significantly during the past few years. They have placed dollar deposits both directly with banks in Europe and indirectly through the intermediary of Canadian banks. Of even greater importance has been the participation of overseas affiliates of U.S. firms through the temporary placement of funds that had previously been borrowed in advance of their needs in European capital markets.

Individuals and business enterprises have chosen to hold larger dollar balances because they can often earn higher rates of interest than those available on deposits in domestic currencies and can obtain greater flexibility with respect to amounts and maturities. For foreign traders the holding of dollars also avoids the costs of conversion to and from domestic currencies. In many countries it is almost a necessity for business firms and individuals to invest their liquid resources abroad because of the lack of a developed domestic money market. The major incentive for the non-banks to place these dollar holdings in the Euro-dollar market rather than in the U.S. money market, however, has been the fact that the market has been able to provide a high degree of liquidity and safety along with higher interest rates.

In attempting to rank the three types of institutions according to their importance as suppliers of Euro-dollars it was conceded during the early years of the market that official institutions (mainly central banks) and non-banks (mainly business enterprises) had made the greatest contributions— with commercial banks playing a relatively small role as suppliers. Some controversy has developed, however, as to whether official institutions or non-banks had been the largest suppliers. Altman has pointed out that:

The proportion of the funds in foreign currency markets which are owned directly or beneficially (in the form of deposits or swap counterparts with domestic commercial banks) by central banks and monetary authorities can be estimated only very roughly. It would be conservative to assume, however, that two-thirds of all the funds in European markets in the summer of 1962 were of this character.[1]

It seems from this statement that Altman considers the official institutions to have been the largest suppliers—at least up until mid-1962.

In its 1963–4 annual report the Bank for International Settlements (B.I.S.), on the basis of fuller information, concluded that central banks were less important as suppliers after this date. In discussing central bank swap arrangements and deposits with their own commercial banks, the B.I.S. states that:

What can be said . . . is that this supply of official funds to the banks, and hence indirectly also to the Euro-market, has declined, and that official sources altogether have therefore become somewhat less

---

[1] Altman, 'Recent Developments . . .', p. 57.

prominent, relatively and absolutely, than they were two or three years ago.[1]

Later on, they conclude that,

Non-banks have now probably become the most important source of Euro-dollar funds.[2]

From these statements by Altman and the B.I.S. it appears that official institutions were the major suppliers up until 1962 or 1963 but that after this date the non-banks took over. This is also pointed out by the B.I.S.:

In summary, all the sources listed have helped to supply the Euro-dollar market, but over the past two years there has been some shift of accent from central-bank to non-bank sources.[3]

This relative decline of official institutions as a source of Euro-dollars was caused by three factors: (1) the decreased use of central bank swap arrangements and direct deposits with their own commercial banks in West Germany, Italy and Switzerland, (2) the requirement during 1964 that West German banks invest any swap dollars in U.S. treasury bills rather than in Euro-dollar deposits, and (3) the exemptio of official deposits from the terms of Regulation Q in October 1962. The first two factors reduced the indirect flow of official dollar deposits into the Euro-dollar market and the third factor, by making it more attractive for central banks to place their deposits in U.S. banks, reduced the direct flow.

For the period 1963–8 the B.I.S. has attempted to determine the sources of Euro-dollars on both a geographical and institutional basis. Geographically, they have distinguished between the Euro-dollar funds supplied by an eight country European area (as defined in the previous chapter) and those supplied by the rest of the world. Within the eight country region, the sources have been broken down institutionally between banks and non-banks; while in the outside area a further geographical breakdown has been attempted—with the United States and Canada, Japan, and Eastern Europe being singled out for

[1] Bank for International Settlements, *Thirty-Fourth Annual Report* (Basle: Bank for International Settlements, 1964), 133.
[2] Ibid., p. 133.
[3] Ibid., p. 134.

special attention. No attempt, however, has been made to provide an institutional breakdown for the outside area. Wit hin the eight country region, the 'banks' category includes t he funds converted into dollars by the commercial banks fr om domestic or third currencies—both on their own initiative and under special swap arrangements with the central banks—for lending as Euro-dollars. In addition, funds rechannelled b y the monetary authorities of the eight European countries into the Euro-dollar market are also included in this category. As a result, both commercial bank and central bank sources are included under this item. The results of this breakdown are summarized in Table 3.

From Table 3 it can be seen that the outside area has been an increasingly important supplier over the four year period; while the inside area was on a declining trend as a supplier until 1968—when the two areas supplied approximately equal quantities of Euro-dollars. In the outside area the U.S. and Canada were the major suppliers—although much of this was accounted for by the depositing of funds raised by U.S. corpora-tions in European financial markets. The 'other' outside countries—mainly the Middle Eastern, Latin American and other Western European countries—have also been significant suppliers of Euro-dollars during this period. Within the eight country European region the commercial and central banks have been the major suppliers in every year except 1967.

The figures in the 'banks' category, however, do not provide a complete picture. First, many of the funds converted into Euro-dollars by the banks have originated from non-bank sources (although it is impossible to separate them from the banks' general pool of resources). Secondly, they do not give a breakdown between commercial and central bank sources. In fact, if we use a series of estimates of central bank participation previously supplied by the B.I.S. for the period 1964-7, we can see that official monetary institutions accounted for $0·8 billion of the total supply in 1964, $2·2 billion in 1965, $2·8 billion in 1966 and $3·1 billion in 1967.[1] This indicates that central banks, through special swap arrangements and direct placements, accounted for virtually all of the $3·1 billion increase in the

[1] Bank for International Settlements, *Thirty-Eighth Annual Report* (Basle: Bank for International Settlements, 1968), 154.

TABLE 3

Geographical and Institutional Sources of Euro-Dollars, 1964–8

| | Quantity Supplied as at end of year | | | | | Change in Quantity Supplied | | | |
	1964	1965	1966	1967	1968	1964–5	1965–6	1966–7	1967–8
					Billions of U.S. Dollars				
Outside Area									
U.S. and Canada	1·5	1·3	1·7	2·6	4·5	−0·2	+0·4	+0·9	+1·9
Japan	—	—	—	—	0·1	—	—	—	+0·1
Eastern Europe	0·3	0·3	0·4	0·5	0·6	—	+0·1	+0·1	+0·1
Other	2·8	3·3	4·0	4·8	6·6	+0·5	+0·7	+0·8	+1·8
Total	4·6	4·9	6·1	7·9	11·8	+0·3	+1·2	+1·8	+3·9
Inside Area									
Non-banks	1·8	2·2	2·8	3·9	5·2	+0·4	+0·6	+1·1	+1·3
Banks	2·6	4·4	5·6	5·7	8·0	+1·8	+1·2	+0·1	+2·3
Total	4·4	6·6	8·4	9·6	13·2	+2·2	+1·8	+1·2	+3·6
Total	9·0	11·5	14·5	17·5	25·0	+2·5	+3·0	+3·0	+7·5

Source: Bank for International Settlements, *Thirty-Ninth Annual Report* (Basle: Bank for International Settlements, 1969)

'banks' category for the period 1964–7.[1] Although no estimate of central bank participation is provided for 1968, it seems reasonable to assume that official monetary institutions contributed substantially to the $2·3 billion increase in the 'banks' item during 1968.

In summary, then, of the total four year increase of $16·0 billion, the outside area has accounted for $7·2 billion (of which the U.S. and Canada provided approximately half) and the inside area $8·8 billion. Within the eight country reporting area banks (including central banks) supplied $5·4 billion and non-banks $3·4 billion over the four year period. Since it seems reasonable to assume that a substantial portion of the Euro-dollar funds supplied by the outside region emanates from non-banks, these figures indicate that non-banks have been the dominant suppliers during the past four years. This is even more true when we consider the fact that some of the funds supplied by the commercial banks actually originate with non-banks. On the other hand, central banks, although they have not been the dominant suppliers over this extended period of time, have been substantial contributors during particular periods— especially at year-end and mid-year 'window-dressing' dates. More will be said about this aspect of official participation in Chapter 10 of this study.

The Users of Euro-dollars

Euro-dollar deposits may be used by any one of the three major types of institutions—official institutions, commercial banks, or non-banks. These institutions employ Euro-dollars in a wide variety of ways and it is, therefore, often difficult to determine exactly the final destination and end-use of these funds. We can, however, determine with a reasonable degree of accuracy the extent to which each type of institution enters the demand side of the market.

Official institutions, although major participants on the supply side, are relatively small users of Euro-dollar deposits.

[1] These B.I.S. estimates, however, since they are year-end figures, overstate the contribution of the official monetary institutions. At the year-end official funds, in order to offset the impact of 'window-dressing' activities, tend to substitute for private funds until the commercial banks reverse their year-end Euro-dollar operations. More will be said about these operations in Chapter 10 below.

There has been considerable borrowing at times by governments but central bank participation on the demand side is all but non-existent. The main governmental borrowing has been by U.K. local authorities, the Belgian treasury, and the Eastern European countries.

In the case of U.K. local authorities, the market provides short-term sterling loans through swaps of dollar deposits at any time that a covered differential favouring these transactions develops. As a result, these investments have become a well recognized medium for interest arbitrage operations between Euro-dollars and the U.K. domestic money market. It should be pointed out, however, that the local authorities have a number of sources from which to choose and obtain funds from the Euro-dollar market only if favourable interest rates and forward exchange rates induce U.K. banks to invest a portion of their Euro-dollar deposits in these securities. In other words, since their financing needs are assured from one source or another, their objective is to obtain the funds they need at the cheapest rate.

The Belgian government, on the other hand, has borrowed Euro-dollars from the market (mainly through the intermediary of Belgian commercial banks) to finance their budget deficits which they are unable to finance in Belgium. Their participation in the market, therefore, is not dependent upon the occurrence of a favourable covered interest rate differential but instead upon their budgetary needs. This unusual situation is the result of the rigid limits placed upon the amount that the Belgian government can borrow from its own central bank and of the tendency of Belgian governments to run chronic budgetary deficits which are beyond the capacity of the domestic capital market. Eastern European countries through their state-owned banks also borrow substantial amounts directly from the market—mainly for the purpose of financing foreign trade.

Central banks, although theoretically able to borrow directly from the market, have made very few attempts to do so. With the expansion of credit facilities available to them through the International Monetary Fund (I.M.F.) and swap arrangements between the major central banks, there has been little need for central banks to borrow in the Euro-dollar market even during severe foreign exchange crises. In addition, the volume of funds that could be attracted in the market would probably be quite limited and would be insignificant in a crisis of this sort. Central banks could also conduct indirect operations on the demand side of the market by offering special swap arrangements to their commercial banks in order to induce them to borrow or withdraw funds from abroad. The size of these operations, however, would be limited by the volume of funds held abroad by the commercial banks and the ability of the banks to borrow abroad. In fact, in the case of Euro-dollar borrowings, the borrowing limits of a country's banks may be reached rather quickly because of the rigid limits placed upon the volume of Euro-dollars that will be lent to the banks of any one country. Partly due to these limitations then and partly due to the fact that there has been no need for them to undertake such operations, central banks have not participated to any significant extent on the demand side of the market.

In assessing the importance of the various institutions as final users of Euro-dollars, Altman states that: 'Most of the dollars and other foreign currencies obtained through the Euro-money market are . . . used by the private sector.'[1] This would indicate that the commercial banks and non-banks are the dominant institutions on the demand side. As on the supply side, these banks and non-banks may be either U.S. or non-U.S. residents.

Commercial banks, as stated earlier, act mainly as intermediaries—standing between the original suppliers and the final users. They also, however, use a significant volume of Euro-dollars for their own purposes—mainly as an additional money market instrument. If commercial banks in countries other than the U.S. are in temporary need of additional domestic liquidity, they may swap dollar deposits rather than discounting with their central bank or selling securities in the open market. In addition, individual U.S. commercial banks can use Euro-dollars as a source of liquidity in a situation where Regulation Q has imposed limitations on their ability to compete for deposits within the U.S. As a result, commercial banks often use Euro-dollars to increase their resources and ability to lend—thereby obtaining greater scope and flexibility in their operations.

[1] Altman, 'Recent Developments . . .', p. 59.

5

Non-banks (mainly business enterprises) are also major users of Euro-dollars. They use them to finance both foreign and domestic trade—although foreign trade financing is probably still the major outlet. Because of the dominance of the U.S. dollar as the international means of settlement, non-U.S. firms engaged in foreign trade must obtain dollar funds to finance their activities. If Euro-dollar rates are lower than the rates on equivalent loans in New York, these firms will use Euro-dollars to meet their dollar loan needs. In addition, U.S. firms engaged in foreign trade may also find it advantageous to finance their activities by means of Euro-dollars—especially since the imposition of the U.S. Voluntary Restraint Programme.

Firms may also use Euro-dollars to finance domestic activities if interest rates and forward exchange rates (or a shortage of domestic credit) are such as to give an incentive to borrow Euro-dollars rather than local currency. This situation applies particularly to non-U.S. firms and foreign affiliates of U.S. firms operating in countries that suffer from a shortage of domestic credit facilities. In many cases, however, it is difficult to say, once they have been absorbed in the pool of corporate assets, which activities are financed by Euro-dollars. As a result, it is hard to tell whether foreign trade or domestic trade financing dominates the non-bank participation in the market.

The B.I.S. has also attempted a geographical and institutional breakdown of Euro-dollar uses similar to that employed in the supply-side analysis of the previous section. The demand for Euro-dollars during the 1964–8 period has been broken down geographically between the uses of Euro-dollars within the eight country European area and the uses in all countries outside this area. From Table 4, in which this breakdown has been summarized, it can be seen that the most striking development on the demand side during this period has been the fact that the outside area has taken over from the inside area as the major user of Euro-dollars from 1966 on. In fact, of the total $16 billion increase in demand over this four year period, the outside area accounted for $13 billion and the inside area for only $3 billion. As a result, the total quantity of Euro-dollars used by the outside area, as at the end of 1968, was more than twice the amount used by the inside area.

Within the reporting area non-banks have been the major

TABLE 4

Geographical and Institutional Uses of Euro-Dollars, 1964–8

	Quantity used as at end of year					Change in Quantity used			
	1964	1965	1966	1967	1968	1964–5	1965–6	1966–7	1967–8
					Billions of U.S. Dollars				
Outside Area									
U.S. and Canada	2·2	2·7	5·0	5·8	10·2	+0·5	+2·3	+0·8	+4·4
Japan	0·4	0·5	0·6	1·0	1·7	+0·1	+0·1	+0·4	+0·7
Eastern Europe	0·5	0·5	0·7	0·8	0·9	—	+0·2	+0·1	+0·1
Other	0·9	1·5	1·9	3·0	4·2	+0·6	+0·4	+1·1	+1·2
Total	4·0	5·2	8·2	10·6	17·0	+1·2	+3·0	+2·4	+6·4
Inside Area									
Non-banks	2·3	3·3	3·7	4·1	4·7	+1·0	+0·4	+0·4	+0·6
Banks	2·7	3·0	2·6	2·8	3·3	+0·3	−0·4	+0·2	+0·5
Total	5·0	6·3	6·3	6·9	8·0	+1·3	—	+0·6	+1·1
Total	9·0	11·5	14·5	17·5	25·0	+2·5	+3·0	+3·0	+7·5

Source: Bank for International Settlements, *Thirty-Ninth Annual Report* (Basle: Bank for International Settlements, 1969)

users of Euro-dollars. Banks (mainly commercial banks) have
played a relatively small role on the demand side of the market
in the eight European countries and even their small participation was probably destined mainly for non-bank uses. In the
outside area the U.S.-Canada region has been the largest user—
especially during 1966 and 1968 when demand from this region
increased by $2·3 billion and $4·4 billion respectively. Japan
also used a significant volume of Euro-dollars during 1967 and
1968. In the outside area, although no institutional breakdown
is given by the B.I.S., it is likely that the majority of Euro-
dollars used by countries other than the U.S. were employed
by non-banks either directly or through the intermediary of
commercial banks.

In the case of the U.S.–Canada region, the major institutions
involved on the demand side have been the U.S. commercial

TABLE 5

Liabilities of U.S. Banks to their Foreign Branches, 1963–8

End of Month	Amount	End of Month	Amount	End of Month	Amount
			Billions of U.S. Dollars		
1964		September	1·6	May	2·8
January	1·0	October	1·7	June	3·2
February	1·1	November	1·7	July	3·7
March	1·0	December	1·3	August	4·0
April	1·1	1966		September	4·1
May	1·1	January	1·7	October	4·3
June	1·0	February	1·9	November	4·2
July	1·0	March	1·9	December	4·2
August	1·2	April	1·9	1968	
September	1·2	May	2·0	January	4·3
October	1·2	June	1·9	February	4·5
November	1·4	July	2·8	March	4·9
December	1·2	August	3·1	April	5·0
1965		September	3·5	May	5·9
January	1·4	October	3·7	June	6·2
February	1·6	November	3·8	July	6·2
March	1·4	December	4·0	August	7·0
April	1·4	1967		September	7·1
May	1·4	January	3·7	October	7·1
June	1·4	February	3·4	November	7·3
July	1·6	March	3·4	December	7·0
August	1·8	April	3·0		

Source: *Federal Reserve Bulletin* (Washington: Board of Governors of the Federal Reserve System, Monthly)

banks. During the periods of tight money in the U.S. during 1966 and 1968 the U.S. banks attracted large volumes of Euro-dollars through their foreign branches. This is best illustrated by examining the liabilities of the U.S. banks to their foreign branches, as presented in Table 5. From this table, it can be seen that these liabilities increased by $2·7 billion during 1966 and by $3 billion in 1968—thereby accounting for all the increase in the U.S.-Canada demand for 1966 and the major part of the 1968 increase. During these two years then U.S. banks took over from non-banks as the dominant users of Euro-dollars.

The 1967 experience, however, as shown in Tables 4 and 5, indicates that under more normal monetary conditions in the U.S. the U.S. banks tend to reduce their demands on the market and non-banks again become the main users of Euro-dollar funds. This fact, along with their dominance on the supply side, means that non-banks (especially business corporations) are usually the dominant institutions in the Euro-dollar market. As a result, the market has become dependent upon the willingness of business firms to hold a substantial portion of their liquid resources in the form of U.S. dollars and upon the ability of other firms to find profitable outlets for these dollar funds in the private sector of the world economy.

The Factors Affecting the Supply of Euro-dollars

The fundamental permissive factor determining the supply of Euro-dollars is the quantity of U.S. dollars made available to the rest of the world by the United States through its balance-of-payments deficit. Without this outflow of dollars from the U.S. there would not have been any substantial accumulation of foreign-owned U.S. dollar deposits—either private or official —on which the creation and development of the market depended. At the same time, of course, the Euro-dollar market has contributed to the U.S. deficit by attracting U.S.-owned dollar deposits. The continuation and size of the U.S. deficit, however, although still important for the long-term growth and development of the Euro-dollar market, are not of such crucial importance now as they were originally because there is already a large stock of foreign-owned dollar deposits in existence. In fact, since this huge stock of foreign-owned dollars can only be eliminated gradually through the re-flow of funds to the U.S., the market could still exist even if the outflow from the U.S. was completely stopped or reversed. In general though, any factor that affects the U.S. balance-of-payments deficit and, hence, the supply of U.S. dollars held abroad, could have at least an indirect impact on the supply of Euro-dollars.

However, since a comprehensive discussion of these factors is beyond the scope of this study, we will deal only with a number of more specific factors that directly determine and affect the supply of Euro-dollars, including:

(1) the differential between Euro-dollar rates and interest rates on time deposits and other money market securities in the United States.
(2) the covered differential between Euro-dollar rates and interest rates on domestic time deposits and money market securities in countries other than the United States.
(3) the covered differential between Euro-dollar rates and other Euro-currency rates.
(4) expectations regarding spot exchange rate movements.
(5) policy measures taken by various countries (including the U.S.) to control short-term capital flows and domestic monetary conditions.
(6) political and other non-economic factors favouring the holding of dollar deposits in Europe rather than in the U.S.

The differential between Euro-dollar rates and interest rates paid on time deposits and money market securities in the United States basically determines whether foreign and U.S.-owned dollar balances will be invested in U.S. securities and time deposits or placed with foreign banks in the form of Euro-dollar deposits. By determining the flow of U.S.-owned deposits to the market this factor not only has a direct impact on the supply of Euro-dollars but also an indirect effect through changing the size of the U.S. balance-of-payments deficit. Similarly, the differential between Euro-dollar rates and interest rates that can be earned on domestic time deposits and money market securities in countries other than the U.S., along with the cost of forward covering, determines whether or not domestic currency balances will be converted into dollars for investment in the Euro-dollar market. These transactions are interest arbitrage operations between domestic securities and Euro-dollars, and, if the covered differential is favourable, they can contribute to the net supply of Euro-dollars. Finally, the covered differential between interest rates paid on Euro-dollars and those paid on other Euro-currencies can also affect the supply of Euro-dollars by determining whether or not arbitrage flows will take place between Euro-dollar and other Euro-currency deposits.

The behaviour of spot exchange rates, or more precisely speculation about their behaviour, can also have an effect on the supply of Euro-dollars. If speculative pressure develops against a foreign currency there could be an uncovered movement out of that currency into U.S. dollars—which, in turn, could find their way into the Euro-dollar market. As a result, there may be net conversions of foreign currencies into Euro-dollars even though there is no covered interest differential to support such conversions. On the other hand, if there is speculation against the U.S. dollar, the supply of Euro-dollars would probably decrease as dollar holders moved into either other currencies or gold.

The policy measures adopted by a number of countries to control short-term capital flows and domestic monetary conditions have also had substantial effects on the supply of Euro-dollars. These measures, taken mainly by the central banks of West Germany, Italy, and Switzerland involve swap arrangements and direct deposits of dollars with commercial banks, special reserve requirements for foreign-owned deposits, and the prohibition of interest payments on foreign-owned deposits. The swap arrangements and direct deposits facilitate the holding of dollar deposits by the commercial banks. The special reserve requirements and the prohibition of interest payments induce the banks to seek foreign outlets for their foreign-owned deposits and discourage foreigners from depositing funds with domestic banks. As a result, these policy measures have had an indirect impact on the supply of Euro-dollars by increasing the volume of privately-held dollar deposits outside the U.S. and by discouraging the conversion of dollars into other currencies for investment in domestic securities. Whether or not these funds find their way into the Euro-dollar market, however, depends primarily on the three interest rate differentials that we have just discussed.

Finally, measures adopted by the U.S. authorities in recent years, although aimed primarily at reducing short-term capital outflows from the U.S., have also had a direct impact on the supply of Euro-dollars. These measures involve a series of voluntary guidelines for controlling the expansion of U.S. bank and non-bank short-term foreign assets. As part of this programme, the U.S. authorities have requested that U.S. banks and non-banks voluntarily not expand and preferably reduce their foreign money market investments (including dollar deposits with foreign banks) from their 31 December 1964 level.[1] These measures then have affected the supply of Euro-dollars both indirectly (by reducing the U.S. balance-of-payments deficit) and directly—by reducing the supply of dollar deposits that had been entering the Euro-dollar market directly from the U.S. On the other hand, this programme has also stimulated U.S. corporate borrowing in European capital markets and a portion of these funds have been deposited temporarily in the Euro-dollar market.

The relative importance of each of these factors has varied over the life of the market. The most important factor throughout, however, has been the Euro-dollar-U.S. interest rate differential. It was especially crucial during the initial stages of development when, due to the existence of exchange controls and the absence of external convertibility in Europe, the supply of Euro-dollars depended almost entirely upon the ownership transfer of already existing privately-held dollar deposits from foreign or U.S. owners to banks operating outside the U.S. Even after the return to convertibility, however, and especially when European central banks adopted policies to facilitate and encourage the private holding of U.S. dollar balances, this differential played a vital role in determining whether the additional U.S. funds now obtainable would be invested in the Euro-dollar market or in the U.S. It was also the instrumental factor in determining the volume of U.S.-owned dollar deposits flowing into the market—although its significance in this respect has now been reduced by the U.S. Voluntary

[1] For complete details of the U.S. Voluntary Restraint Programme see Appendix E.

Restraint Programme. If this differential had not been in favour of the Euro-dollar market it is unlikely that any substantial supply of Euro-dollars would have been created.

The covered differential between Euro-dollar rates and domestic rates in countries other than the U.S., and the Euro-dollar–other Euro-currency covered differential, became significant only after the 1958 return to external convertibility in Europe. Residents of these countries were then freer to move funds out of domestic securities or other Euro-currencies and into Euro-dollars if there was an incentive to do so. They were also important in determining the eventual destination of the funds made available by the European central banks through the dollar swaps and deposits with commercial banks and the funds diverted by the reserve and interest rate regulations. The return to convertibility also opened the door for speculative movements between other currencies and Euro-dollars. These, however, have only been of significance during specific periods —such as the 1966 and 1967 sterling crises.

The second most important factor in determining the supply of Euro-dollars has undoubtedly been the policy measures adopted by the European central banks to encourage the private holding of U.S. dollars. Without these measures these dollar funds would have been retained by the central banks and the supply of privately-held U.S. dollar deposits available for use in the Euro-dollar market would have been greatly reduced. Therefore, during the early 1960's and again in 1965, when they were being used extensively, these measures were undoubtedly the major factor operating to expand the supply of Euro-dollars. Since early 1965 these measures have also been employed by the central banks and the B.I.S. in a conscious effort to control the supply of Euro-dollars on specific occasions —notably at year-end and mid-year 'window-dressing' dates. Although these control measures do not have a long-term impact on the supply of Euro-dollars they do have a significant effect during the specific periods in which they are employed.

The greatest significance of the U.S. Voluntary Restraint Programme has been the fact that it has reduced the importance of the Euro-dollar-U.S. interest rate differential in determining the flow of U.S.-owned dollar deposits into the market. The most important factor determining whether or not U.S. owners will place funds in the Euro-dollar market is now the restrictions imposed by these voluntary agreements. On the other hand, this restraint programme places no restrictions on the transfer of foreign-owned dollar deposits to banks outside the U.S. and, therefore, has no direct impact on the supply of Euro-dollars emanating from foreign owners of dollar deposits. However, by reducing the U.S. balance-of-payments deficit it does have an indirect impact through reducing the volume of foreign-owned dollar deposits available for placement in the Euro-dollar market.

It is apparent then that the supply of Euro-dollars is dependent upon two basic factors: (1) the conditions and official policies that influence the volume of privately-owned U.S. dollar deposits available for placement in the Euro-dollar market, and (2) the existence of a sufficient interest rate differential in favour of the Euro-dollar market to induce holders to place their funds there rather than in New York or other domestic financial markets. In addition, of course, there are a large number of political and other non-economic factors that also enter into the investment decisions of dollar deposit holders—but little new or special can be said about these in the context of an economic analysis of the Euro-dollar market.

The Factors Affecting the Demand for Euro-dollars

The fundamental factor underlying the demand for Euro-dollars is the level of economic activity in the countries (including the U.S.) that participate in the market. If the level of activity is high, the demand for credit for financing both foreign trade and domestic economic activity will also be high. If this demand cannot be met domestically, and, particularly, if anti-inflationary monetary measures are being used, there will be an incentive for residents of these countries to seek additional financing abroad—of which the Euro-dollar market is one source. Any factor then that changes the level of economic activity in the participating countries will have an indirect impact on the Euro-dollar market by changing the credit requirements of these countries.

More specifically, however, there are a number of factors

which directly affect the demand for Euro-dollars by determining the extent to which the Euro-dollar market will be used to meet the financing needs of the participating countries. These include:

(1) the differential between interest rates on Euro-dollar loans and those on bank loans of equivalent risk in the United States.
(2) the availability of credit in the U.S. and the volume of funds that the U.S. commercial banks are willing to make available for foreign lending.
(3) the covered differential between interest rates on Euro-dollar loans and those on domestic bank loans of equivalent risk in countries other than the U.S.
(4) the volume of domestic credit available in countries other than the U.S.
(5) the covered differential between Euro-dollar and other Euro-currency loans.
(6) expectations regarding spot exchange rate movements.
(7) policy measures that restrict the volume of foreign lending by U.S. commercial banks and non-banks.

The differential between interest rates charged on Euro-dollar loans and those charged by U.S. commercial banks on dollar loans of equivalent risk are of major importance in determining whether a business firm will borrow in the Euro-dollar market or in the United States. In order to compete in the market for dollar loans—especially with regard to foreign trade financing—European banks must be prepared to undercut the U.S. interest rates on loans involving the same degree of risk. If they cannot do this, the borrower will obtain his dollar financing in New York. This, of course, is assuming that U.S. commercial banks are able and willing to meet all demands for foreign dollar financing—which is often not the case. Due to their pre-occupation with domestic activities and lack of knowledge of foreign borrowers at the retail level, the U.S. banks are usually unwilling to withdraw funds from domestic uses in order to meet all foreign demands for dollar loans. As a result, foreign borrowers are often forced to find other sources of dollar financing even at higher rates of interest than those available in the U.S. This has been especially true since the imposition of the U.S. Voluntary Restraint Programme, which has severely restricted the ability of the U.S. banks to make foreign dollar loans.

In addition, if there is a shortage of liquidity and interest rates begin to rise in the U.S. as a result of tight money conditions, Euro-dollar borrowings become attractive for U.S. banks. This situation arises from the fact that U.S. banks are restricted in their competition for deposits within the U.S. by the maximum deposit rates imposed under Regulation Q. As a result, they may add to the demand for Euro-dollars during periods of monetary restraint in the U.S. The Euro-dollar-U.S. interest rate differential and the availability of credit in the U.S. then are of importance in determining both the foreign and U.S. demand for Euro-dollars.

The covered differential between interest rates on Euro-dollar loans and those on domestic bank loans in countries other than the United States also influences the demand for Euro-dollars. If it is cheaper to borrow dollars in the Euro-dollar market, on a covered basis, than to borrow domestic currency from local banks, business firms will usually do so, if they can. This differential then determines the extent to which firms in these countries will borrow Euro-dollars rather than domestic currency for financing both foreign trade and domestic activity. Similarly, the covered differential between Euro-dollars and other Euro-currencies determines whether or not covered arbitrage flows will take place between Euro-dollar and other Euro-currency deposits.

If there is a shortage of credit in the domestic economy, due either to the imposition of a contractionary monetary policy or to the under-developed nature of credit facilities, borrowers may go to the Euro-dollar market (if they are allowed to) even if there is no interest rate incentive. In this situation borrowers cannot obtain domestic funds at any price and, therefore, it is not the cheaper interest rates that attract them to the Euro-dollar market but instead the ready availability of credit. This is also the case for commercial banks when they cannot obtain enough domestic liquidity to meet their year-end 'window-dressing' requirements.

The behaviour of spot exchange rates may also affect the demand for Euro-dollars. If the movements of the U.S.

exchange rate give rise to speculative pressure against the U.S. dollar, many firms may decide to borrow U.S. dollars (possibly from the Euro-dollar market) instead of buying them—in anticipation of a further depreciation. If, on the other hand, speculation against other currencies develops, business firms and banks may borrow these currencies and buy dollars, rather than borrow dollars in the Euro-dollar market.

Recently, in order to reduce the volume of capital outflows and improve the balance of payments, the U.S. authorities have taken measures aimed at limiting the volume of foreign lending by U.S. banks and non-banks. These measures have taken the form of an interest-equalization tax and a voluntary programme to limit the volume of foreign bank loans granted by U.S. banks.[1] The Interest-Equalization legislation attempts to reduce the outflow of U.S. capital by imposing a tax on U.S. purchasers of foreign securities. Although it originally applied only to long-term securities, it was extended in February 1965, to include bank loans involving maturities of greater than one year. As a result, it has cut off an important source of medium-term dollar financing.

The voluntary guidelines programme, on the other hand, is aimed primarily at reducing the short-term outflow of capital by means of requesting U.S. banks and non-banks to voluntarily limit the volume of short-term loans granted to foreigners. Under the terms of these guidelines the growth in foreign bank loans is to be limited to a certain percentage of the 31 December 1964 base figure. This programme then has severely limited the ability of U.S. banks to meet the demand for foreign dollar loans. As a result of these two policy measures, therefore, many foreign firms have been forced to seek their short-term dollar financing elsewhere than in New York—with the majority of them turning to the Euro-dollar market.

The most important factor in determining the initial demand for Euro-dollars was the interest differential between Euro-dollar loans and bank loans in the U.S. During the early stages of development the demand for Euro-dollars arose primarily from the need for additional foreign trade financing facilities. At this time exchange controls and the absence of external

---

[1] For details of the Interest-Equalization legislation see Appendix F; and of the U.S. Voluntary Restraint Programme see Appendix E.

convertibility in Europe restricted the conversion of Euro-dollars into domestic currencies for use in financing domestic activity. As a result, the market was competing primarily with U.S. sources of dollar financing and had to undercut the U.S. rates to attract borrowers. If European banks had not been able to do this it is doubtful that any substantial demand for Euro-dollars would have arisen.

With the return to convertibility in 1958, however, the covered differential between Euro-dollar loans and domestic currency loans in countries other than the U.S. became important. Since Euro-dollars could now be converted and used domestically, borrowers in these countries entered the Euro-dollar market (if they were allowed to) to meet some of their domestic financing needs whenever it was advantageous to do so. In particular, the emergence of tight money policies throughout much of Europe in the 1958–60 period made these operations especially attractive—not only because of the interest rate incentive but also because of a general shortage of credit in many European countries.

The other critical factor that has been of great significance throughout the life of the market has been the volume of credit that U.S. banks are willing and able to make available for foreign lending. Even in the early stages, the U.S. banks were not willing to meet all demands for foreign dollar financing and many borrowers were forced to borrow from the Euro-dollar market at higher rates than those available in the U.S. Since the imposition of the U.S. Voluntary Restraint Programme, however, this factor has become even more important. The guidelines laid down under this programme are now the most important factor determining the participation of U.S. banks (and non-banks) in foreign lending activities. As a result, the Euro-dollar-U.S. interest differential has lost much of its importance in determining the non-U.S. demand for Euro-dollars.

The Euro-dollar-U.S. differential, however, is still important in determining the U.S. demand for Euro-dollars. When a restrictive monetary policy causes a shortage of credit and rising interest rates in the U.S. (as it did in 1966), thereby widening the differential between Euro-dollar rates and domestic U.S. lending rates, it is advantageous for the U.S. banks (partly because of Regulation Q) to compete for dollar deposits through the Euro-dollar market. These operations were of major importance in expanding the demand for Euro-dollars during 1966 and 1968. Therefore, although the U.S. Voluntary Restraint Programme and the interest differential between the Euro-dollar market and countries other than the U.S. (along with the availability of credit in these other countries) have taken over as the main determinants of the non-U.S. demand for Euro-dollars, the availability of credit in the U.S. and the Euro-dollar-U.S. differential still have a substantial impact on the demand side of the market through their influence on the U.S. demand for Euro-dollars.

The factors determining the demand for Euro-dollars then can also be broken down, similarly to those on the supply side, into two basic categories: (1) the conditions and official policies that determine the ability of the banks in the participating countries (especially in the U.S.) to meet the demands placed upon them by foreign and domestic borrowers; and (2) the existence of a sufficient interest differential to attract borrowers to the Euro-dollar market rather than to New York or other domestic financial markets. It is also apparent from this analysis that the supply of and demand for Euro-dollars are not determined by the circumstances or policies of any particular country but are instead affected by a wide variety of international factors. The major factor on both the supply and demand sides of the market, however, seems to be the relationship between national interest rates and the international rates existing in the Euro-dollar market. This relationship will be explored more fully in the next chapter.

5

THE RELATIONSHIP BETWEEN NATIONAL AND EURO-DOLLAR INTEREST RATES

As we have seen in the preceding chapter the relationship between national interest rates and Euro-dollar rates is vital to the analysis of the Euro-dollar market and its impact on the economic system. To explore this relationship we will first set up a model showing how the interest rate structure is actually determined in a typical national economy. Next, we will develop a similar model for the determination of Euro-dollar rates which we will compare with the model for national interest rates. From this comparison we will point out the similarities and differences in the determination of national and Euro-dollar rates and assess the degree of interdependence between them. Finally, this theoretical assessment will be tested empirically by observing the behaviour of short-term U.S., U.K., and Euro-dollar interest rates over the five year period 1962–7.

The Determination of a National Interest Rate Structure

Regardless of whether we use the liquidity-preference or the loanable-funds approach to the theory of interest, there are four basic determinants of the equilibrium rate of interest in any economy—the investment-demand function, the saving function, the liquidity-preference function, and the quantity of money. In addition to the equilibrium rate of interest, of course, there is a whole structure of interest rates with a separate rate being determined for each type of security. These differentials between rates, as pointed out by Joan Robinson,[1] arise from the

[1] Joan Robinson, *The Rate of Interest and Other Essays* (London: Macmillan and Co. Ltd., 1953), pp. 5–11.

fact that various types of securities possess to varying degrees the following attributes: (1) convenience—the capacity of an asset to be realized in money; (2) capital-uncertainty—the risk of a capital loss due to a rise in interest rates if the asset has to be liquidated before maturity; (3) lenders-risk—the fear of partial or total failure of the borrower to repay; and (4) income-uncertainty—the risk of a fall in income when funds are re-invested upon maturity should interest rates fall.

The differentials arising between securities of the same term involve mainly the different degrees of lenders-risk attached to the various securities by potential holders. The term structure, on the other hand, involves the opinions of holders regarding the degree of convenience, capital-uncertainty, and income-uncertainty attached to each security. Short-term securities then, which differ from money only in their inferior degree of convenience (assuming them to be free of lenders-risk) involve a low degree of capital-uncertainty but a high degree of income-uncertainty; while long-term securities, if they are readily marketable, will have the same degree of convenience as short-term securities but a higher degree of capital-uncertainty and a lower degree of income-uncertainty. Therefore, short-term interest rates are determined essentially by the convenience yield on holding money, and the long-term rates by adding a risk factor—reflecting the net effect of the higher degree of capital-uncertainty and the lower degree of income-uncertainty —to this convenience yield. Because of the substantial changes in capital values resulting from small changes in interest rates, it is likely in the normal case that capital-uncertainty outweighs income-uncertainty in the determination of these term differentials.

Before turning to the development of our model showing how the interest rate structure is actually determined in a typical national economy we must first look at the concept of liquidity preference. In Keynesian analysis it is defined in a rather narrow sense as being the choice between money and bonds at the margin. When we are considering the structure of interest rates, however, we must, as Hicks points out, define it in a somewhat wider sense:

As soon as one begins to ask questions about the structure of these rates, it becomes apparent that the choice between money and

6

bonds is only one of the many possible choices between forms of asset-holding into which similar considerations of liquidity enter. The demand for money, it used to be said, arises out of the needs for convenience and security; liquidity preference is an elaboration of the security motive; but the security motive in the demand for money is not fundamentally different from the security motive in the demand for safe securities—even though the latter do bear interest while money (it is assumed) does not.[1]

Therefore, for each entity in the economy balance sheet equilibrium not only between money and securities but also between the various types of securities themselves must be achieved through adjustments in the interest rate structure.

In a Closed Economy

The model we will use in this section is similar to one developed by Hicks.[2] This model begins with a simple economy in which there are three types of entities whose balance sheet equilibriums must be considered—firms conducting real investment, individuals who are saving, and the banking system (including the central bank) providing credit money. As a result, savers hold their assets (or wealth) in the form of bank money and securities of the firms; firms hold real assets and bank money while owing debts to the banking system and to savers; and the banking system holds securities of the firms while owing bank money to the firms and savers.

Now, let us examine how liquidity considerations enter into the determination of a national interest rate structure. In the case of savers a switch from bank money to securities of the firms results in a decrease in liquidity. As a result, they will require a higher yield on securities than on bank money to compensate for their loss of liquidity. For firms, the expansion of real assets by borrowing from the banking system or from savers reduces their liquidity, and, therefore, they will be unwilling to pay interest rates that are as high as the returns which they expect from their real investments. The banking system has no problem of shifts among bank liabilities since it can create money—the most liquid asset available. Its assets, however, are made up of debts of the firms whose values are

---

[1] J. R. Hicks, *Capital and Growth* (Oxford: Oxford University Press, 1965), pp. 283–4.
[2] Ibid., pp. 284–7.

uncertain because of uncertainty about the ability of the firms to repay. As a result, the banking system will not always lend at the rates which firms would be willing to pay nor lend the amounts desired by the firms at going rates. In addition, allowances must also be made for bad debts and administrative expenses—which force the banking system to lend at a rate of interest higher than the rate it pays to savers.

In our simple economy then there is a maximum to all rates of interest set by the expected rate of return on real investment and a minimum set by the rate of interest paid by the banking system (which may or may not be zero). All other rates must lie, in equilibrium, between these limits—with their exact positions depending upon the balance of liquidity considerations in the balance sheets of lenders and borrowers. Now, what happens if we introduce a financial intermediary into our model? A financial intermediary can prosper only if it makes use of specialized knowledge about particular kinds of real investment and thereby makes loans that banks would not be able to make; and if it can acquire funds at less loss of liquidity to the saver than would be involved if savers lent the funds directly to the borrower. In addition, it must also cover administrative costs and make a profit—which requires it to borrow at a lower rate than it lends.

In our modified model then the 'in-rate', to use Hicks' terminology, of the intermediary (the rate at which it borrows) must be less than its 'out-rate' (the rate at which it lends) and both rates must fit into the structure of our first model—with the in-rate being higher than the 'previous' minimum (i.e. the minimum before the establishment of the intermediary) and the out-rate being lower than the 'previous' maximum. The in-rate, however, need not be higher than the rates paid by firms to the banks or savers since the intermediary will be able to attract funds from banks and individuals by offering a greater degree of liquidity than the firms do directly. Correspondingly, the out-rate need not be lower than the rate charged by banks since the intermediary will do business with firms which the banks would not do. In general though, the in-rate must be considerably higher than the old minimum and the out-rate must be higher than the in-rate. Finally, if we wanted to approach even closer to reality, we could superimpose a series of intermediaries on our model. In this case each intermediary would specialize even further and the intermediaries of a higher order would become dependent for funds on those of a lower order. This would result in a whole pyramid of intermediaries—with the in-rates of the higher orders being the out-rates of the lower orders—all of which would have to be squeezed in between the minimum and maximum of our first model.

From our model, therefore, it can be seen that there must be a gap, bounded on the top by the rate of profit on real investment and on the bottom by the rate of interest paid by the banking system, which provides scope for a whole structure of interest rates. The extent to which this gap is filled depends on the number and type of financial intermediaries in the system and hence, on the financial maturity of the economy. If the intermediaries did not exist, the lending would have to be done by the banking system or directly by the savers—which would reduce the general liquidity of the system and, thereby, involve wider margins. As a result, the introduction of financial intermediaries into our model makes it possible for the interest rate structure to fit more smoothly into the gap and, thereby, makes it easier for the system to operate.

In this model then we bring together the four basic determinants of interest rates—the investment-demand function, the saving function, the liquidity-preference function (defined in the wider sense), and the quantity of money. The investment-demand function in combination with the liquidity-preference function of the firms determines the rate of interest at which the firms are willing to borrow. In particular, the liquidity-preference function of the firms determines the difference between this rate and the maximum rate in our model (the rate of return on real investment). The saving function and the liquidity-preference function of individuals determine the minimum rate in our model—the rate which the banking system must pay to borrow from savers. In addition, the liquidity-preference function of individuals, firms and banks determines the position of each interest rate in the overall structure of rates. The quantity of money, on the other hand, determines (given the structure of intermediaries) the overall level of liquidity in the system—with increases in the supply of money causing the level of liquidity to rise and decreases causing it to fall. As a result of these changes in the level of liquidity individuals, intermediaries, and banks are either more or less willing to lend at each rate of interest. It is mainly through this factor then that the monetary authorities are able to influence the national interest rate structure.

In An Open Economy

We must now turn to deal with an important abstraction that we have made in our model. So far we have been assuming that our economy is closed and is, therefore, operating in complete isolation from the rest of the world. This, particularly in the context of our present study, is a very unreal assumption. As a result, we must remove this assumption and see what effects it has upon our model.

In considering an open-country situation we will use a two-country model made up of country A and country B (or the rest of the world). The interest rate structures in each of these countries will be built up in the manner described by our closed-economy model. The two structures (if both countries are operating in isolation) will almost certainly be different because of different investment-demand functions, saving functions, liquidity-preference functions, and quantities of money (resulting from different monetary policies) existing in the two countries. In addition, there will undoubtedly be different structures of intermediaries. If both countries are opened to inflows and outflows of capital, these different interest rate structures will cause international flows of capital between the two countries—with funds (normally) flowing from the low-interest rate country to the high-interest rate country.

These capital flows, however, involve an exchange of currencies and, therefore, have an exchange risk attached to them. In the case of short-term capital flows (to which the analysis in this study will be restricted) this exchange risk may be eliminated by entering into a forward exchange transaction equal in amount to the spot transaction but opposite in direction. This, of course, results in an additional cost and, hence, reduces the interest margin that can be earned by transferring funds on a covered basis from one country to the other. As a result, we must take the cost of forward covering into consideration as well as the pure interest rate differential in determining the volume of short-term capital that will flow between the two countries.

In our two-country model the flows of short-term capital between the two countries will affect the short-term interest rate structures of both countries. If country A has a higher interest rate structure, funds will flow from the rest of the world to country A. This will tend to push interest rates in country A down and to pull interest rates in the rest of the world up. As a result, the capital flows will tend to bring the two interest rate structures closer together. However, if these flows are conducted on a covered basis, the forward exchange rate will also adjust simultaneously with the interest rate structures towards its interest-parity value—i.e. to a discount or premium equal to the interest differential between the two countries. This means that the covered arbitrage flow will be cut-off and, hence, have no further impact on the interest rate structures when the cost of covering forward equals the interest rate differential. On the other hand, uncovered arbitrage flows would still have an impact on the interest rate structures because they could continue even though there was no covered differential between the two countries.

The extent to which the short-term interest rate structures will adjust to each other depends upon the volume of short-term capital that will flow between country A and the rest of the world in response to an interest rate differential and upon the impact of these flows on the interest rate structures in both country A and the rest of the world. This, in turn, depends on three basic factors: (1) the elasticity of supply of short-term arbitrage funds in both country A and the rest of the world; (2) the freedom with which short-term capital can move between country A and the rest of the world; and (3) the elasticity of demand for short-term arbitrage funds in both country A and the rest of the world. The first two factors essentially determine the international mobility of short-term arbitrage funds and the last factor the impact of the capital flows on the respective interest rate structures. In addition, in determining the volume of covered arbitrage flows we must also consider the elasticity of supply of forward exchange in response to covered arbitrage demands. This determines how quickly and to what extent the forward exchange rate will adjust to its interest-parity value in response to a given covered arbitrage demand.

The elasticity of supply of short-term arbitrage funds in country A (or the rest of the world) will be defined as the relationship between changes in the quantity of short-term arbitrage capital that country A (or the rest of the world) is willing to supply to the rest of the world (or country A) and changes in the interest rate differential between country A and the rest of the world. Similarly, the elasticity of demand for short-term arbitrage funds in country A (or the rest of the world) is the relationship between changes in the quantity of short-term arbitrage capital demanded by country A (or the rest of the world) from the rest of the world (or country A) and changes in the interest rate differential between country A and the rest of the world. The interest rate differential, of course, would be a net differential after taking into consideration such factors as differences in taxation rates; transactions costs; and, in the case of covered arbitrage flows, the cost of forward covering. These elasticities are basically determined by the size and development of the short-term capital markets involved, the existing credit conditions in each market, and the attitudes held by individuals and institutions regarding foreign short-term investment and borrowing.

These pure elasticity concepts, however, do not include the impact of such factors as exchange controls and administrative techniques that create artificial barriers to the free flow of short-term capital between countries. These factors do not determine the willingness of individuals and institutions to borrow or lend abroad but instead place restrictions on their ability to carry out their desired level of foreign borrowing or investment. As a result, these factors are included under our concept of freedom of movement. Under our definitions then the elasticities of supply of and demand for short-term arbitrage funds determine the willingness of country A (or the rest of the world) to supply or absorb short-term arbitrage capital; while the freedom of movement serves to determine the actual ability of country A (or the rest of the world) to supply or absorb short-term arbitrage capital.

The elasticity of supply of forward exchange in response to

covered arbitrage demands will be defined as the relationship between changes in the quantity of forward exchange supplied and changes in the forward exchange discount or premium (i.e. the differential between the spot and forward exchange rates) caused by the covered arbitrage demand for forward exchange. This elasticity is determined primarily by the extent to which hedgers and speculators are conducting operations through the forward exchange market; and, hence, depends on the volume of exports and imports and the state of expectations regarding changes in the spot exchange rate. It also can be influenced by official intervention in the forward exchange market on the part of the foreign exchange authorities.

Now, let us examine how all of these factors operate to determine the extent to which the short-term interest rate structures in country A and the rest of the world will adjust to each other if interest rates in country A rise relative to those in the rest of the world.[1] The elasticity of supply of arbitrage funds in the rest of the world will determine the potential volume of arbitrage funds available to move from the rest of the world to country A in response to the change in the interest rate differential. If this elasticity is high there would be a large potential increase in the supply of arbitrage funds from the rest of the world in response to a small rise in interest rates in country A relative to those in the rest of the world; while if it is low there would be only a small potential increase.

The actual volume of arbitrage funds that will move from the rest of the world to country A, on the other hand, depends, in the first place, on the freedom with which short-term capital can move from the rest of the world to country A. If the freedom of movement is restricted there would only be a small flow even if the elasticity of supply in the rest of the world was high. Secondly, the volume of covered arbitrage flows from the

[1] The analysis throughout this chapter employs a stock adjustment theory to explain the international movement of short-term capital. This approach, when applied to a constant stock of capital, requires that a constant interest differential between two countries be associated, after an adjustment period, with a zero net capital flow. In a situation where the stock of short-term capital is increasing, however, this adjustment process would still be valid. In this case, the large initial flow, resulting from portfolio switches, would be followed by a smaller but maintained flow allocating the portfolio additions. In our analysis the desired stock adjustment is often frustrated by the degree to which short-term capital is free to move internationally.

rest of the world to country A depends on the elasticity of supply of forward exchange in response to arbitrage demands. If this elasticity is low, the forward rate will quickly and completely adjust to its new interest-parity value and cut-off the flow of covered arbitrage funds. On the other hand, if it is high, the forward rate adjustment would be slow and possibly incomplete—thereby allowing an incentive for covered arbitrage movements to persist.[1] As a result, the elasticity of supply of forward exchange is instrumental in determining the actual volume of covered arbitrage flows from the rest of the world to country A. Uncovered arbitrage flows, however, would not be affected by the forward exchange rate adjustment and could continue even though there was no covered differential.

The impact of the arbitrage funds that do flow from the rest of the world to country A on the short-term interest rate structure in both country A and the rest of the world depends on the elasticities of demand for arbitrage funds in each of the short-term capital markets. If the elasticity of demand in country A is high, an inflow of arbitrage funds could be absorbed without a fall in interest rates; while if it is low the inflow could only be absorbed if interest rates in country A fell substantially. Similarly, if the elasticity of demand in the rest of the world is high there would be a large decrease in the demand for arbitrage funds in the rest of the world in response to the change in the interest differential. This would prevent interest rates in the rest of the world from rising in response to an outflow of arbitrage funds to country A. On the other hand, if the elasticity of demand was low in the rest of the world interest rates in the rest of the world would tend to rise as a result of the outflow of arbitrage funds to country A.

In addition, there would also be a time lag involved in this adjustment process. First there would be a lag in the adjustment of the forward exchange rate to its interest-parity value. The size of this lag would depend primarily on the elasticity of supply of arbitrage funds in the rest of the world (along with the freedom of movement) and the elasticity of supply of forward exchange. The larger the volume of arbitrage funds

[1] Forward exchange theory and the process by which the forward rate adjusts to its interest-parity value will be discussed in detail in the next chapter.

capable of moving from the rest of the world and the smaller the elasticity of supply of forward exchange, the quicker would be the adjustment of the forward rate to interest-parity. Secondly there would be a lag involved in the adjustment of the interest rate structures in response to the actual flows of arbitrage funds. The length of this lag would depend on the volume of funds actually moving from the rest of the world to country A and the elasticities of demand for arbitrage funds in both markets. If the volume of funds is large and the elasticities are low the lag would be relatively short. It is apparent then that this lag is also primarily dependent on the four factors outlined above.

In general then we can conclude that, given the elasticity of supply of forward exchange, the impact of international influences on the national interest rate structure in country A will be substantial if the elasticities of supply of and demand for short-term arbitrage funds in the rest of the world are higher than those in country A. This would be the case if country A possessed a small underdeveloped short-term capital market. However, if the elasticities are higher in country A than in the rest of the world the international influences on national interest rates would be minimal. This, of course, is assuming that short-term capital can move with the same degree of freedom in both cases. Variations in the freedom of movement, on the other hand, could partially (or even completely) off-set the impact of the elasticities.

International influences then could gain complete dominance over national influences in the determination of the short-term interest rate structure in country A only if there was a perfectly elastic supply of and demand for arbitrage funds in the rest of the world—along with complete freedom of movement. This means that all securities would be perfect substitutes, and, therefore, implies that existing exchange rates are expected to remain unchanged. As a result, there would be no need for forward exchange covering and even the insulating effect of the forward exchange mechanism would be removed. Since these conditions are unlikely to exist in the real world we must conclude that, although they are influenced to varying degrees by international factors, national interest rates are to some degree independent of international influences—especially when we take into consideration the insulating effect of the forward exchange mechanism.

The determination of the Euro-dollar Rate Structure

We will now turn to the development of a similar model showing how the structure of interest rates is determined in the Euro-dollar market. To begin with, we will assume that the Euro-dollar market is operating in isolation from other national and international capital markets. In addition, we will assume that there are three types of entities participating in the market: individuals (original-owners) who are wealth-holders (savers); firms (final-users) who are conducting real investment; and banks. The banks, in this case, do not form a national banking system as in our previous model but instead consist of all the commercial banks operating outside the United States. Also, the banks do not have the power to create Euro-dollars in the same way as the banking system could create credit money in our national model. As a result, the banks themselves have a liquidity problem to consider in their Euro-dollar operations.

In this model then participants in the market will have the following items in their balance sheets; individuals will hold their assets in the form of Euro-dollar deposits and Euro-dollar securities of the firms; firms will hold real assets and Euro-dollar deposits while owing Euro-dollar debts to the banks and individuals; and the banks will hold Euro-dollar securities of the firms and owe Euro-dollars to the firms and individuals. Now, how do liquidity considerations enter into the determination of Euro-dollar rates? If savers switch from Euro-dollar deposits to Euro-dollar securities of the firms they suffer a decrease in liquidity and, therefore, will require a higher rate of interest on the securities than on the Euro-dollar deposits. Similarly, if the firms expand their real assets by borrowing Euro-dollars they suffer a decrease in liquidity and will not pay a rate of interest on Euro-dollar loans that is as high as the rate of return expected on their real investments. Finally, the banks, since they cannot create Euro-dollars, also suffer a decrease in liquidity when they make Euro-dollar loans to the firms. This loss of liquidity, along with the allowance for bad debts and administrative costs, makes it necessary for the banks to charge a higher rate on Euro-dollar loans than they pay on Euro-dollar deposits.

In the Euro-dollar market then we also have a maximum to all rates set by the rate of return on real investment (in an international sense) and a minimum determined by the rate paid on Euro-dollar deposits by the commercial banks outside the U.S. All other Euro-dollar rates must be squeezed in between this upper and lower limit with their exact position in the structure depending on the liquidity-preference functions of individuals, firms, and banks. If we now impose a series of financial intermediaries on our system, we find that the intermediaries must, because of liquidity considerations and allowances for bad debts and administrative costs, have higher out-rates than in-rates—as in our national interest rate model. In fact, the same type of specializing and pyramiding of rates will occur in the Euro-dollar market and these rates must be fitted into the gap between the minimum and maximum Euro-dollar rates. The only difference in the Euro-dollar case is that the banks themselves generally play the role of inter-mediaries—accepting deposits and then passing them along to another bank at a slightly higher rate. As in the case of national interest rates, the intermediaries increase the liquidity of the system and thereby enable the Euro-dollar rate structure to fit more smoothly into the gap.

It is apparent then that this structure is determined by the same basic factors as is the national interest rate structure. Because of the international nature of the Euro-dollar market, however, the investment-demand, saving, and liquidity-preference functions must be defined in an international sense and not in terms of the national functions of any particular country. In addition, there is no central monetary authority in the market which can control the quantity of Euro-dollars and, hence, the overall level of liquidity. In fact, in our isolated model the supply of Euro-dollars is fixed at some pre-determined level and cannot be changed. In our isolated Euro-dollar market, therefore, we have a situation in which supply and demand factors within the market are the sole determinants of the interest rate structure—with no outside influence being exerted by a central monetary authority.

We must now remove our simplifying and, because of the international nature of the market, very unreal assumption that the Euro-dollar market is operating in complete isolation. Because of the different investment-demand, saving, and liquidity-preference functions involved, the interest rate structure in the Euro-dollar market and the national interest rate structures in the rest of the world (if all were operating in isolation) would undoubtedly be different. This is particularly so when we take into consideration the influence that can be exerted on national interest rates by national monetary authorities and which cannot be exerted on Euro-dollar rates. If, therefore, we remove our assumption of isolation and allow capital to be mobile between the Euro-dollar market and the national markets, it will result in capital (normally) moving from the lower interest rate market to the higher interest rate market. This process, of course, would tend to raise rates in the low interest rate market and lower rates in the high interest rate market and, thereby, pull the national and Euro-dollar interest rate structures closer together.

In examining the factors that determine the extent to which the national and Euro-dollar interest rate structures adjust to each other we must consider two cases: (1) the adjustment of Euro-dollar and U.S. rates; (2) the adjustment of Euro-dollar rates and rates in countries other than the U.S. The Euro-dollar-U.S. case is a special situation because both markets are dealing in the same currency and, therefore, capital flows between the U.S. and the Euro-dollar market do not involve an exchange risk. As a result, the cost of forward covering does not enter into the determination of the volume of arbitrage funds that will flow between the U.S. and the Euro-dollar market. The volume of arbitrage funds moving between these two markets then depends only on the elasticities of supply of arbitrage funds in each market and the freedom with which funds can move between the two markets; while the impact of these flows will depend, as in our national model, on the elasticities of demand for arbitrage funds in each market.

In the case of flows between the Euro-dollar market and countries other than the U.S., however, an exchange risk is involved. This means that a large volume of the flows between these markets will consist of covered arbitrage flows. As a result, the elasticity of supply of forward exchange will also enter into the determination of the volume of funds flowing between the markets—as it did in our national model. This will serve to cut off the covered arbitrage flow at the point where the cost of covering forward equals the interest-rate differential between the markets—thereby insulating the interest-rate structures from further covered flows.

Since the supply of and demand for short-term arbitrage funds have at least some degree of elasticity in the Euro-dollar market, the U.S., and other countries; there is at least some degree of freedom of movement; and, in the case of other countries, the supply of forward exchange is to some degree elastic, it seems apparent that national interest rates and Euro-dollar rates will be, to some degree, interdependent—as we found national rates to be. It would, as we have seen in our national interest rate model, be unrealistic, however, to assume that the elasticities and freedom of movement would be such as to make this interdependence complete. As a result national and Euro-dollar rates must be, to some degree, independent of each other. This is especially true in the case of Euro-dollar rates and rates in countries other than the U.S. which are insulated from each by the forward exchange mechanism. On the other hand, since this factor is absent in the Euro-dollar-U.S. case, it seems that the degree of interdependence between U.S. and Euro-dollar rates would be greater than that between Euro-dollar rates and rates in other countries. We will now look more closely at the degree to which national and Euro-dollar interest rates are interdependent in both of these cases.

The Interdependence of National and Euro-dollar Rates

In examining the interdependence of national and Euro-dollar rates we must consider two cases: (1) the relationship between Euro-dollar rates and U.S. short-term interest rates and (2) the relationship between Euro-dollar rates and short-term interest rates in countries other than the U.S.—as an example of which we will use the United Kingdom. In our statistical analysis we will use three month Euro-dollar and national interest rates. Three month rates were chosen because of their ready availability and comparability in all markets. Any other short-term rates could have been chosen, of course, if comparable data had been available. The choice of the U.K. as the representative of all other countries was based partly on the ready availability of data and partly on the fact that it has been one of the major participants in the market.

Let us begin by examining the relationship between U.S. and Euro-dollar interest rates. The fact that both markets are dealing in the same currency is particularly important when we are considering the minimum rate in our structure of Euro-dollar rates. Since U.S. dollar deposits are automatically included in the U.S. banking system (regardless of who owns them) the holders of U.S. dollars always have the option of leaving their deposits with U.S. banks as an alternative to placing them in the Euro-dollar market. This means that the Euro-dollar market has a very high elasticity of supply of arbitrage funds vis-à-vis the U.S. and that there is complete freedom of movement for funds moving from the Euro-dollar market to the U.S. short-term capital market. As a result, the minimum rate paid on Euro-dollar deposits must always be higher (ignoring non-economic factors) than the minimum rate paid on equivalent deposits by banks in the U.S. Otherwise, there would be no advantage in placing deposits in the Euro-dollar market. This special situation then provides a direct link between Euro-dollar rates and U.S. short-term interest rates.

On the other hand, the U.S. short-term capital market, because of its immense size, undoubtedly has high elasticities of supply and demand for arbitrage funds vis-à-vis the Euro-dollar market. This means that there would be a large increase (decrease) in the supply of short-term capital moving from the U.S. to the Euro-dollar market and a large decrease (increase) in the U.S. demand for short-term capital from the Euro-dollar market if Euro-dollar rates rose (fell) relative to U.S. rates. As a result, U.S. influences could potentially have a substantial impact on Euro-dollar rates because of the highly elastic U.S. supply; while the impact of Euro-dollar influences on U.S. rates could be off-set by the highly elastic U.S. demand. It seems then that, although Euro-dollar rates are highly dependent on U.S. rates, the impact of Euro-dollar rates on U.S. rates is relatively small.

This does not mean, however, that Euro-dollar rates are completely dominated by U.S. influences. The Euro-dollar market also has a relatively high elasticity of demand for arbitrage funds vis-à-vis the U.S. which serves partially to off-set the impact of the high U.S. elasticity of supply. In addition, artificial barriers could reduce the influence of U.S. factors by restricting the flow of short-term capital from the U.S. to the Euro-dollar market. Therefore, as long as Euro-dollar rates remain higher than equivalent rates in the U.S. (as we have seen they must) it is likely that they will be able to maintain a considerable degree of independence from U.S. rates —especially if the elasticity of demand in the Euro-dollar market remains high and/or the freedom of movement from the U.S. to the Euro-dollar market is restricted.

The close relationship between Euro-dollar rates and U.S. short-term interest rates can be seen quite readily from the data plotted in Chart 5. This chart plots the three-month Euro-dollar, U.S. treasury bill, and U.S. negotiable time certificate rates weekly for the period 1962–7.[1] During the period covered by these data the Euro-dollar rate appears to have followed both U.S. treasury bill and U.S. negotiable time certificate rates fairly closely—with the closest relationship being between the Euro-dollar rates and the U.S. negotiable time certificate rates. This latter situation is quite understandable when we consider that, although there is a difference in negotiability, time certificates and Euro-dollar deposits are very close substitutes. Both are essentially time deposits placed with commercial banks—U.S. banks in the case of the time certificates and non-U.S. banks in the case of Euro-dollar deposits.

Because of this direct competition then, the relationship between Euro-dollar rates and U.S. negotiable time certificate rates is the most valid comparison for testing the interdependence of Euro-dollar and U.S. short-term interest rates. In the first place, the fact that the Euro-dollar rate has usually been higher (even after allowing approximately ½ per cent per annum for the difference in negotiability) than the time certificate rate (which is somewhat higher than the rate currently being paid on time deposits by U.S. banks) seems to prove the contention

---

[1] For details of the statistical series plotted in this chart see Appendix G.

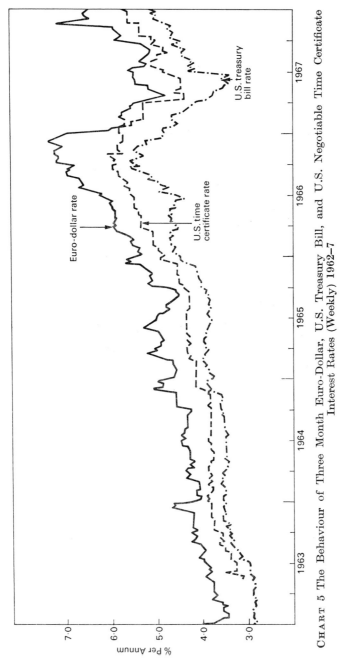

CHART 5 The Behaviour of Three Month Euro-Dollar, U.S. Treasury Bill, and U.S. Negotiable Time Certificate Interest Rates (Weekly) 1962–7

that the time deposit rate paid by U.S. banks imposes a lower limit on the Euro-dollar rate structure. On the other hand, it can be seen from the chart that the differential between the Euro-dollar rate and the time certificate rate has varied considerably over the period being considered. This seems to prove that the degree of dependence of Euro-dollar rates on U.S. short-term rates is considerably less than perfect and that Euro-dollar rates are to some degree independent of U.S. rates.

However, although it indicates that the dependence is not complete, the chart does show that there is a close relationship between Euro-dollar and U.S. short-term rates. Because of the immense size of the U.S. market, as compared to the Euro-dollar market, we have concluded that U.S. rates should have a stronger influence on Euro-dollar rates than Euro-dollar rates have on U.S. rates. As a result, Euro-dollar rates should generally adapt to U.S. rates and not cause U.S. rates to change to any significant extent. This is indicated in the chart by the fact that, although Euro-dollar rates often change to a greater extent than U.S. rates, they generally return, within a short period of time, to some fairly consistent level relative to U.S. rates.[1] This is especially apparent from the behaviour of the differential between Euro-dollar and U.S. negotiable time certificate rates. This indicates then that the degree of independence enjoyed by Euro-dollar rates vis-à-vis U.S. rates is rather limited. This independence, however, seems to have increased somewhat during the last half of 1966—with the differential continuing to widen over a considerable period of time. This resulted primarily from the combination of a strong

---

[1] From a mathematical analysis of this relationship P. H. Hendershott, 'The Structure of International Interest Rates: The U.S. Treasury Bill Rate and the Euro-dollar Deposit Rate,' *Journal of Finance*, XXII (1967), 455–65, has concluded that the Euro-dollar rate adjusted completely to changes in the U.S. treasury bill rate over a period of about a year (during the period 1957–64). This analysis, however, because of the limitations imposed by the availability of data, was conducted on the basis of very simplified and unrealistic assumptions. In particular, it was assumed that the only alternative yield available to Euro-dollar holders and the only alternative cost of funds to Euro-dollar borrowers was the U.S. treasury bill rate. As a result, it is doubtful that the conclusion regarding the adjustment lag is entirely valid. In addition, this conclusion has become even weaker since the imposition of the U.S. Voluntary Restraint Programme in February 1965—especially in a situation where the U.S. treasury bill-Euro-dollar differential widens in favour of the Euro-dollar market.

demand for Euro-dollars on the part of U.S. banks and a decrease in the freedom with which capital can move from the U.S. to the Euro-dollar market due to the U.S. Voluntary Restraint Programme. This reduced mobility was particularly significant in that it prevented an outflow from the U.S. which would have served to off-set the impact of the large U.S. demand for Euro-dollars.

The relationship between Euro-dollar rates and short-term rates in countries other than the U.S., on the other hand, is somewhat different. The two markets are dealing in different currencies and, therefore, Euro-dollar deposits are not included in the banking system of the country involved. As a result, there is no direct link between Euro-dollar deposits and other currency deposits as there was between Euro-dollar deposits and dollar deposits in the U.S. This results then in a lower elasticity of supply of arbitrage funds in the Euro-dollar market and less freedom of movement between the Euro-dollar market and the short-term capital markets of other countries than in the U.S. case. For similar reasons the elasticity of demand for arbitrage funds on the part of the Euro-dollar market would be lower vis-à-vis other countries than it was vis-à-vis the U.S.

The short-term capital markets in countries other than the U.S., moreover, are much smaller than the U.S. market and, hence, have lower elasticities of supply and demand for arbitrage funds. As a result, their impact on Euro-dollar rates and their ability to off-set the impact of the Euro-dollar market would both be smaller than in the U.S. case. In fact, in many cases it is probable that the elasticities in the Euro-dollar market are greater than those in the national short-term capital market concerned—in which case Euro-dollar influences would have a greater impact on national rates than national influences have on Euro-dollar rates. In the case of other countries then national rates are likely, on the basis of the elasticities of supply of and demand for arbitrage funds, to be more dependent on Euro-dollar rates than were U.S. rates and Euro-dollar rates are likely to have a greater degree of independence from national rates than they did vis-à-vis U.S. rates. This would be made even more true by the restrictions that are often placed on the freedom of movement between the markets in countries other than the U.S. and the Euro-dollar market.

This situation, however, is often altered by the insulating effect of the forward exchange mechanism. Since a large proportion of the flows between the Euro-dollar market and countries other than the U.S. are likely to take place on a covered basis, the flows are often cut-off by the forward exchange rate adjustment before they can bring about the adjustment of Euro-dollar and national rates that would be expected on the basis of the elasticities of supply of and demand for arbitrage funds. As a result, the Euro-dollar and national interest rates in countries other than the U.S. are more independent of each other because of the forward exchange mechanism—with the degree of independence depending partly upon the elasticity of supply of forward exchange in response to arbitrage demands.

In Chart 6, using the U.K. as an example, we have attempted to test these conclusions empirically by plotting three month Euro-dollar rates against three month U.K. treasury bill and U.K. local authority deposit rates on a weekly basis for the period 1962–7.[1] Although all three series have followed a general upward trend since the beginning of 1963, it is obvious that the fluctuations of the Euro-dollar rate about this trend have been quite different from those of the U.K. rates—with the amplitude of the U.K. fluctuations generally being greater than that of the Euro-dollar fluctuations. In particular the very modest reaction of the Euro-dollar rate to the large changes in U.K. rates during 1965 should be noted. This indicates that Euro-dollar rates are to a considerable extent independent of U.K. rates.

The closest substitutes for Euro-dollar deposits in the U.K. are the local authority deposits and, therefore, the closest relationship should exist between the Euro-dollar rate and the rate paid on these deposits. This is apparent in the chart from the fact that the two rates rise and fall approximately together —although not to the same extent. The behaviour of the differential between these two rates then seems to show that there is some degree of interdependence between Euro-dollar rates and U.K. short-term rates. However, the fact that U.K. rates have been able to change to a much greater extent than

---

[1] For details of the statistical series plotted in this chart see Appendix G.

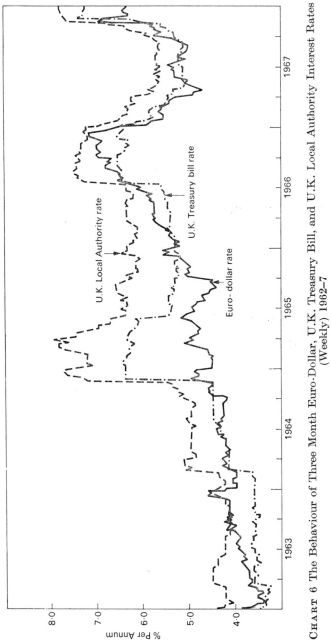

CHART 6 The Behaviour of Three Month Euro-Dollar, U.K. Treasury Bill, and U.K. Local Authority Interest Rates (Weekly) 1962–7

Euro-dollar rates and have, on occasion, even moved in the opposite direction shows that U.K. rates are not greatly dependent on Euro-dollar rates.

The relatively high degree of independence enjoyed by Euro-dollar and U.K. interest rates vis-à-vis each other can be explained by the interaction of the factors outlined on our previous analysis. U.K. rates achieve considerable independence from Euro-dollar rates due to the fact that the elasticities of supply of and demand for arbitrage funds are probably higher in the U.K. than in the Euro-dollar market. On the other hand, the impact of the relatively high elasticity of supply of arbitrage funds in the U.K. on Euro-dollar rates is partially offset by exchange controls which restrict the freedom of capital to move from the U.K. to the Euro-dollar market. Finally, U.K. and Euro-dollar interest rates gain a considerable degree of independence due to the impact of the forward exchange mechanism —especially in the light of substantial official intervention in the forward market on the part of the U.K. authorities in recent years aimed at maintaining the forward rate as close as possible to its interest-parity value. As a result, covered arbitrage flows were cut-off before they could have their full impact on the interest rate structures.

In assessing the degree to which Euro-dollar rates are independent of national rates then the most important consideration is the degree to which they are independent of U.S. rates. It is really this independence that determines the extent to which the Euro-dollar market will have an independent existence. If Euro-dollar rates are not independent of U.S. rates, the Euro-dollar market would merely be an appendage to the U.S. short-term capital market. Prior to the U.S. Voluntary Restraint Programme this independence was very limited and depended primarily on the fact that the Euro-dollar market had a relatively high elasticity of demand for arbitrage funds, and, therefore, could absorb relatively large flows of funds from the U.S. This served to delay the impact of the flows and created a lag in the adjustment of Euro-dollar rates. Since early 1965, however, the degree of independence has been increased by the restrictions imposed by the Voluntary Restraint Programme on the freedom with which funds can move from the U.S. to the Euro-dollar market. It is primarily these restrictions that now provide Euro-dollar rates with their independence from U.S. rates.

On the other hand, Euro-dollar rates have a relatively high degree of independence from short-term rates in countries other than the U.S.—both because the elasticities of supply of and demand for arbitrage funds are more equal in the two markets and because of the insulating effect of the forward exchange mechanism. This is more like the situation that we found in our national interest rate model. This independence, however, is not the only factor determining the impact of the Euro-dollar market on capital flows into or out of these countries (as it is in the U.S. case). In this case the forward exchange mechanism imposes an additional limit on the actual volume of capital that will flow. Therefore, before we can determine the impact of the Euro-dollar market on the volume of capital flowing into or out of a country other than the U.S. we must also examine its impact on the forward exchange mechanism.

6

THE NEW POSSIBILITIES FOR ARBITRAGE, HEDGING, AND SPECULATION

IN our analysis of the relationship between national and Euro-dollar interest rates we found that Euro-dollar rates were at least partially independent of national interest rates. As a result, interest rate differentials between the Euro-dollar market and national short-term capital markets could arise and provide an incentive for international short-term capital flows. These differentials alone, however, are not the only factors involved in determining the direction and magnitude of international short-term capital movements between the Euro-dollar market and countries other than U.S. We must also consider the influence of the Euro-dollar market on the forward exchange mechanism.

In this chapter then we will undertake a detailed analysis of the impact of this additional set of interest rates on the forward exchange mechanism and, hence, on the three main types of operations—covered interest arbitrage, hedging, and speculation—which determine the direction and magnitude of international short-term capital flows. First, we will discuss the ways in which these activities can take place and how they affect international short-term capital flows and form an integral part of forward exchange theory. Next, on the basis of this analysis, we will outline the impact of the Euro-dollar market on the forward exchange mechanism and on covered arbitrage, hedging, and speculative activities. Finally, we will consider our conclusions in the light of the U.K. experience during the five year period 1962–7.

Covered Arbitrage, Hedging, Speculation and Forward Exchange Theory

To begin, let us define the terms covered arbitrage, hedging and speculation. Covered arbitrage will be defined as 'an international transfer of spot funds for short-term investment purposes covered by a simultaneous forward transaction of the same amount in the opposite direction'.[1] The same thing can also be accomplished by means of international short-term borrowing of spot funds and simultaneous forward covering operations. In both cases, the operation is free of exchange risk. Covered arbitrage would occur between two countries if the rate of interest in one country minus the cost of covering forward was greater (or less) than the rate of interest in the other. If this situation developed, investors would place their funds in the market with the highest covered yield and borrowers would borrow their funds in the market providing the lowest covered cost. The factors that determine which of the two centres will yield the highest return (or the lowest borrowing cost) are: the short-term interest rates ruling in each country and the spot and forward exchange rates. It is these four variables then that determine whether or not covered arbitrage will take place between any two countries.

Hedging, as considered from the forward exchange market point of view, can be defined as 'a sale or purchase of forward exchange calculated to reduce the pre-existing exchange risk of the operator—i.e. it covers or reduces his original open position'.[2] For example, an importer, who has a liability denominated in foreign currency, would purchase his foreign exchange requirements forward; while an exporter, who is due to receive a payment denominated in foreign currency, would sell an equal amount of foreign exchange forward. Hedging, however, can also be conducted through the spot exchange market by means of 'leads' in spot transactions. In our example, the importer could have switched his financing from the exporting to the importing country and purchased foreign exchange spot; while the exporter could also have switched his financing from the exporting to the importing country and sold foreign exchange spot.

The hedging importer then would have to choose between

---

[1] S. C. Tsiang, 'The Theory of Forward Exchange and Effects of Government Intervention on The Forward Exchange Market', *International Monetary Fund Staff Papers*, VII (1959), 77.

[2] Ibid., p. 76.

two alternatives: (1) financing in the exporting country and buying its currency forward, or (2) financing in the importing country and buying foreign exchange spot; while a hedging exporter would have the choice of: (1) financing in the exporting country and selling foreign exchange forward or (2) financing in the importing country and selling its currency spot. The trader, if he is going to hedge, would choose the cheapest of these alternatives. Therefore, whether the forward or the spot exchange market will be used for hedging depends on which centre is the cheapest for trade financing. This, in turn, depends on the same factors as those determining which centre offered the highest return on covered arbitrage flows—namely the short-term interest rates in both centres and the spot and forward exchange rates. This process of choosing between spot and forward hedging has been called 'trader-arbitrage'.[1]

Speculation, for the purposes of this study, will be defined as 'the deliberate assumption or retention of a net open (long or short) position in foreign exchange upon consideration of the current forward rate and the probable future spot rate which the operator concerned expects to prevail'.[2] According to this definition a trader who does not fully hedge his known forward commitments is also considered to be a speculator. Under a fixed exchange rate system expectations can be such that speculators, at any particular time, will anticipate either a depreciation or appreciation of the spot rate, i.e. they may anticipate that it will move in one direction only. These expectations arise either as a result of extreme confidence in the spot rate limits—in which case speculators would anticipate a movement of the spot rate away from the upper or lower limit back towards parity; or as a result of lack of confidence in the spot limits—in which case speculators would anticipate a movement of the spot rate beyond either the upper or lower spot limit. The first would be considered stabilizing speculation while the latter would be de-stabilizing.

Whether speculation is conducted through the spot or the forward exchange market depends first of all on whether or not the speculator owns or can obtain funds denominated in

[1] J. Spraos, 'Speculation, Arbitrage and Sterling,' *Economic Journal*, LXXI (1959), 5.
[2] Tsiang, op. cit., p. 77.

the currency against which he is speculating or has trading activities to finance. If the speculator does not own or cannot borrow liquid funds or have trade to finance, he has no choice but to speculate through the forward market by buying or selling forward exchange—buying the currency which he expects to appreciate and selling that which he expects to depreciate. Following Spraos we will call this 'pure speculation'.[1] On the other hand, speculation undertaken in conjunction with trade or short-term investment and borrowing can take place through either the spot or forward exchange markets.

Under a fixed exchange rate system speculation in conjunction with trade financing could lead to a situation of one-sided covering. Importers who owe the currency expected to depreciate and exporters who are due to receive payments in the currency expected to appreciate will not cover their exchange risks; while importers who owe the currency expected to appreciate and exporters who are due to receive payments in the currency expected to depreciate will always cover. Traders who cover their transactions will do so either in the spot or forward exchange markets as described above. If they then wish to adopt a speculative position they must act as pure speculators and sell the currency that is expected to depreciate forward. Traders who do not cover are, according to our definition, speculating; and in adopting their speculative position they can also use either the spot or forward exchange market.

For example, if the currency of country A is expected to depreciate vis-à-vis that of country B, an importer in country B (who owes the currency expected to depreciate) could either: (1) finance in country A and leave the exchange risk uncovered; or (2) finance in his own country and simultaneously purchase the currency expected to depreciate spot and sell it forward— thereby 'leading' his payment. A similar choice would be open to an exporter in country A who is due to receive payment in the appreciating currency. In making his choice between these alternatives then the trader-speculator would have to consider four factors: the short-term interest rates in the two countries and the spot and forward exchange rates.

In the case of speculation involving short-term investment the situation is much the same. Non-residents of the country

[1] Spraos, op. cit., p. 6.

whose currency is expected to depreciate could either: (1) leave
covered funds in the country whose currency is expected to
depreciate (in which case no exchange risk is attached to them)
or (2) withdraw them by selling the depreciating currency spot
and investing the proceeds abroad. These alternatives basically
involve covered arbitrage operations and if the non-residents
then wished to adopt speculative positions they would, under
either of the alternatives, have to sell the depreciating currency
forward. Residents, on the other hand, could either: (1) leave
their funds in the country and sell the depreciating currency
forward, or (2) sell the depreciating currency spot and invest
their funds abroad. Once again covered arbitage considerations
are involved in making the choice between alternatives.

Therefore, the choice made by either a trader or investor, as
to whether he will use the forward or the spot market in adopting his speculative position, depends on the four arbitrage
variables: the short-term interest rates in the two countries and
the spot and forward exchange rates. The speculator—whether
trader or investor—in choosing between the spot and forward
markets would adopt the cheapest means to the same speculative end with the point of indifference between the alternatives
being the same neutrality condition as that involved in covered
arbitrage—i.e. the point where there is no covered differential
favouring the transfer of covered arbitrage funds. This process
of choosing has been called 'speculator-arbitrage'.[1]

We will now examine how each of these types of transactions
affects international short-term capital flows. Covered arbitrage,
by definition, always involves a flow of capital between
countries—with the direction depending upon which country
is favoured by the covered interest differential. If a country is
favoured by the covered interest differential it is advantageous
to invest in that country and to borrow in the other country. As
a result, capital flows into the country favoured by the differential. The effect of hedging on capital flows, on the other hand,
depends on whether the trader hedges through the spot or the
forward exchange market. If hedging is done through the forward market there is no immediate effect on capital flows; while
if the spot market is used the capital flow associated with the
trade transaction will be accelerated. As a result, a switch from

[1] Spraos, op. cit., p. 5.

forward to spot covering would speed up the flow of payments
and receipts and, hence, change the timing of the capital flows
connected with trade transactions. On the other hand, hedging
in the forward market may have an indirect effect on capital
flows by altering the forward exchange rates and, hence,
providing an incentive for covered arbitrage flows.

The effect of speculation on capital flows also depends on
whether it is conducted through the forward or the spot
exchange market. If 'pure' speculators or investor-speculators
adopt their speculative position by selling (or buying) forward
exchange, there is no immediate capital outflow (or inflow)
involved. However, as in the case of forward hedging, speculation
through the forward market could affect capital flows indirectly
by influencing the forward rate and, hence, the incentive for
covered arbitrage flows. The volume of covered arbitrage flows
resulting from this would depend on the impact that the change
in the forward exchange rate had on hedging and speculative
activities. To the extent that it caused more traders to cover
or speculators to partially close their open positions the covered
arbitrage flow would not be as great as the original volume of
forward speculation. Similarly, if a trader speculates by leaving
his exchange risk uncovered, there would be no effect on the
capital flow associated with the trade transaction. However,
speculation through the spot market—whether connected with
investment or trade—always involves an immediate inflow or
outflow of capital to the full extent of the speculative position
adopted.

It is apparent then that the presence or absence of a covered
interest rate differential between countries is vital in determining the direction and magnitude of international short-term
capital flows. It not only determines the direction and magnitude of covered arbitrage flows but also determines whether
hedging and speculation will be conducted in the spot or the
forward exchange market and, hence, the manner in which
these transactions affect international capital flows. In examining how a covered interest rate differential could come into
existence we must consider the behaviour of four variables:
the short-term interest rates in the two countries involved and
the spot and forward exchange rates. If we assume that the
short-term interest rate in each country is determined and

fixed by monetary policy considerations (as is generally the case in the real world) and that, under a fixed exchange rate system, the spot (but not the forward) exchange rate is fixed within relatively narrow limits, this leaves one factor—the forward exchange rate—as the crucial variable in determining whether or not there will be a covered differential between any two countries. Our next step then is to determine how forward exchange market equilibrium is achieved.

The 'interest-parity' theory of forward exchange, originally developed by Keynes,[1] stressed the major importance of covered arbitrage in the determination of forward exchange market equilibrium. The covered arbitrage flows caused the forward exchange rate to adapt to its interest parity[2] (i.e. the short-term interest rate differential between the two countries involved) and to fluctuate in a narrow range about it. The system, therefore, would be in equilibrium when the forward premium (or discount)—i.e. the difference between the spot and forward exchange rates—was equal to the short-term interest differential between the two countries—in which case there would be no covered interest rate differential.

If a covered differential did develop arbitrage operations would tend to remove it through a combination of three possible effects: (1) by raising the spot rate, (2) by lowering the forward rate, and (3) by raising the short-term interest rate in one country and lowering it in the other. Any deviations from interest-parity then would be removed by means of covered arbitrage flows and, therefore, would be only temporary phenomena. This, in turn, would make the arbitrage flows self-eliminating. As a result, the possibility of persistent

---

[1] J. M. Keynes, *Monetary Reform* (New York: Harcourt, Brace and Co., 1924), pp. 125–51.

[2] In practice this adjustment is unlikely to be perfect because of the costs and inconvenience attached to arbitrage operations. In effect, the gain from arbitrage operations must exceed a certain minimum in order to induce arbitragers to take the trouble. This minimum has traditionally, since the time of Keynes, been set at approximately $\frac{1}{2}$ per cent per annum. Commercial banks, however, will undoubtedly take part in arbitrage on the basis of considerably smaller margins than this—especially when large wholesale amounts are involved. In this study, since we are dealing primarily with large wholesale operations on the part of commercial banks, we will consider the forward rate to be at its 'interest-parity' value if the forward premium (or discount) is within $\pm \frac{1}{4}$ per cent of interest-parity.

covered differentials did not arise as long as the supply of funds available for arbitrage was sufficiently elastic.

The conclusions given by the 'interest-parity' theory however, are dependent on three basic assumptions whose validity in the real world must be seriously questioned. These assumptions are: (1) that the supply of arbitrage funds is sufficiently elastic to achieve interest-parity within a short period of time, (2) that expectations regarding the future level of the spot exchange rate do not give rise to speculation, and (3) that there are no artificial barriers—such as exchange controls—which interfere with the freedom with which short-term arbitrage funds can move internationally.

In the real world expectations regarding the future value of the spot exchange rate can obviously give rise to speculation—either in the forward or the spot exchange market. If it takes place through the forward market it results in a forward purchase or sale of the currency under attack and this is reflected in the forward exchange rate by pushing it to a discount or premium (commonly called an intrinsic discount or premium) relative to the 'interest-parity' value. If the supply of arbitrage funds was perfectly (or at least highly) elastic and funds could move freely between money markets this intrinsic premium or discount would be quickly eliminated by arbitrage flows. However, if the supply of arbitrage is not perfectly elastic, it is possible that covered arbitrage flows would be insufficient to restore the 'interest-parity' equilibrium; and, hence, a covered differential could persist between the two countries involved.

Any number of factors, notably various forms of exchange control, could affect the freedom with which short-term arbitrage funds move internationally and thereby make it more difficult for the forward rate to adjust to its interest-parity. However, these factors, by themselves, would not be decisive and the basic validity of the 'interest-parity' theory would remain as long as international capital movements were not stopped completely.[1]

[1] J. Spraos, 'The Theory of Forward Exchange and Recent Practice,' *The Manchester School of Economics and Social Studies*, XXI (1953), 87–117, points out how this took place in the U.K. case during the early 1950's when rigid exchange controls were in force. Basically, he argues that the arbitrage function would be performed by traders reacting to the same factors that determine interest arbitrage flows.

The critical assumption regarding the validity of the 'interest-parity' theory, therefore, is that concerning the supply elasticity of arbitrage funds. Even if speculation was present and there was a considerable degree of interference with international capital flows, a perfectly elastic supply of arbitrage funds could still enable the forward exchange mechanism to function in a manner predicted by the 'interest-parity' theory. The existence of a perfectly elastic supply of arbitrage funds, however, is highly improbable in the real world. The reason for this can be found in the rising opportunity cost of arbitrage compared to the alternative uses of the same funds. This, in turn, arises from the fact that there is a loss of convenience and liquidity and an increase in risk associated with the investment of more and more funds in the same market. In addition, restraints are often placed on arbitrage operations by central banks—both on commercial bank lending for arbitrage purposes and on the participation of the commercial banks themselves— either by reducing commercial bank reserves or by moral suasion.

It is apparent then that, although the tendency towards equilibrium at the interest-parity level is assured by the original assumptions of the 'interest-parity' theory, the actual achievement of parity is challenged by the absence of some of these assumptions in the real world. As a result, in a realistic theory of forward exchange we must consider all the types of operations that give rise to a supply of or demand for forward exchange—namely covered arbitrage, hedging and speculation. It is the interaction of these operations that will determine the forward exchange market equilibrium in the real world.

In this more realistic case the net supply of (or demand for) forward exchange on the part of hedgers and speculators would result in a fall (or rise) in the forward exchange rate. This, in turn, would provide an incentive for outward (or inward) covered arbitrage operations. The net demand for (or supply of) forward exchange on the part of arbitragers then would tend to off-set (or at least partially off-set) the net supply of (or demand for) forward exchange on the part of hedgers and speculators. Equilibrium in the forward exchange market, therefore, would be achieved and the forward exchange rate determined when the total supply of forward exchange equalled the total demand for forward exchange. The question now arises as to whether or not the equilibrium forward rate determined in this manner would always be at the interest-parity level—given the fact that the supply of arbitrage funds is less than perfectly elastic. If it is, then persistent covered differentials between countries would not exist.

In attempting to answer this question, let us look at a specific situation. First, assume that, from the point of view of the country being considered, the forward exchange rate is at a discount relative to the current spot rate and that it is at its interest-parity level. In addition, assume that we are operating, as in the real world, under a system of fixed exchange rates. If a current account deficit now developed there would be a net supply of forward exchange on the part of hedgers and this, in turn, would tend to push the forward rate to a wider discount and away from interest-parity. The excess of imports over exports if not off-set by increased capital inflows could also place downward pressure on the spot rate and this, if it was felt that the current account deficit was going to persist, could cause speculators to anticipate a further depreciation. This would result in a net supply of forward exchange on the part of speculators and cause a further widening of the forward discount. Now, if the supply of arbitrage funds is not highly elastic, the demand for forward exchange on the part of arbitragers would not be sufficient to off-set the increased supply of forward exchange resulting from the hedging and speculative operations. As a result, an equilibrium could be reached in the forward exchange market at a rate below the interest-parity level. In these circumstances then a persistent covered differential could arise.

The possibility of persistent covered differentials developing between countries has given rise to the suggestion that official intervention in the forward exchange market be used to off-set the disturbing influence being exerted on the forward exchange rate. To do this the foreign exchange authorities of the country concerned would buy or sell forward exchange until they had restored the forward rate either to its interest-parity level or to some other level which they consider desirable from a policy point of view. In effect, official intervention could be used for two purposes: (1) to reduce the loss of foreign exchange reserves

8

during a period of speculative pressure by reducing the incentive for covered arbitrage flows and the shifting of speculation and hedging from the forward to the spot exchange market; or (2) to insulate the domestic economy from interest rate changes abroad by removing the incentive for covered arbitrage flows. Although this policy question has been discussed extensively in the recent forward exchange literature, it will not be dealt with in this study. In a later section, however, we will deal briefly with the use of this technique as a monetary policy tool.

Therefore, although there is a tendency for the forward rate to adjust to its interest-parity as predicted by the 'interest-parity' theory, it is apparent that situations could arise which would result in a persistent covered differential between two countries. This possibility, however, is basically dependent on the fact that strong speculative pressures of a destabilizing nature give rise to a highly elastic supply of (or demand for) forward exchange in a situation where there is a less-than-perfectly elastic supply of arbitrage funds. We will now turn to the problems of integrating the semi-independent Euro-dollar market into the system and determining its impact on the forward exchange mechanism. In particular, we will attempt to determine whether the existence of the Euro-dollar market has increased or decreased the possibility of persistent covered differentials arising between financial centres.

The Impact of the Euro-dollar Market on the Forward Exchange Mechanism

Basically, the impact of the Euro-dollar market on the forward exchange mechanism arises from the fact that it has imposed another set of semi-independent interest rates on the international monetary system and, thereby, has opened up an additional channel through which short-term capital can move internationally. This has tended both to increase the supply and mobility of arbitrage funds and to divert arbitrage funds from other channels. In addition, the imposition of an additional set of interest rates has created another interest-parity to which the forward exchange rate can adjust. There are now two basic possibilities—the forward rate can adjust to the differential between U.S. rates and domestic interest rates in the country concerned or it can adjust to the differential between Euro-dollar rates and domestic interest rates.

The Euro-dollar market has tended to increase the supply and mobility of arbitrage funds for a number of reasons. First, as we have seen in Chapter 2, the intermediary functions performed by the commercial banks operating in the Euro-dollar market serve to spread the risks encountered in the international movement of short-term capital. Because of the highly developed network of intermediary banks operating in the market, each bank is in a position to enter into the type of transactions for which its knowledge and experience best suit it. This allows the banks to move funds internationally in accordance with each bank's specialized knowledge in much the same way as financial intermediaries move funds within a national economy. As a result, because they can restrict the types of international transactions that they undertake to those involving the degree of risk that they are prepared to accept, the banks are more willing to move funds internationally. This undoubtedly has broadened the opportunities for interest arbitrage and, hence, tended to increase the supply and inter-national mobility of arbitrage funds.

This impact is particularly evident in the case where foreign or U.S. owners transfer dollar deposits from a bank in the U.S. to a bank operating outside the U.S. The banks outside the U.S. are very likely to move these funds internationally rather than leave them on deposit in the U.S. because of their special-ized knowledge of foreign investment opportunities. The banks in the U.S., on the other hand, because of their pre-occupation with domestic U.S. financing and limited knowledge of foreign borrowers, would undoubtedly have used the majority of these funds for domestic purposes within the U.S. As a result, U.S. dollar funds are more likely to participate in arbitrage activities if they are placed in the Euro-dollar market than if they are left on deposit in a U.S. bank. The best example of this is the case of covered arbitrage flows between Euro-dollars and U.K. local authority deposits. It is unlikely that flows into or out of U.K. local authority deposits would have taken place in such volume if all dollar deposits had been held at U.S. banks. In this case it was the specialized knowledge of the overseas banks and accepting houses in London that led to the creation of this new channel for arbitrage operations.

Residents of countries other than the U.S. also could be more willing to convert domestic funds into U.S. dollars and place them in the Euro-dollar market as opposed to placing funds directly in other national short-term capital markets. This results from the fact that they can hold Euro-dollar deposits with a bank with which they are familiar and in some cases with their own domestic bank—now having their deposits denominated in U.S. dollars rather than in domestic currency. The risk involved in this, in many cases, is considered to be smaller than that involved in transferring funds to a foreign bank or into foreign short-term securities. This then also tends to increase the supply and mobility of arbitrage funds.

Finally, the fact that the Euro-dollar market is international in nature, and, hence, operates outside national exchange controls, cartel arrangements, and regulatory controls serves to increase both the supply of arbitrage funds and the freedom with which they can move internationally. Since there are no artificial barriers to prevent short-term capital from moving into or out of the Euro-dollar market itself, capital flows between an individual country and the Euro-dollar market would only have to overcome the barriers erected by that particular country; whereas in the case of flows between two countries both countries could have barriers restricting inflows and outflows of short-term capital. Similarly, the ability of the Euro-dollar market to operate without regard to the rigidities imposed upon national banking systems by cartel arrangements and regulatory controls, has allowed national commercial banks to use Euro-dollar operations as a means of avoiding these rigidities. This very likely has led to a greater participation on the part of these banks in international short-term capital movements.

For similar reasons, the Euro-dollar market has probably caused a diversion of arbitrage funds from other more traditional channels. Because of the risk spreading techniques employed by the banks in their Euro-dollar operations, funds are more likely to take part (after passing through a series of intermediary banks) in arbitrage flows into or out of the high yielding (although somewhat riskier) domestic securities available to arbitragers than they would have if the Euro-dollar market had not existed. This undoubtedly has diverted arbitrage funds from the lower risk traditional channels—such as treasury bill arbitrage. In fact, this diversion of funds is virtually forced upon Euro-dollar arbitragers because of the relatively high cost involved in obtaining Euro-dollar deposits. If they are to make a profit on their arbitrage operations they must seek out high yielding outlets for their funds—which would probably not be treasury bills.

Empirical evidence as to the extent to which the Euro-dollar market has either increased the supply and mobility of arbitrage funds or diverted arbitrage funds from other channels is virtually impossible to obtain. First it is impossible to determine what the total volume of short-term arbitrage flows would have been or to what extent they would have flowed through the various channels if the Euro-dollar market did not exist. It would be meaningless to compare the volume of flows before the existence of the Euro-dollar market with the volume of flows now taking place because of the fundamental changes— such as the return to convertibility—that have taken place since the creation of the Euro-dollar market. Secondly, the international nature of the market makes it extremely difficult to obtain comprehensive data for the total volume of arbitrage funds flowing through the Euro-dollar market. Finally, the national data that is available regarding the flows of short-term capital into or out of national financial markets is so entangled that it is often difficult to segregate the funds moving through the Euro-dollar channel from those moving through other channels. Later in this chapter, however, we will attempt to analyse the U.K. data and compare the volume of flows into or out of U.K. treasury bills with the volume of funds moving into or out of the U.K. via the Euro-dollar market.

Now let us examine how all of these factors affect the forward exchange adjustment process. The increase in the supply and mobility of arbitrage funds tends to make the achievement of an interest-parity equilibrium in the forward exchange market easier. On the other hand, the imposition of another set of interest rates make it more difficult to determine which interest-parity the forward rate will adjust to—the differential between U.S. and domestic interest rates or that between Euro-dollar and domestic interest rates. If Euro-dollar rates were merely another set of U.S. interest rates they would not create any difficulties in determining a unique interest-parity to which the forward rate could adjust. In any country there are a whole series of interest rates on securities of the same maturity reflecting the different degree of risk attached to each type of security. However, since the short-term interest rate structures in all countries are determined by basically the same factors, these risk differentials should be approximately equal in all countries. Therefore, if we compare equivalent securities between any two countries, the risk differentials should cancel out—thereby enabling the determination of a unique interest-parity between the two countries.

However, as we have pointed out in the preceding chapter, Euro-dollar rates are at least semi-independent of interest rates in any particular country—even those in the U.S.—and are influenced by a large number of international factors. As a result, the difference between U.S. and Euro-dollar rates involves more than a straight risk differential. This raises the possibility of another independent interest-parity to which forward rates can adjust. In fact, if we apply this same reasoning to the other Euro-currency markets, there is the possibility of a further independent interest-parity—the differential between Euro-dollar rates and other Euro-currency rates—to which the forward rate could adjust. Therefore, since the forward rate can adjust to only one interest-parity at a time, the possibility of persistent covered differentials arising between some of the markets involved seems to be more probable.

It is apparent then that either the covered differential between the Euro-dollar market and the country concerned or that between the U.S. and the country concerned could be wiped out by the additional flows of arbitrage funds; but not necessarily both. In reality it is likely that the covered differential between Euro-dollar rates and domestic rates would be wiped out first due to the fact that arbitrage funds have been diverted from other arbitrage channels and now flow into the country concerned through the Euro-dollar market. If the Euro-dollar-domestic interest parity is achieved more quickly than the U.S.-domestic interest parity it would indicate that there has been a substantial diversion of arbitrage funds from other channels and that flows between Euro-dollars and domestic securities have now become the primary means of conducting covered arbitrage movements into or out of a country other than the U.S.

The Effect of the Euro-dollar Market on Covered Arbitrage, Hedging, and Speculative Activities

The existence of the Euro-dollar market has had a considerable impact on covered arbitrage flows. By creating a new channel through which arbitrage funds can flow it has tended both to increase the volume of arbitrage flows and to divert arbitrage flows from other channels. The increased volume of arbitrage flows, as we have seen, has tended to make it easier for the forward rate to adjust to an interest-parity equilibrium; while the diversion of arbitrage flows has tended to push the forward rate to parity with the Euro-dollar–domestic interest differential. This situation, however, since the forward rate can only adjust to one parity at a time, gives rise to the possibility of a persistent covered differential developing between the country concerned and the U.S. which could provide an incentive for further arbitrage flows. Whether or not these flows take place depends upon the availability of arbitrage funds. If they did take place, they would have the effect of pushing the forward rate away from the Euro-dollar–domestic interest parity and, hence, provide a further incentive for covered arbitrage between these markets.

As far as covered arbitrage is concerned then the importance of this new interest-parity is the fact that it has reduced the significance of the forward exchange mechanism in limiting the volume of covered arbitrage flows. If there was only one interest-parity, covered arbitrage flows would be cut-off as soon as the forward rate adjusted to its interest-parity value. Now, however, if arbitrage funds are still available after the forward rate has adjusted to one of the interest-parities, they could be diverted to the other channel and continue to flow. Therefore, on top of the actual increase in covered arbitrage flows that is associated with the Euro-dollar market there may be a potential increase resulting from the fact that it is now difficult to define a unique interest-parity between any two financial centres to which the forward exchange rate can adjust.

The Euro-dollar market can also be used by hedgers and speculators as an alternative to the forward exchange market. As we have already seen, hedgers and speculators have the choice of conducting their activities through either the forward or the spot exchange market—with the choice depending on whether or not there is a covered interest differential between the money markets involved. By providing another source of financing and, hence, the possibility of another covered differential, the Euro-dollar market gives hedgers and speculators a further opportunity to operate through the spot market. They now have the choice of financing their activities in either of the two countries involved or in the Euro-dollar market. They will, of course, choose the cheapest of these alternatives. In addition, the Euro-dollar market has made it more difficult to achieve a unique interest-parity equilibrium in the forward exchange market and, therefore, has increased the possibility of a covered differential arising.

To illustrate the effect of the Euro-dollar market on hedging operations let us use the case of trade between the U.S. and the U.K. A U.S. importer could cover his exchange risk by undertaking any one of the following operations: (1) finance in New York and purchase sterling spot (thereby, leading his payment); (2) finance in London and purchase sterling forward; or (3) finance in the Euro-dollar market and purchase sterling spot (again leading his payment). On the other hand, a U.K. importer could cover by: (1) financing in New York and purchasing U.S. dollars forward; (2) financing in London and purchasing U.S. dollars spot (leading his payment); or (3) financing in the Euro-dollar market and purchasing U.S. dollars forward. Similarly, U.K. exporters would accelerate their receipts if they financed in either New York or the Euro-dollar market; while U.S. exporters would accelerate their receipts by financing in London.

Therefore, if either the covered differential between London and New York or that between London and the Euro-dollar market was in favour of London, U.S. importers and U.K.

exporters would lead their spot transactions. This would result in an acceleration of the capital flow from the U.S. to the U.K. On the other hand, if the covered differential favoured either the U.S. or the Euro-dollar market, the flow from the U.K. to the U.S. would be accelerated. Consequently, the existence of the Euro-dollar market, by making it possible for another covered differential to arise, has provided importers and exporters with a further opportunity for covering by means of 'leads' in their spot transactions. In addition, as we have seen, the probability of a covered differential existing is now greater because of the additional interest parity added by the Euro-dollar market. In effect, the Euro-dollar market has broadened the scope for 'trader-arbitrage'.

In illustrating the effect of the Euro-dollar market on speculation let us continue with the U.S.–U.K. example and assume that speculators are anticipating a depreciation of sterling. In this case an investor could adopt a speculative position by either: (1) leaving funds in London and selling sterling forward; (2) selling sterling spot and transferring the proceeds to New York; or (3) selling sterling spot and investing the proceeds in the Euro-dollar market. In the case of trader-speculation under these assumptions U.K. importers and U.S. exporters would always cover their exchange risks while U.S. importers and U.K. exporters would adopt open positions. U.S. importers and U.K. exporters could do this by either: (1) financing in London and leaving the exchange risk uncovered; (2) financing in New York and simultaneously purchasing sterling spot and selling it forward; or (3) financing in the Euro-dollar market and simultaneously purchasing sterling spot and selling it forward.

Therefore, if either the covered differential between London and New York or that between London and the Euro-dollar market was in favour of London, investors would leave their funds in the U.K. and speculate by selling sterling forward— thereby preventing an immediate outflow of capital from the U.K. On the other hand U.S. importers and U.K. exporters would finance in either New York or the Euro-dollar market and, hence, speculate through the spot market—thereby causing an acceleration in the flow of capital from the U.S. to the U.K. However, if the covered differential favoured either

New York or the Euro-dollar market investors would withdraw their funds from London—thereby creating an immediate outflow from the U.K.—and traders would finance in London and leave the exchange risk uncovered—thereby leaving capital flows unaffected. It is apparent then that the existence of the Euro-dollar market has increased the opportunities for 'speculator-arbitrage' by providing another channel through which speculators can shift their activities between the spot and forward exchange markets. This shifting, as we have seen, has a considerable impact on the direction and volume of international short-term capital movements.

The existence of the Euro-dollar market then has had a substantial effect on international short-term capital flows. In the first place, it has increased the volume and mobility of funds available to take part in these flows. This is especially apparent in the case of covered arbitrage flows—but is also important in the provision of additional financing facilities for hedging and speculative activities. The additional flows of covered arbitrage funds have tended to make the achievement of an interest-parity equilibrium in the forward exchange market easier; while the additional source of financing for trade and speculation has enabled hedgers and speculators to shift their activities between the spot and forward exchange markets more freely.

In addition, however, the Euro-dollar market, by creating another interest-parity, has tended to frustrate the achievement of a unique interest-parity equilibrium in the forward exchange market and hence, has tended to maintain a persistent incentive favouring covered arbitrage flows and trader- and speculator-arbitrage. This persistent incentive gives rise to the possibility of further arbitrage flows (if arbitrage funds are available) and results in 'leads' in trade payments and a higher volume of speculation through the spot market. All of these tend to either increase the volume or alter the timing of international short-term capital flows. We will now examine these conclusions by analyzing the U.K. experience during the period 1962–7.

The U.K. Experience

In testing our conclusions empirically we will examine the

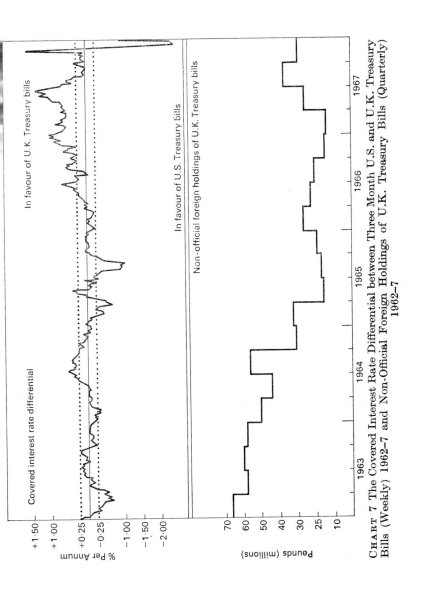

CHART 7 The Covered Interest Rate Differential between Three Month U.S. and U.K. Treasury Bills (Weekly) 1962–7 and Non-Official Foreign Holdings of U.K. Treasury Bills (Quarterly) 1962–7

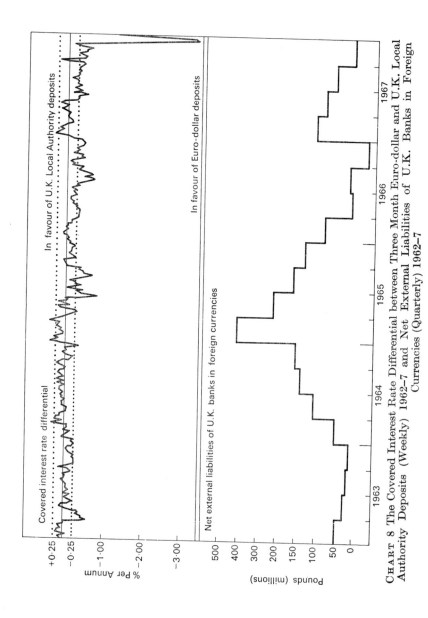

CHART 8 The Covered Interest Rate Differential between Three Month Euro-dollar and U.K. Local Authority Deposits (Weekly) 1962–7 and Net External Liabilities of U.K. Banks in Foreign Currencies (Quarterly) 1962–7

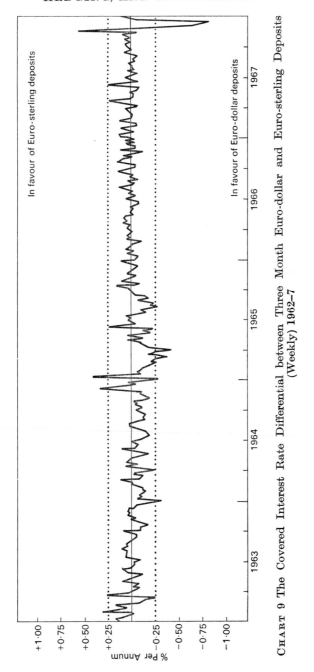

CHART 9 The Covered Interest Rate Differential between Three Month Euro-dollar and Euro-sterling Deposits (Weekly) 1962–7

behaviour of three covered interest rate differentials: (1) the differential between three month U.S. and U.K. treasury bills; (2) the differential between three month Euro-dollar and U.K. local authority deposits; and (3) the differential between three month Euro-dollar and Euro-sterling deposits. These covered differentials are plotted on a weekly basis in Charts 7, 8 and 9 respectively for the period 1962–7.[1] The U.S.–U.K. treasury bill differential has traditionally been considered the interest-parity to which the dollar-sterling forward exchange rate adjusted. As we have seen, the new possibilities added by the introduction of the Euro-dollar market are the Euro-dollar–U.K. local authority and Euro-dollar-Euro-sterling differentials.

In this section then we first want to determine whether or not there is, in the U.K. case (after the introduction of the Euro-dollar market), a unique interest-parity to which the forward exchange rate can adjust. If there is a unique interest-parity, all the covered differentials should move in the same direction and to approximately the same extent. This would mean that any significant covered differential that did develop would be approximately the same for all of the three cases outlined—both in direction and magnitude—and that they would all exist for approximately the same period of time. If the covered differentials do not behave in this manner, it would indicate that the Euro-dollar market has added an independent interest-parity to the system.

If this is so, the forward rate could only adjust to the differential between the securities favoured by arbitragers at any particular time and persistent covered differentials between the securities not favoured by arbitragers could possibly develop. To explore this possibility then, we want to determine which of the three possible interest-parities the forward rate follows most closely. If the forward rate adjusts perfectly to an interest-parity, there will be no covered differential between the securities involved.[2] Therefore, the smaller the covered differential between two securities (of the same risk) the closer the forward rate follows the interest differential between these securities.

---

[1] For complete details of the data underlying these charts see Appendix H.

[2] In this study a covered differential within the limits ± ¼ per cent per annum will be considered equivalent to a zero covered differential.

From the charts it can be seen that at times all three covered differentials, when compared to each other, have moved in different directions and to different degrees. This is particularly evident when we compare the U.S.–U.K. treasury bill differential with the Euro-dollar–U.K. local authority differential. On a number of occasions these differentials have actually moved in opposite directions. In addition, the magnitude of the variations about zero is almost always smaller in the case of the Euro-dollar–U.K. local authority differential. These differences in behaviour are particularly obvious during the last half of 1966 and the first half of 1967 when the U.S.–U.K. treasury bill differential was greater than $+\frac{1}{4}$ per cent (i.e. in favour of U.K. treasury bills) while at the same time the Euro-dollar–U.K. local authority differential was at times greater than $-\frac{1}{4}$ per cent (i.e. in favour of Euro-dollar deposits). Therefore, even though the picture was somewhat clouded during this period by the massive intervention in the forward exchange market on the part of the U.K. authorities, it is apparent that the Euro-dollar–U.K. local authority parity is independent of the U.S.–U.K. treasury bill parity.

In fact the experience during 1966 and 1967 illustrates the difficulties created by the Euro-dollar market with regard to official intervention in the forward exchange market. Even though the U.K. authorities were able to maintain a covered differential favourable to investment in U.K. treasury bills, they were unable or unwilling to maintain a differential in favour of U.K. local authority deposits. As a result, an incentive remained for an outflow of funds to the Euro-dollar market while they were maintaining an incentive for an inflow with regard to treasury bills. It is obvious then that there is no unique interest-parity to which the forward rate can adjust (even with the aid of official intervention) once the Euro-dollar market has been introduced into the system. Consequently, we must now determine which of the three differentials the forward rate follows most closely.

By again looking at the three charts, it can be seen that the smallest covered differential, during the period under review, has consistently been that between Euro-dollar and Euro-sterling deposits (Chart 9). In fact, there have been very few covered differentials between these securities outside the limits of $\pm\frac{1}{4}$ per cent per annum. It seems then that the forward rate has adjusted almost perfectly to the interest differential between Euro-dollar and Euro-sterling deposits. This, however, is a somewhat deceiving conclusion. Because of the relatively small size of the Euro-sterling market there is a strong two-way relationship between the forward exchange rate and Euro-sterling rates; and, as a result, the Euro-sterling rate not only helps in determining the forward exchange rate but is also determined by it. In fact, Euro-sterling rates are basically determined by adding (or subtracting) the forward sterling discount (or premium) to (or from) Euro-dollar rates. In other words, the behaviour of the forward exchange rate affects the Euro-sterling rate more than the Euro-sterling rate affects the forward rate. As a result, the absence of a covered differential in this case does not necessarily mean that the forward rate has adjusted to the interest differential—but more likely means that the interest differential has adjusted to the forward rate. Undoubtedly, the transactions between the Euro-dollar and the Euro-sterling markets do have some impact on the forward rate; but it is certainly not decisive.

We must, therefore, turn to a comparison of the other two differentials in order to determine the differential to which the forward rate adjusts most closely. It is apparent from an examination of Charts 7 and 8 that there have been more covered differentials greater than $\pm\frac{1}{4}$ per cent between U.S. and U.K. treasury bills than there have been between Euro-dollar and U.K. local authority deposits. In addition, the variations in the U.S.–U.K. treasury bill differential have been larger than has been the case for the Euro-dollar–U.K. local authority differential. Finally, the speed with which the covered differential returns to the proximity of zero has been greater in the case of the Euro-dollar–U.K. local authority differential. This has resulted in significant differentials that are more persistent between U.S. and U.K. treasury bills than between Euro-dollar and U.K. local authority deposits. It seems reasonable to conclude then that during most of the period the forward exchange rate has adjusted more closely to the Euro-dollar–U.K. local authority differential than to the U.S.–U.K. treasury bill differential. As a result, there is a greater possibility of a persistent covered differential arising between U.S. and

U.K. treasury bills. This is what we concluded in the previous section.

This would also indicate that there has been a substantial diversion of arbitrage flows from treasury bill arbitrage to the Euro-dollar channel and that arbitrage between Euro-dollar deposits and U.K. local authority deposits has now become the primary means of conducting covered arbitrage operations into or out of the U.K. In order to examine this more closely we will attempt to compare the volume of funds that have moved into or out of the U.K. during the period through each of these channels. As a measure of the volume of flows into or out of U.K. treasury bills we will use the quarterly changes in non-official foreign holdings of U.K. treasury bills; while as a measure of the volume of flows into or out of the U.K. via the Euro-dollar market we will use the quarterly changes in the net external liabilities of U.K. banks in foreign currencies.[1] An increase in either of these will represent an inflow to the U.K.; and a decrease an outflow. These data, for the period 1962–7 are presented in Table 6 and plotted on Charts 7 and 8 respectively.

From Table 6 it can be seen that the flows of short-term capital into or out of the U.K. via the Euro-dollar market have been much larger than those into or out of U.K. treasury bills during the period under review. In addition, from Charts 7 and 8 it can be seen that the inflows and outflows via the Euro-dollar market have corresponded much more closely to changes in the covered differential between Euro-dollar deposits and U.K. local authority deposits than those into or out of treasury bills have with changes in the U.S.–U.K. treasury bill differential—especially during the years 1965–7. The Euro-dollar–U.K. local authority covered differential was in favour of Euro-dollar deposits from the second quarter of 1965 to the end of 1966 and during this period there was a continual outflow from the U.K. to the Euro-dollar market; while during the first half of 1967 when the differential turned in favour of the U.K. there was a significant inflow. This was then followed

---

[1] The net external liabilities of U.K. banks in all foreign currencies were used instead of only those denominated in U.S. dollars because the net external liabilities in U.S. dollars would have overstated the conversions into or out of sterling due to conversions between Euro-dollars and other Euro-currencies.

TABLE 6

Changes in Non-Official Foreign Holdings of U.K. Treasury Bills and
Changes in the Net External Liabilities of U.K. Banks in
Foreign Currencies, 1962–7

Quarter Ending	Non-Official Foreign Holdings of U.K. Treasury Bills		Net External Liabilities of U.K. Banks in Foreign Currencies	
	Total	Change from Previous Quarter Inflow (+) or Outflow (−)	Total	Change from Previous Quarter Inflow (+) or Outflow (−)
		Millions of Pounds		
1963				
March	66	−20	45	+ 17
June	58	− 8	24	− 21
September	60	+ 2	13	− 11
December	58	− 2	11	− 2
1964				
March	50	− 8	46	+ 35
June	44	− 6	101	+ 55
September	56	+12	137	+ 36
December	30	−26	149	+ 12
1965				
March	32	+ 2	305	+156
June	15	−17	209	− 96
September	16	+ 1	155	− 54
December	18	+ 2	128	− 27
1966				
March	26	+ 8	75	− 53
June	22	− 4	9	− 66
September	20	− 2	16	+ 7
December	14	− 6	(34)	− 50
1967				
March	13	− 1	106	+124
June	26	+13	84	− 22
September	37	+11	54	− 30
December	29	− 8	8	− 46

Source: Bank of England, Quarterly Bulletin (London, Bank of England, Quarterly)

by an outflow when the differential swung in favour of Euro-
dollars during the latter part of 1967. The covered differential
between U.S. and U.K. treasury bills, on the other hand, when

it was in favour of the U.S. during the first and third quarter
of 1965 gave rise to a very small inflow to the U.K.; and when
it was in favour of the U.K. during the second quarter of 1965
and the last three quarters of 1966 resulted in a small outflow
from the U.K. During 1967 this situation was again evident
when a significant inflow occurred as the differential in favour
of the U.K. declined to a more modest level. In other words,
the flows into or out of U.K. treasury bills were often not only
very small but actually moved in a direction opposite to that
favoured by the U.S.–U.K. treasury bill differential.

It is apparent then that during the 1965–7 period there was
only a small movement of arbitrage funds into or out of the
U.K. in response to changes in the covered differential between
U.S. and U.K. treasury bills and that the majority of arbitrage
flows took place via the Euro-dollar market in response to
changes in the Euro-dollar–U.K. local authority differential.
This seems to confirm our conclusions that the Euro-dollar
market has added another independent interest-parity and has
caused a diversion of arbitrage flows from other channels.
Although it is impossible to determine from these figures
whether or not the Euro-dollar market has also increased the
total volume of arbitrage flows into or out of the U.K., it
certainly seems possible that the large flows that have occurred
via the Euro-dollar market may not have taken place if the
only channel available for arbitrage had been that between
U.S. and U.K. treasury bills.

7

THE IMPACT ON DOMESTIC CREDIT CREATION

In the preceding chapter we have seen that the Euro-dollar market, by providing another channel through which covered arbitrage, hedging, and speculative activities can take place, has facilitated the international movement of short-term capital. As a result, the volume of short-term funds flowing into or out of a particular country is likely to be greater than it otherwise would have been due to the existence of the Euro-dollar market. We have also seen evidence that covered arbitrage flows into or out of a country have been diverted from the traditional channels and now tend to take place through the Euro-dollar channel. Finally, in addition to the actual increase in the volume of short-term capital flows associated with Euro-dollar activities there could at times be a further potential increase because of the complications created by the market with regard to defining a unique interest-parity equilibrium in the forward exchange market. These actual and potential impacts on short-term capital flows undoubtedly carry with them important implications for domestic credit creation in the countries involved in the Euro-dollar market. It is these implications that we wish to explore in this chapter.

First, we will analyze, the impact of international capital flows in general on domestic credit creation in a typical national economy. On the basis of this analysis we will then determine the effect of the Euro-dollar market on domestic credit creation in a country other than the United States. In particular we will attempt to determine whether or not there is a difference between the impact of flows involving Euro-dollars and the impact of flows moving into or out of a country through more traditional channels. Finally, we will look at the impact of capital movements between the U.S. and the Euro-dollar market on domestic credit creation in the U.S.

Since Euro-dollars merely flow through intermediary countries without changing in form or amount, the only countries in which the domestic credit system will be affected directly by a typical Euro-dollar transaction are the United States and the countries whose currencies are converted into Euro-dollars or into whose currencies Euro-dollars are converted. There may, however, be an indirect effect on domestic credit conditions in an intermediary country due to the fact that domestic foreign investors and traders may be able to obtain their foreign currency requirements by borrowing in the Euro-dollar market rather than by borrowing domestic currency and then converting it into foreign currency. In the analysis that follows though we are only concerned with the case in which there is an exchange between Euro-dollar deposits and domestic currency deposits of the country involved.

Domestic Credit Creation and International Capital Flows

Capital inflows and outflows result in an exchange of one currency for another—with an inflow resulting in a conversion of foreign currency into domestic currency and an outflow resulting in the exchange of domestic currency for foreign currency. As a result, an inflow creates a supply of foreign currency while an outflow creates a demand for foreign currency. Normally, the total supply of foreign currency (resulting from capital flows and trade transactions) is married off by the commercial banks of a country on a daily basis against the total demand for foreign currency. If this cannot be done an excess supply or demand arises—which, in turn, causes the spot exchange rate to appreciate or depreciate. Under a fixed exchange rate system, however, the exchange rate can only be allowed to vary within relatively narrow limits. Therefore, if the spot rate approaches its upper (or lower) limit, the foreign exchange authorities (usually operating through the central bank) must absorb (or supply) the excess supply of (or demand for) foreign exchange.

If supply and demand in the foreign exchange market are equated without official intervention there is no change in the level of domestic bank deposits—since any increase resulting from a sale of foreign currency is exactly off-set by a decrease resulting from a purchase of foreign currency. Therefore, international capital flows can have an impact on domestic credit creation only in the case involving official intervention in the spot exchange market. The need for the foreign exchange authorities to intervene only arises, as we have seen, under a fixed exchange rate system and then only if the exchange rate is at or near one of its support points. These support points, however, need not be the upper or lower limit established for a currency under the International Monetary Fund agreements. In practice, the authorities usually support the domestic currency within a narrower range than that legally required. As a result, the authorities can be absorbing or supplying foreign exchange even though the exchange rate is not at, or even very near, its absolute upper or lower limit.

In order to simplify the analysis that follows we will assume that trade transactions cancel out and that any excess supply of or demand for foreign exchange is due entirely to capital inflows or outflows. In addition, we will deal only with the case of an inflow—although, of course, the same analysis[1] could be applied to the case of an outflow. Finally, the analysis in the first two sections of this chapter will be based, for the sake of convenience and familiarity, on the institutions and practices of the U.K. credit system. However, the analysis, with minor changes, could just as readily be applied to any other final-user country possessing a relatively well-developed credit system.

A surplus of foreign exchange arising from a capital inflow must be purchased by the foreign exchange authorities (the Exchange Equalization Account in the U.K.) if they want to prevent the exchange rate from appreciating beyond a desired level. Normally, this is done by the central bank making a payment in domestic currency to the owner of the foreign exchange (either the original owner or a domestic bank which has purchased the foreign exchange from the original owner).

---

[1] The analysis used in this section is basically similar to that employed in Bank of England, 'Inflows and Outflows of Foreign Funds,' *Quarterly Bulletin*, II (1962), 93–102.

As a result of this transaction there would be an increase in the deposit liabilities and cash reserves of the commercial banks equal to the amount of domestic currency paid out by the central bank in absorbing the excess supply of foreign currency. The commercial banks, in accordance with the maintenance of a fixed cash-reserve ratio, would retain only a fraction of this increase in cash reserves and would employ the surplus cash when it first arose in call money and treasury bills. The net result then of a sale of foreign currency to the foreign exchange authorities is an addition of exactly the same amount to the total liquid assets of the commercial banks. In addition, since most of this increase is in the form of call money and treasury bills, the increase in the total of treasury bills held by the banks and discount market taken together would be nearly as large as the increase in deposits.

The immediate reaction of the banks to the higher liquid-assets ratio (resulting from equal increases in both deposits and liquid assets) would be to buy more investments or make more advances to their customers. This secondary effect would, if nothing else interfered, result in a multiple expansion of domestic bank deposits. The possibility of this occurring, however, is diminished by the fact that the authorities must borrow (usually on the same day) the full amount of the payment made by the foreign exchange authorities. The final impact of a short-term capital inflow on domestic credit creation, therefore, very much depends on how the authorities finance additions to the foreign exchange reserves. In any event there must be an increase in government debt (usually in the form of treasury bills) roughly equal to the domestic currency equivalent of the capital inflow.

The critical factor in determining the impact of a capital inflow on the domestic credit system then is to determine who holds this additional government debt and, hence, finances the additions to foreign exchange reserves. The first possibility would be for the authorities to borrow the whole amount of the inflow (at current interest rates) from the foreign owner of the newly created domestic currency balance. In this case domestic bank deposits and liquid assets would both fall again by the amount of the inflow. As a result, the inflow would be self-financing and there would be no direct effect on domestic credit creation. This would be the case when arbitrage funds are invested directly by the original owner in treasury bills. There are, however, two other basic possibilities: (1) the foreign owner could invest his domestic currency balance himself by purchasing securities other than treasury bills (either government or non-government) from a resident of the country concerned; or (2) the foreign owner could leave his domestic currency on deposit with a domestic bank and let the bank make the investment. We will now analyze each of these in turn.

If the foreign owner invests his domestic currency himself by transferring his deposit to a domestic deposit holder in exchange for a security (other than a treasury bill) there is no further change in the total of domestic bank deposits. There is merely a decrease in foreign-owned deposits and an equal increase in domestically-owned deposits—with the banks still holding their increased quantity of liquid-assets. However, this transaction by affecting relative returns on various securities, could result in a shift in the preferences of domestic investors for various types of securities. These shifts in preferences would undoubtedly be very complicated and difficult to trace—but the important consideration is whether, and to what extent, there is a shift in domestic preferences towards a larger holding of government debt (especially treasury bills). If there is a shift in this direction the inflow would be financed by borrowing from domestic investors—whose bank deposits would fall as they bought government debt. This would also produce a corresponding fall in the liquid assets of the commercial banks —either through selling treasury bills to the public or through a loss of cash reserves (if the public purchased securities directly from the authorities). If there is no shift in favour of government securities, the authorities would have to finance the inflow by borrowing (probably on treasury bills) from the commercial banks. In this case, the equal increases in deposit liabilities and liquid assets caused by the inflow would remain with the banks —thereby enabling them to undertake a secondary multiple expansion of credit.

If, on the other hand, the foreign owner leaves his domestic funds on deposit with a domestic bank, the bank can employ them in two ways: (1) by shifting out of call money and treasury bills (in which they had placed their funds immediately after the inflow) into long-term government securities; or (2) by lending more to other sectors of the domestic economy—namely the private and local government sectors. These transactions again may or may not lead to a shift in preferences on the part of domestic investors for one security against another with the same results as those presented above. Again the crucial factor is the extent of the shift by domestic investors into government securities. If the shift is not as great as the domestic currency equivalent of the original inflow, the deposit liabilities and liquid assets of the commercial banks will both be larger than before the inflow took place and a secondary expansion of credit could occur.

It is apparent then that the major factor determining the impact of international capital flows on domestic credit creation is the degree to which the non-bank public will absorb (or give up) government debt (especially treasury bills) in response to changes in relative rates of return on various securities. Essentially, a short-term capital inflow increases the supply of liquid assets (mainly treasury bills) available to the commercial banks and the public. Whether or not the increase in available liquid assets will result in credit creation depends on the extent to which the public will absorb this increased supply of treasury bills. Credit creation will always occur to some extent unless the public absorbs the total increase in liquid assets.

The extent to which the non-bank public will absorb the additional supply of government securities (usually in the form of treasury bills) basically depends upon three elasticities: (1) the elasticity of demand for government securities (especially treasury bills) on the part of the non-bank public; (2) the elasticity of demand for non-government securities on the part of the non-bank public; and (3) the elasticity of supply of non-government securities. The supply of government securities does not enter into the analysis because normally it is not a function of the interest rate but is instead determined by policy considerations. In fact, in this case, the additional supply of treasury bills is determined automatically by the increase in foreign exchange reserves that must be financed by the foreign exchange authorities as a result of the capital inflow.

When the domestic currency proceeds of a capital inflow are invested—either by the original-owner or by a domestic bank—

in securities other than treasury bills (i.e. in long-term government securities or non-government securities) the interest rate on the particular securities purchased will fall relative to those on treasury bills and other government and non-government securities. In addition, the attempt by the authorities to issue additional treasury bills will cause rates on treasury bills to rise even further relative to the rates paid on the securities in which the inflow proceeds were invested. As a result, domestic investors whose funds have been displaced by the investment of the capital inflow proceeds will tend to shift into other securities which now offer a relatively higher yield than those in which they were originally invested.[1]

Whether or not they shift their funds into government or non-government securities depends on the two demand elasticities outlined above. If the domestic investors involved have a high elasticity of demand for government securities, they will shift a substantial proportion of their funds into government debt. In fact, they would probably shift into treasury bills since these rates have been pushed up relative to other rates by the increased supply of treasury bills issued to finance the inflow. However, if they have a low elasticity of demand for government securities and a high elasticity of demand for non-government securities the shift will be into larger holdings of non-government securities.

This latter possibility, however, depends to a great extent on the elasticity of supply of non-government securities. If it is low, the attempt to purchase more non-government securities will simply push interest rates on these securities down and remove the incentive for shifting funds into them. On the other hand, if it is high, the increased supply of non-government securities (resulting from any decline in interest rates arising from attempts to shift funds into these securities) will tend to maintain relatively high interest rates on non-government securities and the incentive for shifting funds to these securities.

The size of these elasticities is basically determined by the degree to which the markets for securities are developed in the particular country concerned. If the markets are highly

---

[1] The analysis that follows uses the stock-adjustment approach in explaining the process by which equilibrium is achieved in the domestic capital markets.

developed for all types of securities, all of the elasticities are likely to be high. In this case (assuming a given interest rate policy) the extent to which the non-bank public takes up the additional supply of government debt resulting from the inflow depends on the relative size of their demand elasticities for government and non-government securities. If the elasticity of demand for government securities is higher than that for non-government securities, the non-bank public will take up a substantial portion of the additional supply of government debt. In this case the impact of capital inflows on domestic credit creation would be small. However, if the relative sizes of the elasticities were reversed, the non-bank public would not absorb as much of the increased supply of government debt and the impact on domestic credit creation would be greater. This would be the case of a country with poorly developed markets for government securities. In this situation the authorities would be forced to finance changes in the foreign exchange reserves through substantial borrowing from the commercial banks.

In addition, there is a time lag involved in the possibilities depending on a shift in preferences. First, there is a lag before the adjustment in relative interest rates occurs; then there is a lag before the non-bank public reacts to these changes in relative rates. Even in a country with highly developed securities markets these lags could be significant. As a result, there is always (with the exception of flows being invested directly in treasury bills by the original owners) at least a temporary increase in domestic bank liquidity and, hence, a temporary impact on domestic credit creation. Again these lags depend to a great extent on the degree to which securities markets are developed. They also depend, however, on the type of domestic investor affected by the original investment of the capital inflow proceeds. If funds are displaced from high-yielding securities that have some degree of risk attached to them, the investor generally will attempt to re-invest his funds in similar high-yielding securities—which are usually non-government securities. This will make the size of the eventual shift into government securities dependent upon the elasticities of investors further along the chain of shifts and, thereby, serve to delay the eventual shift into government securities.

The Impact of the Euro-dollar Market on Domestic Credit Creation in a Country Other Than the United States

As we have seen in the previous chapter the Euro-dollar market—by providing another channel through which short-term capital can move internationally—has tended to increase the volume of short-term capital movements into or out of a particular country and to divert arbitrage flows from other channels. These capital flows involving Euro-dollars are similar to any other short-term capital flows and, therefore, have much the same impact on domestic credit creation in a country other than the U.S. as that outlined in the above analysis. In one sense then the Euro-dollar market has merely increased the impact of international capital flows on domestic credit creation in any particular country by increasing the volume of these flows.

This has resulted from the fact that the increased volume of capital flows has forced the foreign exchange authorities of the country concerned to finance larger accumulations (or de-cumulations) of foreign exchange reserves. This, in turn, increases the volume of government debt that must be absorbed (or given up) by the non-bank public in order to neutralize the impact of these flows on domestic credit creation. As a result, it has increased the likelihood that a portion of the flows will not be off-set by increased (or decreased) holdings of government securities on the part of the non-bank public. Whether or not this actually occurs depends primarily on the elasticities discussed in the above analysis.

In addition, however, in order to determine the impact of the diversion of flows from other channels, we must also look more specifically at the type of domestic securities involved in the short-term capital flows emanating from (or destined for) the Euro-dollar market and attempt to determine whether this makes the impact of these flows any greater or less than the impact of ordinary short-term capital flows between countries —especially the traditional type of flow involving covered arbitrage between treasury bills. To do this we will examine, in detail, the effect of an inflow involving Euro-dollars on credit creation in the U.K. and compare this with the impact of an inflow involving covered treasury bill arbitrage.

Almost all Euro-dollar funds flow into the U.K. through the overseas and foreign banks and accepting houses in London. The clearing banks, although they operate through subsidiaries, do not, as a rule, participate directly in Euro-dollar transactions. The overseas and foreign banks and accepting houses are not governed by the rates paid on deposits by the clearing banks and, therefore, are able to pay higher rates on foreign-owned deposits (whether denominated in sterling or in foreign currencies). In addition, they do not follow the conventional 30 per cent minimum liquidity ratio used by the clearing banks —although, of course, they do maintain a relatively high degree of liquidity. This latter difference enables them to expand credit by a larger amount than the clearing banks could for any given increase in liquid assets or cash reserves.

The transactions leading to an inflow from the Euro-dollar market begin then with the deposit by the original-owner or a foreign bank (acting as an intermediary) of funds denominated in U.S. dollars with an overseas or foreign bank or accepting house in London. In order to attract this deposit the London bank would, normally, have to pay a relatively high rate of interest. It now has the choice of investing the U.S. funds abroad or of converting them into sterling and investing the proceeds in the U.K. A distinguishing characteristic of capital inflows emanating from the Euro-dollar market is that they nearly always take place via the conversion of Euro-dollars into domestic currency by domestic commercial banks. Euro-dollars are very seldom converted and invested directly by the original-owners. As a result, virtually all switching from Euro-dollars into sterling is covered by a forward exchange transaction. Therefore, since any conversion into sterling would have to allow for the cost of forward cover in addition to the high rate of interest paid on the deposit, there is unlikely to be scope for interest arbitrage unless the sterling proceeds are employed in a relatively high-yielding security—such as loans to local authorities or to finance houses.

If an overseas or foreign bank or accepting house did convert Euro-dollars into sterling there would be an initial increase in both their liquid assets and deposit liabilities equal to the amount of the inflow and, hence, an increase in their liquid-assets ratio. As we have just seen, they must employ this additional liquidity in ways that offer a good return—normally by increasing their loans to local authorities, finance houses, and other domestic customers (usually in the form of bank loans). These transactions will increase the total of domestic deposits. However, since most domestic deposits are held at the clearing banks, some of the additional liquidity will now be transferred to these banks—which, because they work to conventional liquidity ratios, will react by increasing their domestic lending. Potentially then the inflow could lead to a multiple expansion of bank deposits.

The extent to which this occurs, however, depends on how much of the newly acquired liquid assets the banks lose along the way through shifts of domestic investors into government debt—particularly into treasury bills. If the overseas and foreign banks and accepting houses employ the proceeds from their Euro-dollar conversions in loans to local authorities (as seems likely from the relatively small variations in the covered differential between Euro-dollar and local authority interest rates found in the previous chapter), the local authorities would usually react by borrowing less from other sources—primarily from domestic investors. They would react in this way because local authority spending and borrowing requirements are primarily determined by long-term policy considerations and not by the availability and cost of money. Interest rates on loans to local authorities then would fall relative to rates on other comparable securities. As a result, domestic (and foreign) investors would tend to shift their funds to other securities offering a higher yield.

In shifting out of local authority loans investors would basically have two choices: (1) to shift into treasury bills and government bonds; or (2) to shift into loans to finance houses, into deposits or shares in building societies, or into equities. In general it is unlikely that the funds withdrawn from the high yield local authority loans will be invested in securities offering a very much lower return—with the actual choice depending very much on market circumstances at the time. As a result, they are unlikely to be invested in treasury bills and government securities unless the rates of interest on these securities are relatively high. If funds are diverted into government debt they will, of course, finance the inflow for the foreign exchange authorities—in which case there would be no impact on domestic credit creation. However, if funds are diverted anywhere else the inflow will have to be financed by borrowing from the banks—thereby leaving the banks free to carry out a multiple expansion of credit.

Although it is apparent from the above analysis that their impact is basically the same, it does seem that short-term capital inflows emanating from the Euro-dollar market could have potentially more impact on domestic credit creation in the final-user country than capital flows involving treasury bill arbitrage. This results from the fact that Euro-dollar inflows are almost always invested in non-government securities—such as local authority loans—by a domestic bank; while a great deal of treasury bill arbitrage involves direct investment in treasury bills on the part of the original-owners. The direct placement of funds by the original-owners in treasury bills makes the inflow self-financing—with the original-owners taking up the additional supply of treasury bills offered by the foreign exchange authorities. As a result, no change in relative interest rates and no shift in the preferences of domestic investors are necessary to off-set the impact of the capital inflow.

In the case of Euro-dollar inflows, however, the investment decision is made by the domestic banks and the inflow proceeds are usually invested in non-government securities. This then throws the whole weight of reducing the impact of the inflow onto the shift in preferences of domestic investors. Since reliance on a shift in preferences is unlikely to be as effective as direct investment in treasury bills by the original-owner in off-setting the impact of a capital inflow, it is probable that a capital inflow emanating from the Euro-dollar market would have a greater impact on domestic credit creation than an inflow of the same size involving treasury bill arbitrage.

In addition, there is likely to be a substantial time lag involved in the shift of preferences in the case of a Euro-dollar inflow because of the high-yield nature of the securities sought by the banks for their Euro-dollar proceeds. The domestic investors whose funds are displaced by the Euro-dollar proceeds would probably have a relatively low elasticity of demand for treasury bills and, therefore, would seek out other high-yield securities in the private or local government sectors of the economy rather than government securities. Consequently, there could be a long chain of shifts in the case of a Euro-dollar inflow before there was any shift towards a greater holding of treasury bills on the part of the non-bank public and, hence, a considerable time lag involved in the adjustment process.

Finally, the shift into government securities on the part of domestic non-bank investors is not likely to be as great in other countries as it is in the U.K. This results from two things: (1) the fact that markets for securities (especially government securities) in these countries are not as highly developed as in the U.K.; and (2) the fact that Euro-dollars are used in these countries mainly for commercial credit purposes rather than for investment in local authority securities as in the U.K. As in the case of all capital flows the degree to which relative interest rates change and the extent to which these changes have an impact on domestic investors' preferences depends very much on the depth and efficiency of the markets involved. In particular, if the markets for government securities are underdeveloped domestic investors will probably have a low elasticity of demand for government securities and, as a result, are unlikely to shift towards additional holdings of government debt.

This tendency is further enhanced in the case of Euro-dollar inflows by the fact that Euro-dollar proceeds in these countries are often used by the domestic banks to extend commercial credit to the private sector of the economy. Very often this is an addition to the available supply of commercial credit in these countries which does not (at least directly) replace other funds previously used for commercial credit purposes. In these circumstances there is unlikely to be a shift (or at least as great a shift) in the preferences of domestic investors towards larger holdings of government securities. In the U.K. case, on the other hand, there is likely to be a significant shift of domestic funds out of local authority securities because of the relatively low elasticity of supply of these securities.

It is apparent then that short-term capital flows involving the Euro-dollar market could, in the same way as other capital flows, have a substantial impact on domestic credit creation in a country other than the U.S. This impact is made primarily through the effect of these flows on the supply of liquid assets available in the country concerned. If the increase (or decrease) in the supply of liquid assets is absorbed (or released) mainly by the non-bank public there would be very little impact on the domestic credit system; however, if it is absorbed (or released) by the domestic commercial banks the impact would be substantial. Therefore, to the extent that it has increased the volume of short-term flows into or out of a country, the Euro-dollar market has tended to increase the impact of international capital flows on domestic credit creation.

In addition, it is probable that Euro-dollar flows have a greater impact than short-term flows involving treasury bill arbitrage because the required investment (or disinvestment) in government securities, necessary to off-set the impact of a flow, is entirely dependent on the shift in preferences on the part of domestic investors towards a larger (or smaller) holding of government debt. As in the case of any shift in preferences, this shift is unlikely to be very uniform or complete—especially in countries with poorly developed securities markets. As a result, the Euro-dollar market could also have a significant impact on domestic credit creation due to the fact that it has diverted short-term flows away from treasury bill arbitrage and into arbitrage between Euro-dollar deposits and domestic securities.

The Impact of the Euro-dollar Market on Domestic Credit Creation in the United States

We must now look at the impact on the U.S. credit system of short-term capital flows between the Euro-dollar market and the United States. These flows are different from those between the Euro-dollar market and other countries because they do not involve an exchange of currencies. The funds are denominated in U.S. dollars both before and after the flow has taken place. As far as the U.S. credit system is concerned they are simply inflows and outflows of already existing bank deposits involving neither creation nor destruction of credit.

In the case of an outflow a foreign or U.S. owner of a U.S.

10

dollar deposit held at a U.S. bank simply transfers his deposit to a commercial bank outside the U.S. (either a foreign bank or a foreign branch of a U.S. bank). This means that ownership of the dollar deposit has been transferred from the original owner to the bank outside the U.S. Although the bank outside the U.S. may hold this deposit at a different U.S. bank from that at which the previous owner held it, the deposit itself still remains as part of the U.S. credit system (as do all U.S. dollar deposits). This transaction then does not change the total volume of deposits or cash reserves of the U.S. banking system but merely re-allocates them among the various U.S. commercial banks—decreasing the deposit liabilities and cash reserves of some and increasing them for others. A similar series of events occur when there is an inflow from the Euro-dollar market. In this case a foreign bank or a foreign branch of a U.S. bank transfers ownership of a deposit to a U.S. bank —which, of course, may be different from that at which the bank outside the U.S. held the deposit. Again there could be a re-allocation of deposits and cash reserves among the U.S. commercial banks.

From the point of view of the U.S. credit system then the Euro-dollar market has much the same impact as the Federal Funds market within the U.S. This market has the principal function of re-distributing cash reserves from those banks which have an excess to those which have a deficiency of reserves— thereby making fullest use of the cash reserves available to the U.S. commercial banks. As we have seen, the Euro-dollar market could also cause a re-allocation of reserves in a similar manner. This re-allocation of reserves could result in credit creation if the banks losing deposits and reserves already had excess cash reserves and the banks receiving them could use additional reserves to advantage.

In addition, however, there may be a shift between time and demand deposits within the U.S. banking system associated with flows between the Euro-dollar market and the U.S. If a foreign or U.S. owner, who previously held a time deposit at a U.S. bank, transfers the ownership of his deposit to a bank outside the U.S. the deposit at the U.S. bank (now owned by the foreign bank) becomes a demand deposit. The opposite could occur if a Euro-dollar deposit is transferred back to a

U.S. bank and placed as a time deposit. Because of the different cash reserve requirements attached to time and demand deposits by the U.S. authorities, these transfers could result in a change in the cash reserve requirements of U.S. banks and, hence, in their capacity to create credit. This effect is even more pronounced in the case of a flow of Euro-dollar funds into the U.S. through the foreign branches of U.S. banks. Due to the fact that there are no reserve requirements on deposits received by a U.S. bank from its own foreign branches, an inflow of this type could result in an increase in both deposits and cash reserves of the bank concerned; while leaving cash reserve requirements unchanged. Flows between the Euro-dollar market and the U.S., therefore, could also have an impact on domestic credit creation in the U.S. by altering the reserve requirements of U.S. banks.

8

THE CONSEQUENCES FOR
NATIONAL MONETARY POLICY

WE have seen in the last chapter that short-term capital flows between the Euro-dollar market and a country other than the U.S. could, if their effect was not off-set by counter-measures taken by the monetary authorities, have a substantial impact on domestic credit creation. In this chapter we want to look at the extent to which the monetary authorities can use monetary policy to off-set such effects and, in general, at the extent to which monetary policy can be used for internal stabilization purposes in an open economy. In this discussion we will deal only with the case of a country operating under a fixed exchange rate system.

In the first section of this chapter we will examine the effectiveness of monetary policy as an internal stabilization weapon in a country operating with fixed exchange rates under various assumptions regarding the international mobility of capital. In the light of this analysis we will then determine the impact of the Euro-dollar market on the effectiveness of monetary policy in a country other than the U.S. In the final section we will examine a number of alternative methods of making monetary policy effective in an open economy—particularly after taking into consideration the existence of the Euro-dollar market.

The Effectiveness of Monetary Policy Under
Fixed Exchange Rates

In examining the effectiveness of monetary policy in an open economy operating under fixed exchange rates let us begin with a simplified model developed by Mundell.[1] In this model Mundell makes two basic assumptions: (1) that there is perfect international mobility of capital, and (2) that the country concerned is too small (e.g. has capital markets which are too small or poorly developed) to influence events in the rest of the world. The first assumption by meaning that all securities are perfect substitutes implies that existing exchange rates are expected to remain unchanged indefinitely and that spot and forward rates are identical. This eliminates any complications arising from speculation and the forward exchange market. The second assumption means that events in the country concerned (such as interest rate changes) will not have any impact on the rest of the world and, hence, will not result in any feed-back effects on the domestic economy from the rest of the world. In other words we are dealing with a partial equilibrium model.

Under these assumptions Mundell points out that any attempt to expand the money supply would lead to the following series of events:

A central bank purchase of securities creates excess reserves and puts downward pressure on the interest rate. But a fall in the interest rate is prevented by a capital outflow, and this worsens the balance of payments. To prevent the exchange rate from falling the central bank intervenes in the market, selling foreign currency and buying domestic money. The process continues until the accumulated foreign exchange deficit is equal to the open market purchase and the money supply is restored to its original level.[2]

Similarly, an attempted contraction of the money supply would result in upward pressure on the interest rate and a capital inflow. This would force the authorities to buy foreign currency and sell domestic money until the impact of the original money supply contraction was eliminated.

Under conditions of perfect international capital mobility then monetary policy in a small country would be completely ineffective as an internal stabilization weapon. If, on the other

[1] R. A. Mundell, 'Capital Mobility and Stabilization Policy under Fixed and Flexible Exchange Rates,' *Canadian Journal of Economics and Political Science*, XXIX (1963), 475-85.
[2] Ibid., p. 479.

hand, we assumed complete immobility of capital there would
be no capital flows in response to interest rate changes and,
consequently, no purchase or sale of foreign currency on behalf
of the foreign exchange authorities. Under these conditions
monetary policy would be as effective as it would have been if
the economy had been closed. It is apparent then that the
degree of international capital mobility is the crucial factor in
determining whether or not domestic monetary policy will be
effective in a country operating under fixed exchange rates. In
general, we can conclude that the higher the degree of international capital mobility the less effective monetary policy will
be as an internal stabilization weapon.

Now let us look more closely at Mundell's concept of capital
mobility. There are basically two factors involved in this
concept: (1) the freedom with which capital can move between
countries (i.e. the extent to which artificial barriers prevent the
free flow of capital between financial centres); and (2) the
elasticity of supply of arbitrage funds both in the country
concerned and the rest of the world.[1] These are the same
factors that we discussed at length in Chapter 5 of this study.
In the case of a capital outflow from the country concerned
(resulting from an attempt to expand the money supply) the
important factor is the elasticity of supply of arbitrage funds
in that country; while in the case of an inflow (resulting from
an attempted contraction of the money supply) it is the elasticity of supply of arbitrage funds in the rest of the world. In his
assumption of perfect capital mobility then Mundell was
assuming that there was a perfectly elastic supply of arbitrage
funds in both the country concerned and the rest of the world
and that there were no restrictions on the movement of capital
between financial centres. Therefore, according to Mundell's
analysis, monetary policy will be relatively ineffective in a
country operating under fixed exchange rates if capital is
allowed to move freely and if the elasticity of supply of arbitrage

[1] These two factors have been distinguished by Ira O. Scott Jnr. and Wilson
E. Schmidt, 'Imported Inflation and Monetary Policy', *Banca Nazionale del
Lavoro Quarterly Review*, XVII (1964), 390–403; and subsequently discussed
by Peter M. Oppenheimer, 'Imported Inflation and Monetary Policy: A
Comment', *Banca Nazionale del Lavoro Quarterly Review*, XVIII (1965), 191–7
and Ira O. Scott Jnr. and Wilson E. Schmidt, 'Imported Inflation and
Monetary Policy: A Reply', ibid., pp. 197–200.

funds is high in both the country concerned and the rest of the world.

If we now remove Mundell's simplifying assumption of perfect capital mobility and look at the more realistic case in which capital is less-than-perfectly mobile, we come up against the problem of integrating the forward exchange mechanism into our analysis. In this situation exchange rates are not expected to remain unchanged and, therefore, an exchange risk is involved in the international movement of short-term capital. If an arbitrager wants to be free of this exchange risk he must cover his arbitrage operations with a forward exchange trans-action in the opposite direction. This, of course, results in an additional cost to the arbitrager. As a result, the covered arbitrage flow will be cut-off when the cost of forward covering (i.e. the difference between the spot and forward exchange rates) equals the interest differential between the two markets involved. This occurs, as we have seen, when the forward exchange rate adjusts to its interest-parity value. When we are considering the less-than-perfect mobility case then the operation of the forward exchange mechanism serves to make monetary policy more effective for internal stabilization by cutting-off the covered arbitrage flows at the point where an interest-parity equilibrium is achieved in the forward exchange market.

We will now remove the assumption that the country con-cerned has capital markets so small that changes in the domestic interest rates have no impact on their counterparts in the rest of the world and examine the effectiveness of monetary policy in a country with large well developed capital markets.[1] The important characteristic of such a country is that it would have a highly elastic supply of arbitrage funds relative to the rest of the world. Therefore, if it attempted to implement an expansionary monetary policy a large outflow of capital would occur. The impact of this large outflow on interest rates in the rest of the world would depend on the ability of the rest of the world to absorb large arbitrage inflows—which, in turn, would

[1] This has been discussed by R. A. Mundell. 'A Reply: Capital Mobility and Size', *Canadian Journal of Economics and Political Science*, XXX (1964), 421–31, and by M. C. Kemp, 'Monetary and Fiscal Policy Under Alternative Assumptions about International Capital Mobility', *The Economic Record*, XLII (1966), 598–605.

depend on the elasticity of demand for arbitrage funds in the rest of the world.[1]

If the elasticity of demand in the rest of the world was low the flow could only be absorbed if there was a fall in interest rates in the rest of the world. This, in turn, would decrease the incentive for outflows from the country concerned and, therefore, make the expansionary monetary policy more effective. If, on the other hand, the elasticity of demand in the rest of the world was high, there would be very little change in interest rates in the rest of the world and the monetary policy measures taken in the country concerned would be relatively ineffective. Similarly, in the case of a contractionary monetary policy the size of the inflow would depend primarily on the elasticity of supply of arbitrage funds in the rest of the world. If it was relatively low the inflow would be small and the domestic monetary contraction could be relatively effective. The final result, however, would again depend on the elasticity of demand for arbitrage funds in the rest of the world. If it is also relatively low then the outflow of capital would result in a rise in interest rates in the rest of the world and this, in turn, would reduce the incentive for capital flows. As a result, monetary policy would probably be more effective in a country with large capital markets than in a country with small markets.

When we consider the general equilibrium case involving two countries then there are three basic factors determining the effectiveness of monetary policy in an open economy operating under fixed exchange rates: (1) the freedom with which capital can move internationally; (2) the elasticity of supply of arbitrage funds in both the country concerned and the rest of the world; and (3) the elasticity of demand for arbitrage funds in the rest of the world. It is the size of these elasticities that basically determines the extent to which the use of monetary policy as an internal stabilization weapon is constrained by international capital flows. If they are all perfectly elastic we would have Mundell's perfect mobility case without any feedback effect. In general, we can conclude that any factor that causes any of these elasticities to increase or which increases

---

[1] This elasticity has also been discussed more thoroughly in Chapter 5.

the freedom with which short-term capital can move internationally will tend to decrease the effectiveness of national monetary policy for internal stabilization purposes. In addition, any factor that either prevents the forward exchange rate from adjusting to interest-parity or reduces the speed with which it adjusts will also tend to make monetary policy less effective in the country concerned.

We will now consider the possibility that monetary policy could be made more effective by increasing the volume of open-market operations in the country concerned in order to off-set the monetary impact of the capital flows. This is attempted automatically in the U.K. system where the foreign exchange authorities must either buy or sell treasury bills in order to finance the changes in foreign exchange reserves resulting from the capital flows. We have seen in the preceding chapter that the success of such attempts depended on the willingness of the non-bank public to absorb or release government debt (especially treasury bills).

For example, if the monetary authorities of the country concerned attempted to impose a contractionary monetary policy and a capital inflow occurred, they would have to sell even more treasury bills in an attempt to off-set the neutralizing impact of the capital inflow. If they could sell the treasury bills to the non-bank public the expansionary impact of the capital inflow would be off-set by an equal reduction in the money supply as a result of the public purchasing additional treasury bills from the authorities. If, however, they had to sell them to the commercial banks the expansionary impact of the capital inflow would remain—thereby off-setting the impact of the initial contractionary monetary policy.

The degree to which this internal constraint restricts the use of monetary policy depends primarily on the factors determining the willingness of domestic non-bank investors to change their holdings of government debt (especially treasury bills) in response to changes in relative interest rates—namely their elasticity of demand for government securities, their elasticity of demand for non-government securities, and the elasticity of supply of non-government securities. If the elasticity of demand for government securities is higher than that for non-government securities, domestic investors whose funds were displaced by the capital inflow proceeds would increase their holdings of government debt and take up a substantial portion of the additional treasury bills offered by the monetary authorities. However, if the elasticity of demand for non-government securities is higher, domestic investors would not take up many of the additional treasury bills. This internal constraint then is likely to be of considerable importance in countries with poorly developed markets for government securities. In these countries then, the ability of the authorities to off-set the monetary impact of capital flows by means of additional open-market operations would be severely restricted.

The Euro-dollar Market and the Effectiveness of National Monetary Policy

As we have seen in Chapter 6, the main impact of the Euro-dollar market on the international financial system has been to increase the quantity of short-term funds that will move internationally in response to changes in relative interest rates between financial centres and to divert short-term capital flows from traditional channels to the Euro-dollar channel. This has resulted mainly from the risk-spreading techniques employed by the banks participating in the market and from the fact that the market operates outside national cartel arrangements and regulatory controls. The major effect of the increased supply of arbitrage funds in the present context is to increase the elasticity of supply of arbitrage funds both in the country concerned and in the rest of the world. At the very least, even if it does not increase the elasticities of supply, the existence of the Euro-dollar market will increase the range over which the supply elasticities are high. In either case, the effectiveness of national monetary policy for internal purposes would be reduced.

The existence of the Euro-dollar market could also increase the elasticity of demand for arbitrage funds in the rest of the world by increasing the ability of the rest of the world to absorb or release capital in response to small changes in relative interest rates. For example, if a large outflow from a country occurred it could be more readily absorbed because of the existence of the additional demand on the part of the Euro-dollar market. This, of course, would reduce the impact of domestic monetary measures on interest rates in the rest of the world. As a result, the feed-back effect on the domestic economy would be reduced and, along with it, the effectiveness of national monetary policy.

In addition, the Euro-dollar market has probably increased the freedom with which short-term arbitrage funds can move internationally. Since it is truly international in nature and, hence, can operate outside national exchange controls there are no artificial barriers to prevent short-term capital from flowing into or out of the market itself. As a result, capital flows could have fewer barriers to overcome in moving between the Euro-dollar market and a particular country than in moving between two countries. This impact would also tend to reduce the effectiveness of national monetary policy. It is apparent then that the Euro-dollar market has tended to increase all of the elasticities mentioned in the above analysis and the freedom with which short-term capital can move internationally. The effect of this has been to reduce the effectiveness and inde-pendence of national monetary policy by increasing the external constraint.

We have also seen (in the less-than-perfect mobility case) that the forward exchange mechanism tended to cut-off the flow of covered arbitrage funds when the forward rate adjusted to its interest-parity value—thereby, making national monetary policy more effective for internal purposes. Here again, the Euro-dollar market, by making it more difficult to determine a unique interest-parity to which the forward rate can adjust, has had a significant impact. Now, even if the forward rate does adjust to one of the possible interest-parities, the flow of arbitrage funds could continue (if arbitrage funds are still available) through the other channel. As a result, the import-ance of the forward exchange mechanism in cutting-off covered arbitrage flows has been reduced.

Now let us look at the impact of the Euro-dollar market on the ability of the monetary authorities to off-set the monetary impact of short-term capital inflows and outflows. In our analysis in the preceding chapter we found that the monetary effects of short-term capital flows involving Euro-dollars tended to be more difficult to off-set than those of capital flows involving treasury bill arbitrage. This resulted from the fact that the whole adjustment process was dependent on a shift in the preferences of domestic investors towards greater holdings of government debt; whereas in the treasury bill case a substantial amount of government debt was absorbed by foreign investors investing their funds directly in treasury bills. Therefore, to the extent that it has diverted arbitrage funds from treasury bill arbitrage to arbitrage involving Euro-dollars, the Euro-dollar market has tended to increase the internal constraint on the use of monetary policy as an internal stabilization weapon.

The Euro-dollar market then, by increasing the volume of arbitrage funds and the freedom with which they can move internationally, has increased the financial integration of the countries involved in the market. The impact of this increased financial integration has been made more powerful by the fact that the market has also diverted arbitrage funds to the Euro-dollar channel and, hence, made it more difficult for domestic monetary authorities to off-set the monetary impact of capital flows. This combination of effects has served to decrease the possibility of a country being able to follow an effective independent national monetary policy under a fixed exchange rate system. This means, therefore, that either monetary policy will become less important as an internal stabilization weapon and will be relegated to the role of external stabilizer; or that methods will have to be found to make monetary policy more effective in a world in which there is an increasing tendency towards financial integration under a system of fixed exchange rates. It is this latter approach that we will discuss in the next section.

Alternative Methods of Making National Monetary Policy Effective

There are basically two ways of increasing the effectiveness of monetary policy in a country operating under fixed exchange rates and conditions of high capital mobility: (1) by raising artificial barriers that restrict the freedom with which capital can move internationally; or (2) by changing the incentive for international capital flows either by means of non-market regulatory techniques or by official intervention in the forward exchange market. The first method is aimed primarily at reducing the overall volume of international capital flows and usually involves some form of exchange control—which if carried to the extreme by all countries would eliminate international capital flows completely. In addition to ordinary exchange control techniques such controls as the U.S. Voluntary Restraint programme could also be included in this category. The second method is not aimed primarily at reducing the total volume of international capital flows but more at influencing the direction and magnitude of capital flows from the point of view of a particular country. In other words, they are used mainly to divert or re-direct capital flows from one country to another without necessarily reducing the overall level of flows.

Since they are essentially administrative in nature the techniques involved in the first method will not be discussed in this study. In fact, the imposition of exchange controls is likely to be associated with a balance-of-payments crisis rather than with the problem of making monetary policy more effective—although, of course, this would be a side-effect. As a result, we will discuss only those techniques which are aimed at altering the incentives for the international flow of capital between countries. In particular, we will limit our discussion to those techniques involved in influencing short-term capital flows—with special reference to their impact on flows involving Euro-dollars.

As we have pointed out, the techniques used to influence the incentives for international short-term capital flows can be roughly broken down into market techniques and non-market administrative techniques. The latter techniques, which we will discuss first, usually involve selective discriminatory measures aimed at changing the yield that can be earned by moving short-term capital into or out of a particular country. For example, the authorities of the country concerned could adopt any of the following measures: (1) establish special interest rates to be paid on foreign-owned bank deposits or securities (or prohibit interest payments altogether); (2) establish special taxes to be applied in the case of foreign purchases or sales of domestic securities; (3) establish special reserve requirements for foreign-owned bank deposits; or (4) issue directives to limit the external positions of domestic banks. The first two methods would be aimed primarily at discouraging foreigners from moving funds either into or out of a country; while the last two would be designed to either discourage or encourage domestic banks in their attempts to obtain funds from abroad.

In practice, especially in West Germany and Switzerland,[1] these techniques have been used mainly to restrict short-term capital inflows—although it seems that they could be used just as readily to restrain outflows (as in the case of the U.S. Interest Equalization tax). Because they are administrative in nature and vary greatly from country to country these techniques are very similar to exchange controls. As a result, we will not discuss them in any detail in this study but instead will concentrate on the forward market techniques which are more amenable to economic analysis.

As we have already seen the direction and magnitude of short-term capital flows depends not only on the pure interest rate differential between financial markets but also on the cost of covering the exchange risk involved in an international transfer of short-term capital. Since the cost of covering is dependent on the behaviour of the forward exchange rate, it is possible to off-set part or all of the interest rate differential between financial centres by influencing the forward exchange rate. It seems probable then that official intervention in the forward exchange market could be a potent weapon in determining the magnitude and direction of international short-term capital flows from the point of view of a particular country. In practice, official intervention has taken two forms: (1) direct intervention in the forward market aimed at changing the overall volume of short-term capital flowing into or out of a particular country; and (2) indirect intervention by means of swap arrangements between the central and commercial banks of a country aimed at the narrower purpose of controlling the external positions of the commercial banks and thereby the

---

[1] For a discussion of the German and Swiss experience with these techniques see E. Brehmer and G. S. Dorrance, 'Controls on Capital Inflow: Recent Experience of Germany and Switzerland', *International Monetary Fund Staff Papers*, VIII (1961), 427–38.

magnitude of short-term flows taking place through commercial banking operations.[1]

Direct official intervention in the forward exchange market is designed to off-set part or all of the interest rate differential between two financial centres in order to discourage either short-term capital inflows or outflows. By influencing the covered interest rate differential these operations will determine the direction and magnitude of covered arbitrage movements and also whether speculative operations will be conducted through the spot or forward exchange markets. As a result, these operations may be conducted primarily either for balance-of-payments purposes—for example, to off-set the impact of speculative pressure on the forward exchange rate and, hence, prevent persistent capital inflows or outflows—or for the purpose of increasing the effectiveness and independence of national monetary policy. We are concerned only with the latter purpose in this chapter.

If, for example, a country attempted to impose a contractionary monetary policy by raising interest rates, the immediate impact would be to create a covered interest differential favouring the country concerned (assuming that the forward rate had been at its interest-parity before the change in monetary policy). This would give rise to a covered arbitrage inflow which, as we have seen, would tend to neutralize the impact of the contractionary monetary policy. The extent to which this happens, however, depends on how quickly the forward exchange rate adjusts to its new interest-parity value. If it adjusted quickly the capital inflow would be cut-off and monetary policy would become effective. On the other hand, if speculative pressures prevented it from adjusting the inflow would be sustained—thereby making monetary policy relatively ineffective.

To make the contractionary monetary policy more effective then the authorities of the country concerned could intervene in the forward exchange market in order to cause the forward rate to adjust to its interest-parity value as quickly as possible.

[1] For a discussion of the recent experience with both of these forms see Arthur I. Bloomfield, 'Official Intervention in the Forward Exchange Market: Some Recent Experiences' *Banca Nazionale del Lavoro Quarterly Review*, XVII (1964), 3–42.

By doing this the monetary authorities could maintain domestic interest rates that were higher than those prevailing abroad without inducing short-term capital inflows. In a similar manner they could also increase the effectiveness and independence of an expansionary monetary policy. The existence of the Euro-dollar market, however, by creating a set of independent international interest rates and, hence, making it more difficult to determine a unique interest-parity to which the forward rate can adjust, has made the use of this technique somewhat more complicated and unreliable. The authorities must now either decide which interest-parity they will adjust the forward rate to in order to have the greatest impact on the flows of capital into and out of the particular country concerned or find a forward rate that is sufficient to cover all margins.

Forward market intervention, however, can also take the form of swap arrangements at special forward rates between the central bank and the commercial banks of the country concerned. For example, let us consider the situation in a country where the implementation of a contractionary monetary policy is being frustrated by capital inflows. In this situation the central bank would sell foreign currency (usually U.S. dollars) to the commercial banks in exchange for domestic currency and agree to buy it back at a fixed rate sometime in the future. Under this swap agreement the commercial banks would agree to invest the foreign currency obtained from the central bank abroad—thereby causing a capital outflow which would off-set the initial inflow. These operations then would have the effect of neutralizing the monetary impact of the inflows attracted by the contractionary monetary policy. In addition, the central bank could make the terms of the swap arrangements sufficiently attractive to encourage the banks not to withdraw funds from abroad. As a result, swap arrangements could have the impact of both discouraging flows from taking place and of off-setting the effect of flows that do occur by inducing a flow in the opposite direction.

These swap arrangements have been used extensively as a monetary weapon by West Germany. In the West German case they were used mainly against a background of domestic inflationary pressures coupled with a large balance-of-payments surplus and disequilibrating speculation. In this situation the restrictive monetary policy needed for internal purposes was ineffective because it simply attracted short-term inflows—which, in turn, only added to the balance-of-payments surplus. In addition, the poorly developed German money market made it difficult for the monetary authorities to off-set the monetary impact of these flows by means of additional open-market operations. As a result, the German authorities turned to a programme of U.S. dollar swap arrangements with the commercial banks—thereby inducing a short-term outflow which reduced the balance-of-payments surplus and mopped up the excess liquidity in the German economy resulting from the inflows.

The problem with this technique—as the Germans discovered —was that it created two markets for forward exchange—the closed market involving only the central bank and the commercial banks and a free market in which all other transactions took place. As a result, funds that were induced to leave the country through operations in the closed market were often re-invested back in Germany by converting foreign currencies back into domestic currency on a covered basis through the free market. This, of course, resulted in a circular flow of funds from West Germany to a foreign financial centre and then back into West Germany again. This was particularly so in the early stages of the programme when many of the U.S. dollars obtained by the banks through swap arrangements found their way into the Euro-dollar market. The foreign banks receiving the swap dollars from the German banks had complete freedom to use these funds in any way that they desired. Therefore, if either the free market or speculative incentive was still sufficient to attract funds into Germany they often re-invested them in Germany. To overcome this (and to help the U.S.) the German authorities later required the commercial banks to invest swap dollars only in U.S. treasury bills—which were held by the banks until the swap arrangements matured.[1] More recently, the Germany authorities have used direct forward intervention along with these swap arrangements in order to remove the incentive for reflows through the free market.

[1] For complete details of the West German experience with this technique see E. Brehmer, 'Official Forward Exchange Operations: The German Experience', *International Monetary Fund Staff Papers*, XI (1964), 389–413.

It is apparent then that direct forward market intervention and swap arrangements could increase the effectiveness of national monetary policy. Swap arrangements, in particular, could be useful as a supplement to open-market operations in off-setting the monetary impact of an inflow of capital to a country with a poorly developed money market. They do this by encouraging the commercial banks not to repatriate funds from abroad—thereby, reducing the size of the inflow—and by inducing an outflow that off-sets the impact of the inflows that do occur. The induced outflow shifts the holding of foreign exchange reserves from the central bank to the commercial banks and, therefore, reduces the need to finance additions to the official foreign exchange reserves. As a result, this policy can be said to reduce both the external and internal constraints to the use of monetary policy.

The Euro-dollar market, however, has added complicating factors in the use of both direct and indirect forward intervention. In the case of direct intervention it has made it more difficult for the authorities to determine a unique interest-parity to which they can adjust the forward exchange rate. In the case of swap arrangements it has played a double role. First, it has been very useful in that it has supplied an outlet for the swap dollars at relatively high rates of return—thereby reducing the incentive needed to induce the commercial banks to enter into swap agreements and making it easier for the central banks to control the external positions of their commercial banks. Secondly, however, it has restricted the use of swap arrangements by making it very easy for funds to flow back into the country concerned—thereby creating a circular flow of funds. Despite these complications though, the increased international mobility of capital—partly due to the existence of the Euro-dollar market—will make official forward market intervention, and particularly swap arrangements, an increasingly important tool for domestic monetary management. This will be especially true in those countries with poorly developed money markets where the monetary impact of capital flows cannot be off-set by means of traditional monetary operations. The only alternative for these countries—if we exclude exchange controls—would be to increase the efficiency and depth of their domestic money markets, which is a slow long-term task.

9

THE EFFECTS ON EXCHANGE RATES, THE BALANCE-OF-PAYMENTS, AND INTERNATIONAL LIQUIDITY RESERVES

Up to this point in our study we have been discussing the impact of the Euro-dollar market on the internal sector of the national economies involved in the market. In particular we have analyzed the impact on the U.S. economy and on the economy of a country other than the U.S. In order to complete our analysis, however, we must now turn to examine the impact of the Euro-dollar system on the external sectors of these national economies and on the international financial system as a whole. In doing this we will first analyze the effects of the market on exchange rates and then its impact on the balance-of-payments—in the case of both the U.S. and countries other than the U.S. Finally, we will look at its impact on the volume of official international liquidity reserves available to these countries and to the world as a whole.

The Effects on Exchange Rates

In analyzing the effects of Euro-dollar transactions on exchange rates we must consider their impact on both spot and forward rates. The only time that spot rates are affected directly by a Euro-dollar transaction is when a domestic (or third) currency is converted into Euro-dollars or Euro-dollars are converted into a domestic (or third) currency. There would be no direct impact if Euro-dollars merely flow into and out of a country in the form of U.S. dollars. The conversion of Euro-dollars into other currencies puts downward pressure on the U.S. dollar spot rate and strengthens that of the other currency involved; while the conversion of other currencies into Euro-dollars has the opposite effect. Forward rates, in turn, are affected directly only if these conversions are done on a covered basis—with the forward rate for both currencies moving in the opposite direction to that of the spot rate.

It is apparent then that only a portion of the total volume of Euro-dollar transactions has any direct impact on exchange rates. As a result, the large volume of transactions involved in the withdrawal of U.S. dollar deposits from U.S. banks and the placement of these funds with non-U.S. banks and the borrowing and re-lending of Euro-dollars in the form of U.S. dollars does not concern the foreign exchange authorities of either the U.S. or other countries in any direct sense. The only transactions that are important in this respect then are those involving an exchange between Euro-dollars and a currency other than U.S. dollars. These transactions could take the form of either conversions into or out of a domestic currency in accordance with domestic financing needs or conversions into or out of a third currency for the purpose of financing international trade or investment. The impact of either of these types of transactions on the spot exchange rate (and forward rate, if the transaction is conducted on a covered basis) is the same as that of any other transaction involving a currency conversion.

In addition, as we have seen in Chapter 6, the existence of the Euro-dollar market could have an impact on both forward and spot exchange rates by providing another channel through which arbitragers, speculators, and hedgers can operate. This has had the effect of increasing the scope for covered arbitrage and of providing another method by which speculation and hedging can be conducted through the spot exchange market rather than the forward market. To the extent that this has occurred then the volume of conversions between U.S. dollars and other currencies has increased. In particular, the impact of speculative and hedging operations would have been shifted from the forward to the spot market—which would have the effect of increasing the pressure (either upward or downward) on the spot rate while decreasing it on the forward rate. As we have also seen, the possibility of this occurring has also been increased by the difficulties involved, after the introduction of the Euro-dollar market, in defining a unique interest-parity to which the forward exchange rate can adjust.

The existence of the Euro-dollar market, however, if looked at from another point of view, may also have had indirect effects on spot exchange rates. These have resulted from the fact that it has stimulated the holding of private U.S. dollar balances—thereby preventing the conversion of these balances into other currencies. The main effect of this on the U.S. spot rate has been to strengthen the U.S. dollar vis-à-vis other currencies by preventing the conversion of these dollar balances at the time they were accumulated by non-residents of the U.S. or sent abroad by residents of the U.S. In other words, it has made many private individuals and institutions more willing to hold their liquid funds in the form of U.S. dollars rather than in other currencies. However, these Euro-dollar balances, since they remain readily convertible into other currencies or gold still pose a threat to the U.S. spot rate and could be used to exert substantial speculative pressure if devaluation of the U.S. dollar was anticipated by speculators.

Other currency spot rates, on the other hand, could be weaker on balance vis-à-vis the U.S. dollar than they would have been without the Euro-dollar market because of the non-conversion of U.S. dollars into other currencies. The existence of a large volume of Euro-dollar deposits, however, is not a very great threat to the other currencies since, if they are converted, it would strengthen (rather than weaken) them vis-à-vis the U.S. dollar. This, of course, could be troublesome if an upward revaluation of a currency was anticipated by speculators. Finally, the Euro-dollar market has probably removed some of the pressure of trade transactions from spot rates by making it possible for foreign traders to conduct their activities by means of borrowing and lending Euro-dollars without recourse to the foreign exchange market. This has had the effect of reducing the number of conversions between U.S. dollars and other currencies.

On balance it is difficult to say whether the existence of the Euro-dollar market has increased or decreased the stability of the foreign exchange market. It is probable that stability has been increased during normal periods due to the larger volume of stabilizing capital flows associated with the existence of the market; while it has probably been decreased during abnormal times because of the larger volume of de-stabilizing movements

that could take place. As a result, it could make it easier for
the foreign exchange authorities of a country during normal
periods but could also increase their problems when a change
in exchange rates was anticipated by speculators.

The Impact on the Balance-of-Payments

The impact of the Euro-dollar market on the balance-of-
payments accounts of any particular country very much
depends on the method used by that country in calculating
its balance-of-payments deficit or surplus. Ideally, the balance-
of-payments should be broken down into two major parts:
(1) the net balance resulting from autonomous transactions;
and (2) the net balance of compensatory financing transactions.
These two balances must be equal but opposite in sign. In
practice, the problem arises, however, as to which transactions
should be considered autonomous (i.e. included 'above the
line'). Most countries include the net balance on trade in goods
and services, direct investment, non-commercial transfers, and
long-term capital movements above the line; and changes in
official gold and foreign exchange reserves (and, in some cases,
changes in the net IMF position) below the line.

The difficult item to allocate between the autonomous and
financing sections is the movement of short-term capital. Some
countries include both short-term inflows and outflows above
the line; while others include them below the line; and still
others include outflows above the line and inflows below the
line. It is these differences in the treatment of international
short-term capital flows that make it difficult to compare the
official balance-of-payments deficit (or surplus) of one country
with that of another country. As a result, the impact of Euro-
dollar flows on the balance-of-payments of any particular
country will have to be considered in the light of the particular
accounting method employed by that country with regard to
short-term capital movements.

Let us begin our analysis by considering the impact of the
Euro-dollar market on the U.S. balance-of-payments. If a U.S.
resident places a dollar deposit in the Euro-dollar market there
is an increase in the volume of private short-term assets held
abroad by U.S. residents; while if he withdraws a deposit from

the Euro-dollar market there is a decrease. These transactions, if the dollar deposit continued to be held at a U.S. bank by a private foreign owner, would also result in an increase (or decrease) in the volume of private short-term assets held in the U.S. by foreigners. In this situation then private short-term assets held abroad by U.S. residents and private short-term assets held in the U.S. by foreigners would increase by equal amounts. As a result there would be a short-term outflow from the U.S. off-set by an equivalent short-term inflow from abroad.

On the other hand, if a foreign owner of a dollar deposit placed his deposit in the Euro-dollar market there is merely a shift in ownership from one foreign owner to another and, hence, no impact on the volume of private short-term assets held in the U.S. by foreigners. Similarly, there would be no change if a foreign owner withdrew a dollar deposit from the Euro-dollar market and placed it with a U.S. bank. Consequently, there would be no short-term capital flow into or out of the U.S. associated with the movement of foreign-owned dollar deposits between the U.S. and the Euro-dollar market. Of course, if a foreign owner used his dollar deposit to make a payment to a U.S. resident there would be a fall in the private short-term assets held by foreigners in the U.S. and a capital flow into the U.S.

Now we want to examine how these transactions show up statistically in the 'official' measure of the U.S. balance-of-payments deficit or surplus. The measure most commonly used by the U.S. authorities—the liquidity balance—treats the movement of private short-term capital (including commercial bank funds) differently according to whether it is initiated by a resident or a non-resident of the U.S. Changes in private short-term assets held in the U.S. by non-residents are included below the line as compensatory financing items; whereas similar assets held abroad by U.S. residents are classified as autonomous items and included above the line. In other words, an increase (or decrease) in private short-term assets held by foreigners in the U.S. is not considered to be a capital inflow (or outflow) and, therefore, does not affect the size of the official U.S. balance-of-payments deficit or surplus; while an increase (or decrease) in private short-term assets held abroad by U.S. residents is counted as an outflow (or inflow) and does affect the deficit or surplus. In this measure of the U.S. balance-of-payments then private short-term capital movements are treated asymmetrically.

As a result, the placement of funds in the Euro-dollar market by a U.S. resident would worsen the 'official' U.S. balance-of-payments; while a withdrawal would improve it. This results from the fact that the increase (or decrease) in private short-term assets held abroad by U.S. residents would be included in the calculation of the deficit or surplus above the line; while the equal increase (or decrease) in private short-term assets held in the U.S. by foreigners would be included as a financing item below the line. This is the only way in which Euro-dollar transactions can affect the 'official' U.S. balance-of-payments deficit or surplus when calculated on the liquidity basis. On the other hand, if the U.S. surplus or deficit is calculated on an official settlements basis both of the above items would be included in the calculation above the line and the transaction would have no net impact on the surplus or deficit.

As we have seen, if a foreign owner withdraws a U.S. dollar deposit from a U.S. bank and places it in the Euro-dollar market there would be no impact on the U.S. balance-of-payments since these funds are already owned by non-residents before their withdrawal. Similarly, the placement of these funds back in the U.S. would also have no impact. Even if Euro-dollar funds are repatriated through the foreign branches of U.S. banks there would be no impact since these foreign branches are treated in the same way as other foreigners. Finally, even though the foreign owner used his dollar deposit to make a payment to a U.S. resident there would be no impact on the U.S. surplus or deficit under the liquidity approach because this transaction would be included as a financing item below the line.

In the case of countries other than the U.S. the impact of Euro-dollar transactions on the official balance-of-payments accounts again depends on how private short-term capital flows are accounted for by each country. If all short-term capital flows are included as autonomous items above the line, any increase or decrease in net private short-term claims on foreigners will change the size of the balance-of-payments deficit or surplus—with an increase increasing a deficit (or decreasing a surplus) and a decrease decreasing a deficit (or increasing a surplus). However, if all short-term capital movements are included below the line as financing items neither an increase nor decrease in net private short-term claims on foreigners would have any impact on the official balance-of-payments deficit or surplus.

In examining the impact of the Euro-dollar market on the balance-of-payments of a country other than the U.S. there are two basic cases to be considered: (1) that in which a non-resident places a Euro-dollar deposit with a domestic commercial bank; and (2) that in which a resident places a Euro-dollar deposit with a domestic commercial bank. In either of these cases the domestic bank involved can re-lend the Euro-dollar deposit to either a resident or a non-resident of the country concerned.

In the first case, if the domestic bank chooses to re-lend the deposit to a non-resident there would be no impact on the balance-of-payments even if short-term flows were included above the line because liabilities to and claims on non-residents would both increase by equal amounts. This would be the situation for a country acting as an intermediary in Euro-dollar transactions. On the other hand, if the domestic bank re-lends the deposit to a resident it could be used either in the form of U.S. dollars (to pay for imports, for example) or converted into domestic currency (in which case either someone else uses the dollars to make a payment abroad or the foreign exchange authorities purchase the dollars). In either case the liabilities of the domestic bank to non-residents and claims on residents both increase by equal amounts; while claims on non-residents remain unchanged. In this situation then, if private short-term capital movements are included above the line, a balance-of-payments deficit would be decreased (or surplus increased) by the Euro-dollar transactions. However, if short-term flows were considered to be financing items and included below the line there would be no impact on the official balance-of-payments deficit or surplus.

Now let us look at the impact when a resident places a Euro-dollar deposit with a domestic commercial bank. If the bank then re-lends the deposit to a non-resident it has the effect of increasing the bank's claims on non-residents and liabilities to residents by equal amounts; while leaving its liabilities to non-residents unchanged. This would result in a capital outflow and an increase in the balance-of-payments deficit (or decrease in the surplus) if private short-term capital flows were included above the line. However, if they were included below the line, there would be no impact. If, on the other hand, the bank re-lends the deposit to another resident of the country concerned, claims and liabilities of the domestic bank with respect to residents increase by equal amounts; while those vis-à-vis non-residents remain unchanged. As a result, there would be no impact on the balance-of-payments accounts even if private short-term flows were included above the line.

Transactions involving Euro-dollars then would have an impact on the balance-of-payments of a country other than the U.S. only if Euro-dollar deposits received by domestic banks from non-residents are re-lent to residents or if Euro-dollar deposits received from residents are re-lent to non-residents. In addition, of course, the domestic banks can move their own funds back and forth between residents and non-residents in the form of Euro-dollars—with the impact again depending on the presence or absence of the above conditions. It is readily apparent then that not all Euro-dollar transactions carry with them balance-of-payments implications and that the statistical impact of those that do can vary from country to country depending upon the accounting methods used in calculating the balance-of-payments deficit or surplus in each country.

The Impact on International Liquidity Reserves

For the purposes of this study international liquidity reserves will be defined as the official gold and foreign exchange reserves (mainly U.S. dollars and sterling) held by an individual country; or, in an aggregate sense, by the world as a whole. For an individual country the size of these reserves can be determined quite readily by merely determining the total amount of gold and foreign exchange held by the foreign exchange authorities of that country. The aggregate volume of international liquidity reserves for the world as a whole, however, is somewhat more difficult to define and measure.

The aggregate volume of gold held by the exchange authorities of all the countries in the world can be readily measured but the volume of foreign exchange holdings is more difficult to determine—since foreign exchange held as an asset by one country is at the same time a liability of the reserve-currency country.[1] In practice though the liability aspect of foreign exchange reserves is usually ignored and the aggregate world supply of international liquidity reserves is calculated by adding the gold holdings of the reserve currency countries to the gold and reserve currency holdings of all other countries. This measure, although theoretically incorrect, will be the one employed in this study.

Under this definition then the aggregate volume of international liquidity reserves available at any particular moment of time in the world as a whole (assuming U.S. dollars and sterling to be the only reserve currencies) will be the sum of: (1) the gold and sterling holdings of the U.S.; (2) the gold and U.S. dollar holdings of the U.K.; and (3) the gold, U.S. dollar, and sterling holdings of all other countries. The aggregate volume of world reserves then will increase if countries accumulate greater quantities of the reserve currencies in their official gold and foreign exchange reserves; but will decrease if they convert some of their reserve currency holdings into gold by purchasing gold from the U.S. If, on the other hand, they purchase newly produced gold from sources other than the U.S. they leave world reserves, at least in the first instance, unchanged—merely exchanging official holdings of foreign exchange with private individuals in return for gold. These transactions, however, could increase the aggregate supply of reserves if these individuals, in turn, sold their newly acquired foreign exchange holdings to the foreign exchange authorities of a country and if these authorities did not use this foreign exchange to purchase gold from the U.S.

Now let us turn to examine how the existence of the Euro-dollar market has affected the volume of official international liquidity reserves available to individual countries and to the

---

[1] For a detailed discussion of the problems involved in defining international liquidity and determining the aggregate volume of international liquidity reserves available to the world as a whole see Fritz Machlup, *International Monetary Economics* (London: George Allen & Unwin Ltd., 1966), pp. 245–59.

world as a whole. As far as aggregate world reserves are concerned, the Euro-dollar market, to the extent that it has stimulated greater holdings of private U.S. dollar balances, has probably decreased the statistical total of official reserves. If these funds had been converted into domestic currencies and accumulated by the foreign exchange authorities of various countries the aggregate volume of foreign exchange held by the authorities would have been greater, at least temporarily. However, to the extent that these additional foreign exchange holdings were used to purchase gold from the U.S. the volume of official world reserves would have been reduced again. It is probable then that official international liquidity reserves for the world as a whole (as we have defined them) are smaller than they would have been in the absence of the Euro-dollar market—due to the fact that it has stimulated larger private holdings of U.S. dollar balances.

From the U.S. point of view, however, these additional private holdings of U.S. dollars have taken some pressure off the U.S. gold reserve by preventing these U.S. funds from being accumulated by the foreign exchange authorities in the rest of the world and, hence, from being used to purchase gold from the U.S. As a result, the Euro-dollar market has served to strengthen the U.S. gold reserve position. In the case of countries other than the U.S., although their official reserves may be lower than they would have been in the absence of the Euro-dollar market, the pressure on the present level of reserves may be reduced by the fact that a greater volume of private U.S. dollar funds has been mobilized to finance international trade. In fact, a substantial amount of international trade is financed through this revolving fund of privately-owned dollars without any conversions to and from domestic currencies— and, hence without resort to official reserves. The Euro-dollar market then has tended to reduce the pressure of trade financing on the official reserves of these countries.

The Euro-dollar market, in addition to stimulating the use of private dollar holdings for international trade financing, has also increased the international velocity of circulation of private U.S. dollar holdings. It has done this by causing dollar balances held in the U.S. to be switched from time to demand deposits and by providing broad market facilities for lending and borrowing these dollar deposits internationally. This has resulted in a greater turn-over of U.S. dollar deposits and has allowed them to be used to finance many more international transactions during any given period of time than would have been the case if they had been left as time deposits in U.S. banks. This again has served to relieve the pressure of trade financing on official reserves.

In addition to these effects, however, if looked at from another point of view, the Euro-dollar market may have increased the need for larger official reserves in countries other than the U.S. This arises as a result of two factor: (1) the fact that domestic banks may now have larger positions denominated in U.S. dollars which might have to be met by the official reserves; and (2) the fact that the Euro-dollar market has increased the volume and mobility of international short-term capital and, hence, the potential volume of short-term capital movements into or out of any particular country—especially during periods of speculative activity. In this sense the existence of the Euro-dollar market may have increased the pressure on the official reserves of these countries.

From the above analysis then it is apparent that, although it has affected official international liquidity reserves in a number of apparently conflicting ways, the greatest impact of the Euro-dollar market to date has been to ease the international liquidity problem by providing additional private facilities for financing a large portion of international trade—thereby shifting the impact of trading activities away from the official reserves. The dangers to which international liquidity reserves are exposed by the possibility of a greater volume of capital flows or a breakdown in the Euro-dollar system, however, cannot be ignored. These will be discussed in the next chapter.

10

THE NEED FOR CONTROL [1]

In this study we have seen that the Euro-dollar market, because of its international nature and the freedom with which it operates, has been able to mobilize a large volume of short-term capital and distribute it in accordance with pure supply and demand considerations on a world-wide scale. This, in general, has been a beneficial development. However, this freedom to operate in a truly international manner has also involved the participants in the market in additional risks and problems. In this chapter we will examine these risks and problems from the point of view of an individual bank operating in the market, an individual country whose banks are participating in the market, and the international financial system as a whole. We will then discuss the desirability of bringing the market under some form of international control and the difficulties involved in doing so. Finally, we will discuss the steps that have been taken to control the market up to the present time and attempt to assess their importance.

The Risks and Problems Associated with the Market

The risks and problems associated with the Euro-dollar market make themselves felt at three levels: (1) the individual bank; (2) the individual country; and (3) at the level of the international financial system as a whole. Although the risks and problems at each level are caused by essentially the same factors and result from the same characteristics of the Euro-dollar system, their impact and consequences at each level can

[1] This chapter is a revised and up-dated version of an article by the author entitled 'Euro-Dollars: The Problem of Control' first published in *The Banker*, CXVIII (1968), 321–9 and later re-printed in *Readings in the Euro-Dollar*, Eric Chalmers, ed. (London: W. P. Griffith & Sons, 1969), pp. 110–25.

be quite different. In addition, the methods available to deal with them are different at each level. We will now discuss the risks and problems involved at each of these levels and how they relate to the underlying characteristics of the Euro-dollar market.

For an individual bank the main risk is the possibility that a borrower may not repay his Euro-dollar loan. This, of course, is always a risk facing any bank in its commercial banking operations. However, the Euro-dollar market, because of its international nature and the long chain of transactions involved in most Euro-dollar operations, has added a new dimension to this risk. In their domestic operations (and even in foreign operations in their own currency) most commercial banks lend directly to their own customers with which they are in close contact. As a result, they have at their disposal considerable information about the financial standing of these borrowers and the proposed use of the borrowed funds. In many cases these loans are also secured by some form of collateral.

In the case of their Euro-dollar operations, however, the commercial banks are dealing in large unsecured loans denominated in U.S. dollars. These Euro-dollar funds are obtained through accepting a short-term dollar deposit from either a resident or non-resident of the country in which it operates and then re-lent to other residents or non-residents usually on a short-term basis (although sometimes on a longer term basis than the term of the deposit). These Euro-dollar funds may be used by the borrower for any number of purposes—over which, because of their unsecured nature, the lending bank has very little control. This type of operation undoubtedly involves the banks in a somewhat greater risk of default than that involved in their ordinary domestic banking operations.

This risk is compounded by the fact that the market is international in nature. As a result, it is difficult for an individual bank in any one country to determine the soundness of their Euro-dollar borrowers. Although they can easily determine how much they have lent to any particular borrower, it is virtually impossible to tell how much that borrower has also borrowed from other banks either in the form of Euro-dollars or in other currencies. Furthermore, Euro-dollars usually pass through a long chain of transactions between the initial placement of the deposit by the original-owner and the eventual employment of the funds by a final-user. This makes it even more difficult for an individual bank to determine the eventual destination of the funds that it lends—let alone the use to which they will be put. Consequently, the individual banks must rely on the financial standing of the borrower to which it directly lends the deposit and hope that, if a breakdown does occur through a default somewhere in the chain, this borrower will still be able to meet his Euro-dollar obligations.

The risk facing any particular bank then will depend partly on its position in the chain of transactions. If it is near the beginning of the chain and has re-lent the deposit to another financially sound bank, the risk of that borrower defaulting is unlikely to be very great. In some cases, however, the risk of operating near the end of the chain may not be as great as that involved further back along the chain because of the more detailed knowledge concerning the final use of the funds available to the bank at the end of the chain. In other words the bank nearest to the final-user may have a better opportunity to assess the risks involved in lending Euro-dollars to various final-users and to choose the lowest risk borrowers; whereas a bank acting only as an intermediary must rely entirely on the financial standing of the immediate borrower without any knowledge of the intentions of this borrower or the final destination of the funds.

There is also the risk that borrowers in certain countries may take on too many obligations denominated in U.S. dollars. If large amounts of Euro-dollars are converted into domestic currency for employment domestically or if the borrowers of Euro-dollars defaulted on a large scale, the banks of the country concerned may have to obtain U.S. dollars through the foreign exchange market to meet their Euro-dollar obligations. If the foreign exchange reserves of the country are not adequate to meet the demand, exchange controls are liable to be imposed—thereby freezing the outflow of Euro-dollars and preventing the banks in other countries from repatriating their Euro-dollar deposits. This again would have the impact of breaking the chain of transactions and causing a scramble for Euro-dollars among banks in the rest of the world.

To minimize the risks involved in dealing in the Euro-dollar market an individual bank limits its volume of lending to any individual borrower and to the borrowers of any particular country. However, since borrowers can obtain funds from a wide variety of sources, it is difficult for an individual bank to establish these limits and to know whether or not they are realistic. As a result, many banks have tended to create a second line of defence by entering into stand-by arrangements (such as lines of credit), with other banks—especially U.S. banks—to cover themselves in case they are not able to collect their Euro-dollar loans and meet their obligations. Consequently, many banks involved in the market may have both a direct and an indirect exposure to risk in the market, the total of which is difficult to quantify.

Since the market is so international in character and there is no central agency keeping account of the amounts borrowed or lent by participants in the market, the banks must make their lending decisions on the basis of a loose system of contacts and exchanges of information between individual banks. This is unlikely to be a very accurate or reliable basis for determining the creditworthiness of many borrowers. In addition, because their Euro-dollar loans and liabilities are denominated in U.S. dollars and the market is international in nature, there is no single institution to which individual banks can turn automatically as a lender of last resort. As a result, the individual banks themselves must be prepared to accept the risks involved and suffer the consequences if errors of judgement are made. These errors can be particularly damaging in the case of Euro-dollar operations because of the chain reaction that could be set off by a default at any link in the chain of transactions. If a major breakdown did occur it would create a scramble for Euro-dollar liquidity among the commercial banks operating outside the U.S.

For an individual country the problems created by the Euro-dollar market are two-fold: (1) the danger that the domestic banks involved in the market may overextend themselves and, thereby, place demands on the official foreign exchange reserves; and (2) the fact that the existence of the Euro-dollar market has provided another channel through which short-term capital can flow internationally and, hence, has tended to increase the volume of short-term capital moving into or out of any particular country. The first situation is similar in nature to the risk encountered by an individual bank, only it is extended to a national scale; while the second poses a direct threat to both the foreign exchange reserves and the independence and effectiveness of domestic economic policies.

The first problem arises if the commercial banks of the country concerned have converted a large volume of Euro-dollars into domestic currency for use in the domestic economy or if foreign borrowers of Euro-dollars default on their payments to the banks in the country concerned. In either case the domestic banks would probably have to obtain U.S. dollars through the foreign exchange market to meet their Euro-dollar obligations. This would put downward pressure on the exchange rate and could deplete the foreign exchange reserves. If this occurred in substantial volume and the exchange reserves of the country concerned were not large, speculative pressure against the domestic currency could also develop which would further deplete the exchange reserves. This situation, if carried far enough, would force the country to seek international assistance or, if this failed, to devalue its currency. This would only occur, of course, in an extreme situation but it does underline the additional risk involved for a country if its commercial banks have large Euro-dollar positions and there was a major break-down in the chain of Euro-dollar transactions.

The problem of increased capital flows, however, is probably of greater importance for a country than the possibility of the domestic banks overextending themselves. As we have seen, the Euro-dollar–domestic securities interest rate differential has become crucial in determining the direction and magnitude of covered arbitrage and whether speculation and hedging will take place through the spot or the forward exchange market. In general, the addition of this new interest differential has tended to increase the opportunities for highly mobile short-term capital to move between financial markets. This has been further enhanced by the fact that this differential has added a new interest parity to which the forward exchange rate can adjust and, hence, has made it more difficult to achieve a unique equilibrium in the forward exchange market. The combined impact of these two factors then has increased the possibility of larger capital flows into or out of any particular country.

The major impact of these additional short-term capital movements involving Euro-dollars has been to increase the degree of interdependence between the national capital markets and monetary policies of the countries involved in the market. In addition, they have increased the pressures on exchange rates and official foreign exchange reserves in these countries. Consequently, the possibility of a country being able to institute an independent national monetary policy and to isolate itself from monetary developments abroad has been significantly reduced by the existence and operation of the Euro-dollar market.

By means of these capital flows, then, the Euro-dollar market has served to transmit interest rate competition from one country to another and to spread any scramble for liquidity that develops in one country to the other countries involved in the market. It is an important vehicle for doing this because of its uncontrolled international nature. Thus, if interest rates rise and a liquidity shortage develops in one country (especially in the U.S.), this will cause funds to flow into this country from the Euro-dollar market. Euro-dollar rates, because they are uncontrolled and basically determined by pure supply and demand conditions, will tend to rise sharply in response to any significant outflow of funds. This, in turn, will attract funds into the Euro-dollar market from other countries—thereby forcing rates up in these countries and spreading the scramble for liquidity.

This was precisely the case during certain periods of 1966, 1967 and 1968 when liquidity became very tight in the U.S. The resulting competition for deposits among the U.S. banks, because of the limitations imposed by Regulation Q, spilled over into the Euro-dollar market. This had the effect of bidding up Euro-dollar rates and, hence, attracting funds from other financial centres—notably London. As a result, the monetary policies of these countries became more dependent upon monetary conditions in the U.S. and balance-of-payments problems were intensified. Similarly, in a reverse situation where Euro-dollar rates are forced substantially above those in the U.S. by factors in the rest of the world, there could be a flow of U.S. dollar deposits from the U.S. to the Euro-dollar market. This could create balance-of-payments problems for the U.S. and place additional pressure on the U.S. gold reserve.

As far as the international financial system as a whole is concerned the Euro-dollar market has, in one sense, been very useful in that it has eased the international liquidity problem by mobilizing large volumes of privately-owned U.S. dollar funds for use in financing international trade. However, in another sense it has posed a threat to the system by providing another channel through which short-term capital movements can be financed. As in the case of all short-term capital movements, these flows could be of a de-stabilizing nature—thereby increasing the pressures on exchange rates and official foreign exchange reserves. In this way the market could add to the need for international liquidity. If these additional reserves were not readily available during a time of crisis it could result in the devaluation of a number of currencies. If this occurred the stability, and even the existence, of the gold-exchange standard could be threatened. By adding to the potential volume of short-term capital available to finance these flows, the Euro-dollar market has contributed to this threat.

The Need for International Control

The problems created by the existence and operation of the Euro-dollar market result from two characteristics of that market: (1) the fact that there is no single institution to which participants can turn automatically as lender of last resort; and (2) the fact that the market has created a set of semi-independent international interest rates over which no single country or institution has control. It is these characteristics then that must be dealt with and altered if the problems associated with the market are to be solved successfully. If this can be accomplished, the risks facing individual banks, individual countries, and the international financial system would be materially reduced.

As far as an individual bank is concerned the role of lender of last resort could, in most cases, be adequately filled by the central bank of the country in which it operates. If a bank encounters a shortage of Euro-dollars as a result of a borrower not being able to repay, it usually would not cause any difficulty if the bank could obtain, on short notice, a supply of U.S. dollars to meet its own Euro-dollar obligations. Normally, it could do this by either borrowing further in the Euro-dollar market or purchasing U.S. dollars in the foreign exchange market—from either private holders or the central bank. Alternatively, the central bank could arrange to swap or deposit U.S. dollars on a temporary basis with its commercial banks in order to see them through a Euro-dollar stringency. By making U.S. dollars available to its own commercial banks the central bank could prevent a disastrous chain reaction from developing which would undoubtedly involve the banks of a number of countries. However, this role could be played by a central bank only as long as it had an adequate supply of gold and foreign exchange reserves. If it did not, then the problem would escalate to one of national importance.

If it reached the point at which the foreign exchange reserves of a country were not sufficient to meet the shortage of Euro-dollars encountered by their commercial banks, either additional reserves would have to be borrowed from the IMF or through inter-country swap or loan arrangements; or the Euro-dollar chain would have to be allowed to break down. Any defaulting on this scale, however, would undoubtedly involve the banks of many countries and would create a shortage of Euro-dollars in the whole market and not just with respect to the banks of any one country. The best method of averting a shortage of this magnitude would be to provide some form of international assistance for the Euro-dollar market as a whole. In other words, it would be necessary to create an international lender of last resort for the market.

The problem of controlling the volume of short-term capital flowing through the medium of the Euro-dollar market also seems to require some form of international control if it is to be solved successfully. This problem arises because the Euro-dollar market has created a set of semi-independent international interest rates that are affected primarily by pure supply and demand conditions within the market. These supply and demand conditions are influenced by a great number of international factors and, therefore, are beyond the control of the authorities of any particular country. However, if control (or at least influence) over the supply of Euro-dollars could be instituted through international co-operation, Euro-dollar rates could be brought under some degree of control—particularly during periods of stringency. This would aid in controlling the volume of short-term capital flowing through the market—especially during abnormal periods when de-stabilizing flows could develop—and help to reduce the spread of interest rate competition and liquidity scrambles.

There are difficulties, however, in establishing a mechanism that can bring about the necessary degree of international control over the Euro-dollar market. The most important is the fact that there is no single institution — either national or international—that can control the market and act as an international lender of last resort in the same way that a national central bank can in the case of a national money market. Although their ability may be restricted by international influences at times, it is usually possible for a national central bank to maintain a significant degree of control over national money market rates and, in any case, to act as lender of last resort to its own commercial banks.

The central banks of countries other than the U.S., although they may be able to exert some influence over Euro-dollar rates by placing U.S. funds in the market either directly or indirectly (through the intermediary of their commercial banks), are restricted in their attempts to control the market by the volume of foreign exchange reserves which they are free to place in the market and, ultimately, by the size of their reserves. Because of the size of the Euro-dollar market it is doubtful that any one country (other than the U.S.) could be successful in controlling the market even if they decided to use a substantial portion of their reserves for this purpose.

The U.S. Federal Reserve is in the best position among the central banks of the world to control the market because it has the power to create U.S. dollar deposits. However, to accomplish this the U.S. authorities must also be in a position to cause these newly created deposits to flow into or out of the Euro-dollar market. This would involve the maintenance of a substantial position in the market either directly or indirectly through the intermediary of U.S. commercial banks. In addition, it would result in capital flows between the U.S. and the Euro-dollar market, with balance-of-payments implications.

Finally, there is no single international institution with both the resources and authority to effectively control the Euro-dollar market. The IMF, although it could conceivably obtain the resources, does not, under its present constitution, have the power to participate in the market let alone control it. The Bank for International Settlements (BIS) has the ability to participate—and in fact does—but not sufficient resources. It has at times had some influence over Euro-dollar rates but its own resources would certainly not be adequate to check a sustained disruptive trend in Euro-dollar rates or to allow it to act as a lender of last resort in a crisis situation.

Since there is no single national or international institution with the ability to control the Euro-dollar market, the only effective method of achieving this must involve some form of international co-operation either between the national central banks themselves or between the national central banks and the existing international institutions. This would be a natural outgrowth of the present system of dealing with speculative runs on currencies, involving the extension of inter-country swaps and loans in accordance with pre-arranged stand-by agreements. These arrangements, although far from perfect, have been able to cope successfully with a number of exchange rate crisis in recent years. There seems to be no reason why these types of arrangements could not be employed to stabilize the Euro-dollar market—at least during periods of acute stringency.

The national central banks of countries other than the U.S. are unlikely to place any substantial portion of their official foreign exchange reserves directly in the Euro-dollar market because of their desire to maintain the highest possible degree of liquidity and safety. However, they could operate through the intermediary of either their own commercial banks or an international institution such as the B.I.S. In this way they are free to swap or deposit U.S. dollars with these institutions at any time they desire without maintaining a permanent position in the market themselves. This would not tie up any of their resources unnecessarily and gives them a high degree of flexibility.

The Federal Reserve could also participate in this system of control and, in fact, would be the cornerstone of any such arrangements. Since the U.S. authorities have the power to create U.S. deposits they are not limited in their participation by any lack of U.S. dollar reserves, as could be the case for other countries, and, therefore, could act as the ultimate lender of last resort for the market. Without the participation of the U.S. authorities any such system of control would undoubtedly be inadequate during a period of severe crisis. The most direct way in which the Federal Reserve could participate would be through negotiating a stand-by swap or loan arrangement with an international institution. By doing so the U.S. authorities would be assured that the funds provided by the swaps are used for the desired purpose; whereas if they participate by depositing funds with their own commercial banks the leakage could be substantial and the impact delayed.

The most appropriate existing international institution through which the national central banks could operate in controlling the market would be the B.I.S. It already participates in the market on a substantial scale and, therefore, has the necessary experience to undertake this stabilizing role. In addition, it has been in the forefront in collecting data and analyzing the behaviour and trends of the market. As a result, it is in the best position to determine the needs of the market and the quantity of U.S. funds required to ensure stability during periods of stringency. Finally, its contacts with the central banks are highly developed and of long standing. This should make it easier to negotiate the necessary stand-by agreements and institute co-ordinated action during a time of crisis.

Recent Developments

During the past four years a loose system of control involving the intervention of national central banks either directly or through the intermediary of the B.I.S. or their own commercial banks has steadily evolved. The central banks—notably those of the U.S., Switzerland, West Germany, and Italy—have been acting in a co-ordinated manner and have placed a considerable volume of U.S. dollar resources at the disposal of the Euro-dollar market whenever upward pressures on Euro-dollar rates become too great. This system of informal understandings among the central banks seems to have arisen initially as part of their co-operation in fighting exchange crises and has now developed to the point where events in the Euro-dollar market are regularly discussed at the monthly meetings of central bankers in Basle. As a result, central bankers are increasingly prepared to undertake operations that will reduce pressures in the Euro-dollar market—especially those caused by the shifting of liquid funds on the part of their own commercial banks. In fact, these operations have become routine at mid-year and year-end when seasonal strains on the Euro-dollar market are at their height.

The particular measures employed in these operations have been designed to take into consideration the prevailing circumstances and the institutional requirements of the central bank involved. Some central banks (notably the Swiss National Bank) place funds directly in the market or through the B.I.S. The Federal Reserve has negotiated a stand-by swap facility with the B.I.S. from which the B.I.S. can obtain U.S. dollars for investment in the Euro-dollar market. Others—most notably those of Germany and Italy—have employed swap arrangements with their own commercial banks to channel funds back into the Euro-dollar market and have taken steps to reduce the withdrawal of funds by their commercial banks at year-end. In addition, a number of central banks—including the Federal Reserve and the Deutsche Bundesbank—have intervened directly in the forward exchange market in order to reduce the incentive for shifting funds out of the Euro-dollar market.

These stabilizing operations[1] first became apparent during the early part of 1965 when the imposition of the U.S. Voluntary Restraint programme threatened to disrupt the Euro-dollar market by cutting off the supply of dollar deposits entering the market from the U.S. and stimulating the demand for U.S. dollar loans to replace those previously obtainable from the U.S. On this occasion, Italy swapped substantial sums of U.S. dollars with their commercial banks—which were then used to decrease the banks' net indebtedness in the Euro-dollar market. This action was taken partly to benefit the Euro-dollar situation and partly to improve the foreign positions of the Italian

[1] For details of these operations throughout the 1965–8 period see the Annual Reports of the Bank for International Settlements and a continuing series of articles by Charles A. Coombs published semi-annually in the March and September issues of the *Federal Reserve Bank of New York Monthly Review*.

banks. Fortunately, both of these objectives were desirable at the appropriate time. In addition, the B.I.S. also shifted a portion of its own resources into the Euro-dollar market during this period.

Since 1965, these techniques have been expanded and used on a number of occasions—especially at year-ends when 'window-dressing' requirements of the commercial banks increase the demand for U.S. dollar funds and often place a substantial strain on the Euro-dollar market. At the end of 1966 direct support involving approximately $800 million was given to the market. This included $470 million re-channeled to the Euro-dollar market through deposits from the Swiss National Bank and $275 million placed in the Euro-dollar market by the B.I.S. (of which $200 million was obtained through the swap arrangement with the Federal Reserve). In addition, the German and Italian central banks took measures to limit their banks' year-end repatriations.

These 1966 year-end operations appeared to be the first real attempt to stabilize the Euro-dollar market by means of a co-ordinated programme of central bank actions. This also indicated that central bankers were becoming increasingly aware of the important role played by the Euro-dollar market in the international financial system. During 1967 a number of disruptive events occurred on the international scene which, unfortunately, placed considerable pressure on the Euro-dollar market at a time when seasonal strains were also present in the market. In mid-1967 the Middle East War, combined with mid-year liquidity requirements, forced the B.I.S. to draw $143 million on its swap line with the Federal Reserve for use in the Euro-dollar market. This was followed in July by an increase in the Federal Reserve swap arrangement with the B.I.S. from $400 million to $550 million.

After the devaluation of sterling in November 1967 the major central banks initiated a co-ordinated programme in the forward exchange market aimed at inducing reflows into the Euro-dollar market of short-term funds that had gone into continental European markets during the flight from sterling. The German authorities alone rechanneled $850 million through swap operations with their commercial banks. Towards year-end, however, 'window-dressing' requirements placed additional pressure on the market and forced the implementation of further stabilizing measures. In fact, from the time of devaluation to the year-end, total central bank and B.I.S. operations in the Euro-dollar market amounted to approximately $1·4 billion—of which $346 million came from the B.I.S. swap facility with the Federal Reserve. This swap arrangement was also expanded during this period to a total of $1 billion.

Continued uncertainties in the gold and foreign exchange markets and heavy demands on the part of U.S. banks combined to keep considerable pressure on the Euro-dollar market during the first half of 1968. This was partly met during the early months by extensive swap operations on the part of the Deutsche Bundesbank which resulted in an outflow of nearly $800 million from Germany. Later, in June, the Swiss National Bank and the B.I.S. placed $430 million and $111 million respectively in the market to reduce the impact of mid-year 'window-dressing' operations. During the last half of the year the large speculative flows into Germany resulted in renewed pressure on the market. This, however, was quickly offset by re-channeling on the part of the Deutsche Bundesbank. At the year-end, the B.I.S. drew $80 million on its swap facility for use in the market and the Swiss National Bank re-channeled $746 million through swaps with the Swiss commercial banks.

These stabilizing operations on the part of the national central banks and the B.I.S. have been instrumental in maintaining the Euro-dollar market as a viable and orderly short-term credit market—despite the occurrence of major disruptive events. Although the measures employed are of an ad-hoc informal nature and are dependent upon the policy decisions of individual central banks, their effectiveness in both smoothing the impact of major international currency developments and relieving seasonal strains has been amply demonstrated over the past four years. Without this stabilizing intervention it is doubtful that the Euro-dollar market could have come through the currency crises of 1967 and 1968 completely unscathed. Undoubtedly then this programme has been an important beneficial development which has reduced the risks and problems facing the individual banks, the individual countries, and the international financial system during this period.

The nature of these arrangements, however, does create some uncertainty as to their effectiveness under some circumstances. Because of their informality, these arrangements, with the possible exception of the U.S. swap arrangement with the B.I.S., are dependent upon the policy decisions of individual central banks and not solely on decisions taken by a central authority—such as the B.I.S. As a result, the volume and type of assistance available to the Euro-dollar market cannot be determined before the disrupting events occur. In addition, in circumstances where the needs of the Euro-dollar market conflict with other policy objectives of the central banks, the danger arises that the national central banks may not give priority to the Euro-dollar market. Fortunately, on the occasions when assistance has been required by the market neither of these factors caused any difficulties. These are, however, the basic weaknesses of the present arrangements.

In order to avoid this situation the U.S. dollar funds needed to stabilize the Euro-dollar market would have to be made available on a more formal basis—such as by means of pre-arranged swaps and stand-by agreements between the national central banks and the B.I.S. In this situation the B.I.S. should be allowed to call on these swap funds in accordance with the needs of the Euro-dollar market. In addition, to meet these requirements during a period of crisis, the volume of U.S. funds at the disposal of the B.I.S. would have to be substantial. Undoubtedly, the major portion of these funds would have to originate from the Federal Reserve System. Although the recent expansion of the swap arrangements between the Federal Reserve and the B.I.S. to a total of $1·6 billion has gone a long way towards remedying the weaknesses of the present control arrangements, there still remains the need for more formal commitments on the part of the European central banks.

In normal circumstances, of course, these control arrangements are not activated and the market is left free to find its own level; but the mere fact that this large volume of funds is behind the market and can be used by a lender of last resort, acts as a stabilizing influence and has probably prevented a serious disruption of the market on a number of occasions during the past four years. The main benefit from this approach is that it allows the market to operate as freely as possible during normal times and thereby encourages its use in the financing of trade; while at the same time limiting its use for financing de-stabilizing short-term capital flows during abnormal periods.

11

THE SIGNIFICANCE OF THE MARKET

FROM our analysis we have seen that the Euro-dollar market has had a considerable impact on both the individual countries involved in the market and the international financial system as a whole. In the case of individual countries the market has affected a number of areas—but of greatest significance has been its impact on monetary theory and policy. For the international financial system the most significant impact has been the role played by the market in stimulating the forces of international financial integration. This, in turn, has strengthened the tendency towards greater international financial cooperation among the major countries of the world. We will now examine the significance of the market in each of those areas in more details.

The Significance for Monetary Theory and Policy

Monetary theory has traditionally been developed within the framework of a closed economy. In this situation changes in the money supply must be instituted through the shifting of asset holdings between money balances and other financial assets on the part of individuals, businesses, and financial institutions. Hicks,[1] in his analysis, breaks financial assets (and assets in general) down into three categories: running assets, reserve assets, and investment assets. In addition, he points out that money balances may be held as part of all three categories. Money balances held as running assets (due to the transactions demand for money) are involuntary holdings needed to finance a given level of economic activity. On the other hand, money

[1] Sir John Hicks, *Critical Essays in Monetary Theory* (Oxford: Oxford University Press, 1967), pp. 38–60.

balances held as reserve assets (due to the precautionary demand for money) and as investment assets (due to the speculative demand for money) are purely voluntary holdings which can be shifted into or out of other financial assets in accordance with the desires of the holder. It is primarily through these latter holdings then that shifts into or out of money balances can be induced by the monetary authorities.

In his analysis Hicks lays the greatest importance on the changes that can be instituted in the money balances held as reserve assets—especially those held by financial institutions. He reaches this conclusion from the fact that there is a high degree of substitution between the various assets (including money) which can be held as reserve assets. Therefore, a change in relative interest rates on reserve asset securities—which induces holders to take up either a more or a less liquid position —would result in a shift over the whole spectrum of reserve assets (including a shift into or out of money balances). It is in this way, he maintains, that the operation of liquidity preference has its greatest impact.

In the case of investment assets a shift into or out of money would result only if there was a change in expectations about future interest rates—that is, only if investors became more or less bearish in their outlook. This change may occur as a result of changes in current relative interest rates but does not necessarily take place. As a result, the shift into or out of money balances held as investment assets is unlikely to be as great as the shift into or out of money held as a reserve asset. This is especially true if we take into consideration the role played by financial institutions—whose assets are largely made up of reserve assets. These large volumes of reserve assets are particularly liable to be involved in liquidity shifts—both between various securities and between securities and money balances.

It is primarily through these liquidity shifts between reserve assets (including money) then that changes in the money supply can be instituted. For example, if the monetary authorities sell readily marketable securities (such as treasury bills) that can be held as reserve assets, they will be absorbed into reserve assets in exchange for money taken from a reserve balance. In order to induce this shift to a less liquid position on the part of reserve asset holders, the price of the securities issued by the authorities must fall (i.e. the interest rate on them must rise). This, in turn, will result in a general fall in the money value of reserve assets held in the economy. As a result, some reserve asset holders will feel that their reserves are insufficient and will attempt to obtain a greater volume of reserve assets. If there is a general shortage of liquidity and reserve assets cannot be borrowed from others, money balances from running assets must be absorbed into reserve assets—thereby lowering the level of economic activity that can be financed.

In reality commercial banks are likely to play an instrumental role in this process. When the monetary authority attempts to contract the money supply by causing a shift between money balances and other reserve asset securities it is the commercial banks who feel the direct pressure on their reserve assets. The banks attempt to relieve this pressure by contracting their credit to the other sectors of the economy; which, in turn, forces a withdrawal of money from running assets and a consequent decline in the level of economic activity. An attempted expansion in the money supply would operate in a similar manner but the pressure on the banks and other sectors of the economy to employ the excess reserve assets for transactions purposes would be much less compelling than the need to withdraw money from running assets to meet a reserve asset shortage. As an alternative they could place this excess money among investment assets. This is the main reason for the asymmetrical impact of monetary policy.

In order to determine the impact of the Euro-dollar market on this process, however, we must consider an open economy situation. When a country is operating under fixed exchange rates and the foreign exchange authorities are being forced to accumulate (or decumulate) foreign exchange reserves in order to maintain the exchange rate at a support point, monetary theory becomes somewhat more complicated. First, we have the possibility that foreign securities may be held by asset holders alongside domestic securities as part of their reserve assets. As a result, changes in relative interest rates on domestic reserve assets (brought about by the domestic monetary authorities) could possibly lead to shifts between domestic and foreign securities rather than between domestic securities and money balances. If the foreign exchange authorities bought (or sold) the foreign exchange involved in these operations, the total volume of domestic money balances would be unchanged. Although this would still result in a fall (or rise) in the total money value of reserve assets held by asset holders and consequently lead to an additional demand for (or supply of) reserve assets, the direct pressure on domestic bank reserves (resulting from the shift out of or into reserve money holdings) would be reduced.

More importantly, even if there is an additional need for (or supply of) reserve assets in the economy, there is now another alternative to the withdrawing from (or adding to) transactions money balances in order to adjust reserve assets to their desired level—namely the ability to either borrow or lend money balances abroad. This is particularly important in allowing commercial banks to replenish their reserve assets in a contractionary period—thereby preventing the need for a contraction of credit and a consequent shift of money balances from running assets to reserve assets in other sectors of the economy. Similarly, in the case of an expansionary monetary policy the need to transfer excess reserve assets to running assets (which is already weak) would be much less compelling because they could now be transferred abroad as well as into investment assets. In addition, these flows could also take place at the initiative of foreigners. As a result, the impact of domestic monetary policy could be neutralized even if residents of the country concerned were not deliberately initiating the international flows.

We must now determine the significance of the Euro-dollar market in this situation. The movement of funds between domestic currencies and Euro-dollars has exactly the same impact on the domestic money supply as any other capital inflows or outflows. However, Euro-dollars do add something in that they are a very flexible device with which residents of a country can alter their foreign positions. Because of the broad market facilities transactions in Euro-dollars are readily arranged on short notice—with maturities for both loans and deposits being very flexible. In addition, there are no restrictions on entry to or exit from the Euro-dollar market itself. As a result, the ease with which liquid funds can be transferred to or from abroad has been substantially increased by the existence of the market.

13

The Euro-dollar market then has added a very flexible foreign liquid asset which asset holders (especially domestic financial institutions) can hold as a reserve asset. If this is the case and relative interest rates on domestic securities are changed by the monetary authorities, there could very easily be a shift between Euro-dollars and domestic securities rather than the desired shift into or out of money balances. Since Euro-dollar deposits are very liquid and, hence, close substitutes for money balances this shift may be sufficient to adjust the liquidity preferences of reserve asset holders to the new situation. As a result there would only be a small (if any) shift between money balances and domestic securities.

This factor is likely to be of greater significance in the case of Euro-dollars than it would be for other foreign securities because the difference in liquidity between foreign securities (such as treasury bills) and domestic securities would probably be very small. As a result, even if there was a shift between foreign and domestic securities it would probably still be accompanied by some shifting into or out of money balances in order to adjust the liquidity preferences of reserve asset holders. The Euro-dollar market, therefore, by minimizing this adjustment, has served to reduce the possibility of an initial shift into or out of money balances and, hence, to decrease the immediate impact on domestic bank reserves.

In particular, the Euro-dollar market has provided a very convenient and highly liquid alternative in which commercial banks of a country can invest excess reserves during periods of monetary ease and from which they can obtain funds during times of monetary restraint. This allows the banks to easily adjust their domestic reserve position through changes in their foreign position without the necessity of contracting (or expanding) the volume of credit supplied to other sectors of the domestic economy. As a result, the possibility of money balances being transferred into or out of running assets in order to adjust the total money value of reserve assets in the economy to their desired level has been decreased. In addition, we have also seen that the Euro-dollar market has made it easier for residents (especially banks) to borrow or lend liquid funds abroad through increasing the elasticities of supply of and demand for short-term arbitrage funds facing any particular country and the freedom with which short-term capital can move internationally. Consequently, the volume of short-term funds moving into or out of a country in response to changes in domestic interest rates has been increased. Because of these increased flows the monetary authorities of a country would have to take stronger monetary measures in order to achieve a given change in the domestic money supply.

The Euro-dollar market then (under a fixed exchange rate system) has served to make monetary policy less effective as an internal stabilization weapon. At the same time, however, it has made it somewhat more potent for external stabilization. This means that the Euro-dollar market has strengthened the trend towards the substitution of fiscal policy for monetary policy as the major internal stabilizer. On the other hand, if monetary policy is still to be used for internal stabilization the Euro-dollar market has made it more imperative that changes in monetary policy be either conducted by means of foreign exchange operations—such as foreign swaps or deposits with commercial banks—or, at least, accompanied by foreign exchange operations—such as forward market intervention. In particular, it has made it necessary for the central bank of a country to control the foreign positions of their commercial banks as well as their domestic positions (especially in countries with poorly developed domestic money markets). This undoubtedly is one of the most significant consequences of the Euro-dollar market.

The Significance for International Financial Integration

Since the return to convertibility and the general dismantling of exchange controls in the late 1950's there has been a growing tendency towards international financial integration. Even so, two major obstacles still tend to limit this process—the existence of operating rigidities and cartel arrangements in banking operations and the continuing presence of exchange controls. It is these factors that limit the volume of short-term capital available to finance international trade and international short-term capital flows—the two aspects of international finance through which the forces of international integration can have the greatest impact. In limiting the amount of short-term capital available for these purposes, however, these impediments have also created interest rate differentials both within countries and between countries. This, in turn, provides an incentive for devising means of circumventing these impediments—of which the development of the Euro-dollar market has been of particular significance.

The Euro-dollar market, because of its international nature, has been able to operate outside the remaining exchange controls and generally without regard to the operating and control rigidities existing in any particular country. This has allowed it to mobilize a large volume of short-term capital and distribute it on a world-wide scale in accordance with pure supply and demand considerations. By being able to circumvent a great many of these impediments then the Euro-dollar market has been able to increase the volume of funds available to finance both international trade and international short-term capital movements. In addition, it has served as a stimulus to international banking operations which in itself tends to break down operating and cartel rigidities and make banking operations more competitive throughout the world.

By expanding the use of private dollar holdings for financing international trade the Euro-dollar market has provided a cheaper and more plentiful supply of trade finance. The main impact of this has been to expand international banking operations and, hence, break down cartel arrangements and rigidities in national banking systems. Now domestic banks not only have to compete among themselves in foreign trade financing but also with a large number of foreign banks which are willing to provide dollar credits at very competitive rates. The market also allows the domestic banks to compete with each other outside national legislative and cartel controls. The effect of this has been to adjust national interest rates (at least on foreign trade financing) closer to the international level existing in the Euro-dollar market.

Of even greater importance has been the use of these additional Euro-dollar funds for financing international short-term capital flows between the Euro-dollar market and national short-term capital markets. In addition to providing additional funds, the Euro-dollar market has also facilitated the international movement of short-term capital—thereby increasing the sensitivity of short-term funds to changes in international interest rate differentials. The consequence of this has been an increase in the volume of short-term capital movements. These larger capital flows, which have a direct impact on interest rates in both the Euro-dollar market and the national markets, have tended to push interest rates throughout the world towards a common level. If there were no impediments in the way of short-term capital flows and a sufficient supply of capital with which to finance them, international financial integration could be complete. Even though it has not had an impact great enough to bring this about, the Euro-dollar market has certainly contributed substantially to this tendency.

These additional capital flows involving Euro-dollars are of particular significance because they can actually operate to off-set the impact of domestic monetary policies. This makes the monetary policies of the countries involved in the market more interdependent and leaves each individual country less room for independent action. Through these flows then the market has served to spread the impact of monetary changes in one country to the other countries involved in the market. This has substantially increased the interdependence of the whole international financial system and provided a stimulant for the forces of international financial integration.

As a significant side-effect of its integrating impact the Euro-dollar market has also strengthened the tendency towards international financial co-operation. Because of its international nature the major central banks have been forced to take collective action to bring Euro-dollar rates under some degree of control—particularly on occasions when severe strains within the Euro-dollar market could have been spread to other financial markets or when disturbing influences in one financial market could have been transmitted to other markets via the Euro-dollar market. In addition, it has made it more imperative for them to co-ordinate their monetary policies and to consult each other prior to making any major changes in domestic or international policies.

APPENDIX A

Regulation Q

THE responsibility for regulating the maximum rates of interest payable on time and savings deposits by member banks of the Federal Reserve System was vested in the Board of Governors of the Federal Reserve System by the United States Congress in 1933. The Board of Governors acted on this responsibility by establishing Regulation Q. This prohibits the payment of interest on demand deposits (i.e. deposits placed for thirty days and less) and sets the maximum permissible rates of interest that can be paid on time and savings deposits by the U.S. banking system.

The maximum permissible rate payable on time deposits was set at 3 per cent in 1933 and then reduced to 2½ per cent in 1935 where it remained until 1 January 1957, when it was again raised to 3 per cent. Since 1957 the maximum rates permissible on deposits of varying maturities have been altered from time to time by the Board of Governors. These alterations are outlined in the table below.

On 15 October 1962 an amendment was made exempting the time deposits of foreign governments, of monetary and financial authorities of foreign governments, and of certain international financial institutions from the terms of Regulation Q for a period of three years. In October 1965 this exemption was renewed for a further three year period ending 15 October 1968. Effective 15 October 1968 official time deposits were exempted permanently from the terms of Regulation Q.

Regulation Q applies only to the banks and branches of U.S. banks operating within the United States. This permits the foreign branches of U.S. banks to pay interest on demand deposits and higher rates on time deposits than those allowed under the terms of Regulation Q. As a result, the U.S. banks have been able to enter the Euro-dollar market through their European branches by paying rates of interest which are competitive with those paid on U.S. dollar deposits in Europe.

Maximum Interest Rates Payable on U.S. Time Deposits

Effective Period	30 days to 60 days	60 days to 90 days	90 days to 180 days	180 days and over
Prior to 1 January 1957	1%	1%	2%	$2\frac{1}{2}$%
1 January 1957 to 31 December 1961	1%	1%	$2\frac{1}{2}$%	3%
1 January 1962 to 16 July 1963	1%	1%	$2\frac{1}{2}$%	$3\frac{1}{2}$%
17 July 1963 to 23 November 1964	1%	1%	4%	4%
24 November 1964 to 5 December 1965	4%	4%	$4\frac{1}{2}$%	$4\frac{1}{2}$%
6 December 1965 to 19 July 1966	$5\frac{1}{2}$%	$5\frac{1}{2}$%	$5\frac{1}{2}$%	$5\frac{1}{2}$%
20 July 1966 to 25 September 1966				
Multiple-maturity	4%	4%	5%	5%
Single-maturity	$5\frac{1}{2}$%	$5\frac{1}{2}$%	$5\frac{1}{2}$%	$5\frac{1}{2}$%
26 September 1966 to 17 April 1968				
Multiple-maturity	4%	4%	5%	5%
Single-maturity				
Over $100,000	$5\frac{1}{2}$%	$5\frac{1}{2}$%	$5\frac{1}{2}$%	$5\frac{1}{2}$%
Under $100,000	5%	5%	5%	5%
18 April 1968 to 31 December 1968				
Multiple-maturity	4%	4%	5%	5%
Single-maturity				
Over $100,000	$5\frac{1}{2}$%	$5\frac{3}{4}$%	6%	$6\frac{1}{4}$%
Under $100,000	5%	5%	5%	5%

APPENDIX B

Overseas Deposits and Advances of Overseas Banks and Accepting Houses in London, 1956-1968

THE statistical series involving non-resident deposits and advances of overseas banks and accepting houses in the U.K. have been published by the Bank of England annually from 1951 to 1959, semi-annually for 1959 and 1960, and quarterly thereafter. For the purposes of this study, however, only the series from the end of 1956 to the present will be used. The data includes deposits and advances denominated in both sterling and foreign currencies and do not segregate those denominated in U.S. dollars or any other specific currency. From June 1966 they also include issues of negotiable certificates of deposit. In Table 1 the data have been converted into U.S. dollars at the rate of £1 = $2.80 until September 1967 and at the rate of £1 = $2.40 thereafter.

The banks covered under each heading in Table 1 are as follows:

(1) British Overseas Banks—contributors are members of the British Overseas and Commonwealth Banks Association.
(2) U.S. Banks—contributors are members of the American Banks in London.
(3) Other Foreign Banks—contributors are members of the Foreign Banks and Affiliates Association.
(4) Accepting Houses—contributors are members of the Accepting Houses Committee.
(5) Other Banks—contributors are a group of other foreign banks with offices in London, including the Japanese banks and the Moscow Narodny Bank. Of these banks, 25 began contributing in September of 1962, 10 in March of 1964 and 13 in December of 1967—thereby causing discontinuities in the data at these dates.

The names of the banks included under the first three headings are given in Bank of England, *Quarterly Bulletin*, I (1961), 23 and the names of the banks included in the 'Other Banks' category are given in *Quarterly Bulletin,* VIII (1968), 97. In addition, the statistics for September 1962 and subsequent dates differ to some extent from those for earlier dates, as explained in *Quarterly Bulletin,* II (1962), 267–9.

TABLE 1

Overseas Deposit Accounts and Advances of Overseas Banks and Accepting Houses in London, 1956–68

(Millions of U.S. Dollars)

A. Deposit Accounts

Period Ending	British Overseas Banks	U.S. Banks	Other Foreign Banks	Accepting Houses	Other Banks	Total
1956—December	1,023	96	216	236		1,570
1957—December	965	145	247	224		1,582
1958—December	1,145	189	408	313		2,056
1959—June	1,393	304	465	406		2,568
December	1,357	361	455	407		2,580
1960—June	1,412	808	502	532		3,254
December	1,554	812	703	700		3,768
1961—March	1,593	909	732	680		3,914
June	1,633	988	663	663		3,947
September	1,644	1,000	579	714		3,937
December	1,612	908	636	798		3,954
1962—March	1,690	955	774	904		4,323
June	1,833	1,051	705	937		4,526
September	2,059	1,166	660	899	714	5,498
December	2,257	1,017	734	968	778	5,754
1963—March	2,412	1,270	694	930	767	6,073
June	2,532	1,353	661	1,042	731	6,319
September	2,636	1,363	697	1,187	857	6,740
December	2,589	1,364	703	1,075	915	6,646

TABLE 1 (continued)

Overseas Deposit Accounts and Advances of Overseas Banks and Accepting Houses in London, 1956–68

Period Ending	British Overseas Banks	U.S. Banks	Other Foreign Banks	Accepting Houses	Other Banks	Total
1964—March	2,688	1,471	843	1,025	1,156	7,183
June	2,793	1,672	784	1,162	1,322	7,733
September	2,936	1,833	907	1,246	1,414	8,336
December	2,736	1,994	935	1,218	1,616	8,499
1965—March	2,747	2,220	925	1,156	1,532	8,580
June	2,713	2,383	823	1,084	1,494	8,497
September	2,786	2,685	789	1,064	1,610	8,943
December	3,049	2,828	1,000	1,114	1,520	9,511
1966—March	3,077	3,208	899	1,210	1,439	9,833
June	3,396	3,685	865	1,173	1,405	10,524
September	3,058	4,138	863	1,134	1,509	10,702
December	3,195	4,505	960	1,215	1,666	11,541
1967—March	3,262	4,788	1,047	1,411	1,705	11,972
June	3,351	4,863	926	1,408	1,806	12,336
September	3,570	5,462	966	1,369	1,920	12,804
December	3,355	5,520	866	1,325	2,126	12,600
1968—March	3,460	6,580	926	1,420	2,133	13,999
June	3,984	7,999	1,195	1,610	2,544	16,408
September	4,008	8,486	1,233	1,764	2,767	16,900
December	4,180	9,348	1,454	1,824	2,877	18,254

TABLE 1 (continued)

Overseas Deposit Accounts and Advances of Overseas Banks and Accepting Houses in London, 1956–68

B. Advances

Period Ending	British Overseas Banks	U.S. Banks	Other Foreign Banks	Accepting Houses	Other Banks	Total
1956—December	187	45	54	55		342
1957—December	199	81	52	58		389
1958—December	275	74	66	77		493
1959—June	340	142	125	125		732
December	336	188	153	123		801
1960—June	404	668	153	185		1,410
December	495	654	241	249		1,639
1961—March	661	776	221	181		1,839
June	676	849	256	318		2,099
September	625	828	244	322		2,019
December	634	706	249	345		1,934
1962—March	702	775	257	340		2,074
June	702	853	255	445		2,255
September	841	894	235	504	577	3,051
December	930	695	330	608	650	3,213
1963—March	1,044	1,025	344	529	700	3,642
June	1,106	1,044	286	714	644	3,794
September	1,118	1,060	308	804	680	3,970
December	1,168	1,117	324	638	683	3,930

TABLE 1 (continued)

Overseas Deposit Accounts and Advances of Overseas Banks and Accepting Houses in London, 1956–68

Period Ending	British Overseas Banks	U.S. Banks	Other Foreign Banks	Accepting Houses	Other Banks	Total
1964—March	1,197	1,204	308	498	935	4,142
June	1,228	1,198	283	577	927	4,213
September	1,290	1,366	321	619	1,033	4,629
December	1,330	1,596	375	694	1,169	5,164
1965—March	1,277	1,688	311	613	1,140	5,029
June	1,305	1,750	280	661	1,105	5,101
September	1,308	2,117	283	633	1,210	5,551
December	1,450	2,310	409	672	1,215	6,056
1966—March	1,282	2,875	249	644	1,162	6,212
June	1,456	3,366	305	733	1,204	7,064
September	1,358	3,914	319	714	1,296	7,601
December	1,548	4,326	417	806	1,436	8,533
1967—March	1,498	4,166	324	770	1,464	8,232
June	1,657	4,401	299	856	1,531	8,750
September	1,682	5,160	375	907	1,629	9,760
December	1,752	5,510	338	960	1,843	10,406
1968—March	1,833	6,722	381	993	1,898	11,834
June	2,028	8,791	403	1,077	2,152	14,462
September	2,028	9,031	460	1,236	2,354	15,115
December	2,376	9,895	626	1,384	2,431	16,718

Source: Bank of England, *Quarterly Bulletin* (London: Bank of England, Quarterly).

APPENDIX C

External Liabilities and Claims of U.K. Banks in U.S. Dollars, 1962-1968

THE statistical series involving the external claims and liabilities of U.K. banks denominated in U.S. dollars have been published by the Bank of England on a quarterly basis since December of 1962 and are part of two larger series involving the external claims and liabilities of U.K. banks denominated in all foreign currencies. The U.K. banks covered by these series include the domestic banks, the accepting houses, and the London offices and branches of British overseas and foreign banks.

External liabilities of U.K. banks include deposits and advances received from overseas residents and some commercial bills drawn on U.K. residents and held by the banks on behalf of their overseas customers. Similarly, external claims of U.K. banks include deposits with, and advances to, overseas residents; notes and coins; treasury bills and similar short-term paper; commercial bills drawn on overseas residents and owned by the reporting institutions or held by them on behalf of their U.K. customers; and claims on overseas customers arising from acceptances.

The figures for U.K. banks' external claims and liabilities in U.S. dollars are gross figures as shown in the reporting banks' books at the close of business on the last working day of the period—with the U.S. dollar amounts being calculated in sterling terms at the middle closing rate for that day. For the purposes of this study, the data in Table 1 have been converted back into U.S. dollars at the rate of £1 = $2.80 until September 1967 and at £1 = $2.40 thereafter. As a result of rounding, the figures for individual countries in Table 1 may not add exactly to the total figure.

TABLE I

External Liabilities and Claims of U.K. Banks in U.S. Dollars by Countries, 1962–8

(*Millions of U.S. Dollars*)

A. External Liabilities

Period Ending	Overseas Sterling Countries	United States	Canada	Latin America	Western Europe	Middle East	Japan	Other	Total
1962—December	50	288	448	126	1,257	196	6	104	2,475
1963—March	59	291	554	137	1,512	193	6	126	2,878
June	78	319	526	157	1,484	305	6	134	3,010
September	90	358	529	162	1,529	322	14	154	3,158
December	104	384	356	174	1,456	300	12	218	3,002
1964—March	118	319	375	196	1,596	291	12	193	3,100
June	148	490	470	159	1,560	339	14	249	3,430
September	165	493	520	171	1,966	347	17	213	3,892
December	213	535	739	216	2,005	392	17	263	4,379
1965—March	252	501	613	213	2,237	454	20	266	4,556
June	302	501	392	255	2,187	504	28	241	4,410
September	305	524	420	258	2,453	493	31	269	4,752
December	325	529	468	252	2,853	512	25	297	5,261
1966—March	361	652	417	269	2,898	524	31	294	5,446
June	431	868	425	314	3,186	563	31	260	6,079
September	512	997	484	316	3,598	627	28	325	6,888
December	529	952	543	355	4,211	580	28	392	7,591
1967—March	543	1,033	462	378	4,230	674	28	414	7,764
June	467	960	632	411	4,659	504	30	459	8,125
September	543	1,010	610	422	5,446	523	30	484	9,072
December	667	1,384	768	427	5,191	537	36	549	9,561
1968—March	849	1,744	866	465	5,839	540	45	753	11,104
June	1,070	2,486	921	492	7,099	528	72	751	13,420
September	1,168	2,385	938	544	7,353	511	69	1,154	14,126
December	1,207	2,568	1,173	573	8,186	537	60	1,072	15,379

TABLE 1 (continued)

External Liabilities and Claims of U.K. Banks in U.S. Dollars by Countries, 1962–8

B. External Claims

Period Ending	Overseas Sterling Countries	United States	Canada	Latin America	Western Europe	Middle East	Japan	Other	Total
1962—December	6	904	25	70	940	11	185	106	2,248
1963—March	3	1,271	22	70	949	14	235	90	2,654
June	3	1,061	20	81	1,257	22	227	112	2,783
September	3	1,005	67	81	1,352	22	272	171	2,974
December	8	795	70	75	1,453	36	246	185	2,870
1964—March	8	1,072	53	73	1,140	33	277	157	2,814
June	11	986	50	75	1,274	62	302	165	2,926
September	20	1,184	42	78	1,285	62	347	193	3,220
December	11	1,210	42	84	1,686	70	389	204	3,696
1965—March	22	1,464	25	101	1,154	64	414	185	3,430
June	25	1,425	50	151	1,221	62	406	196	3,536
September	42	1,688	104	190	1,308	73	417	202	4,024
December	64	1,596	112	199	1,795	98	465	218	4,547
1966—March	70	2,220	53	182	1,526	84	473	272	4,880
June	84	2,467	75	204	1,887	89	518	294	5,620
September	104	3,125	73	182	1,963	89	568	272	6,375
December	106	3,466	187	201	2,349	117	624	257	7,311
1967—March	115	3,253	84	226	2,128	129	765	268	6,963
June	232	3,318	176	333	2,203	168	826	394	7,652
September	193	4,132	201	364	2,248	151	851	375	8,517
December	232	4,065	276	388	2,539	196	991	499	9,189
1968—March	237	5,164	290	451	2,611	211	1,120	494	10,581
June	268	7,125	300	532	2,613	196	1,322	597	12,958
September	331	7,346	307	544	2,884	273	1,406	614	13,708
December	410	7,243	417	664	3,698	266	1,588	688	14,978

Source: Bank of England, *Quarterly Bulletin* (London: Bank of England, Quarterly).

APPENDIX D

Non-Resident Short-Term Liabilities and Assets of Ten Countries' Commercial Banks in U.S. Dollars, 1963-1968

THE statistical series covering the short-term U.S. dollar liabilities and assets of ten countries' commercial banks vis-à-vis non-residents have been published by the Bank for International Settlements since September 1963—on a semi-annual basis until September 1964 and quarterly thereafter. These series have been presented in two different ways—with one set of series including the positions of the banks vis-à-vis the United States and the other set excluding their positions vis-à-vis the United States. The figures included in the series are gross in the sense that they include interbank positions between countries but exclude positions vis-à-vis bank and non-bank residents.

The banking systems covered by these series include those of Belgium, Canada, France, West Germany, Italy, Japan, the Netherlands, Sweden, Switzerland, and the United Kingdom. As a result, the figures cover the major suppliers and users of Euro-dollars; although by no means all of them. In addition, it should be noted that the Euro-dollar assets of the B.I.S. are included in the figures for Switzerland.

TABLE 1

Non-Resident Short-term Liabilities and Assets of Ten Countries' Commercial Banks in U.S. Dollars, 1963–8

(Millions of U.S. Dollars)

A. Including Positions vis-à-vis the U.S.

1. Liabilities

Period Ending	Belgium	Canada	France	Germany	Italy	Japan	Netherlands	Sweden	Switzerland	U.K.	Total
1963—September	360	2,350	650	270	1,540	1,820	270	80	1,060	3,160	11,560
1964—March	380	2,170	610	220	1,240	2,110	280	80	1,220	3,100	11,410
September	290	2,440	620	290	1,250	2,230	310	110	1,370	3,890	12,800
December	420	2,590	810	440	1,530	2,380	360	110	1,590	4,380	14,610
1965—March	400	2,370	730	230	1,340	2,500	360	130	1,450	4,560	14,070
June	400	2,220	770	250	1,280	2,540	400	150	1,480	4,410	13,900
September	480	2,470	920	270	1,230	2,460	400	130	1,580	4,750	14,690
December	560	2,370	1,070	370	1,710	2,550	530	150	1,700	5,260	16,270
1966—March	560	2,040	770	290	1,220	2,570	570	140	1,490	5,440	15,090
June	530	1,960	810	300	1,230	2,590	650	150	1,760	6,080	16,060
September	570	1,830	1,100	330	1,630	2,460	670	150	1,730	6,890	17,360
December	670	2,150	1,330	330	1,930	2,550	790	190	1,890	7,590	19,420
1967—March	680	2,040	1,170	260	1,640	2,820	690	210	1,920	7,760	19,190
June	750	2,250	1,020	270	1,640	3,130	730	210	2,100	8,130	20,230
September	790	2,170	1,290	250	1,820	3,180	780	230	2,260	9,070	21,840
December	890	2,370	1,700	280	2,140	3,490	810	170	2,430	9,690	23,970
1968—March	990	2,320	2,150	280	2,010	3,640	910	160	2,680	11,100	26,240
June	1,120	2,430	1,890	330	1,920	3,660	870	180	2,630	13,420	28,450
September	1,180	2,550	2,040	420	2,050	3,600	880	200	2,840	14,130	29,890
December	1,310	2,700	3,040	510	2,630	3,930	970	210	2,820	15,380	33,500

TABLE 1 (continued)

Non-Resident Short-term Liabilities and Assets of Ten Countries' Commercial Banks in U.S. Dollars, 1963–8

A. Including Positions vis-à-vis the U.S.

2. Assets

Period Ending	Belgium	Canada	France	Germany	Italy	Japan	Netherlands	Sweden	Switzerland	U.K.	Total
1963—September	260	2,790	670	510	950	1,660	360	150	1,660	2,970	11,980
1964—March	310	2,360	710	510	780	1,780	330	180	1,960	2,810	11,730
September	310	2,780	720	420	810	2,020	280	200	2,110	3,190	12,840
December	360	3,180	860	440	870	2,210	390	230	2,180	3,670	14,390
1965—March	440	2,770	890	510	800	2,290	420	180	2,270	3,410	13,980
June	440	2,440	830	460	900	2,470	380	220	2,360	3,520	14,020
September	460	2,740	980	400	1,340	2,600	360	220	2,380	4,000	15,480
December	470	2,670	1,220	440	1,570	2,620	420	260	2,660	4,550	16,880
1966—March	530	2,440	1,160	440	1,280	2,600	360	230	2,520	4,880	16,440
June	520	2,360	1,280	470	1,330	2,640	450	220	2,370	5,620	17,260
September	590	2,490	1,570	660	1,880	2,840	440	230	2,310	6,380	19,390
December	740	2,890	1,860	400	2,090	2,870	550	330	2,780	7,310	21,820
1967—March	680	2,550	1,620	760	1,690	2,890	470	300	2,780	6,960	20,700
June	730	2,810	1,660	790	1,670	3,000	480	320	3,280	7,650	22,390
September	800	2,950	1,780	810	1,980	3,120	600	440	3,310	8,520	24,310
December	970	3,440	1,890	1,030	2,260	3,340	650	350	3,520	9,210	26,660
1968—March	1,020	3,350	2,390	1,140	2,140	3,350	780	370	3,850	10,580	28,970
June	1,320	3,580	2,690	750	2,250	3,580	820	430	4,340	12,960	32,720
September	1,370	3,880	2,980	1,160	2,540	3,740	880	420	4,370	13,710	35,050
December	1,460	4,130	3,430	1,490	3,200	4,090	990	490	4,390	14,980	38,650

TABLE 1 (continued)

Non-Resident Short-term Liabilities and Assets of Ten Countries' Commercial Banks in U.S. Dollars, 1963–8

B. Excluding Positions vis-à-vis the U.S.

1. Liabilities

Period Ending	Belgium	Canada	France	Germany	Italy	Japan	Netherlands	Sweden	Switzerland	U.K.	Total
1963—September	280	890	600	220	1,420	300	230	70	920	2,800	7,730
1964—March	290	860	590	190	1,060	250	240	70	1,060	2,780	7,390
September	220	860	590	260	1,010	330	270	80	1,210	3,400	8,230
December	330	910	730	390	1,250	350	320	80	1,440	3,840	9,640
1965—March	350	1,010	660	190	1,030	380	300	90	1,290	4,060	9,360
June	330	1,110	650	200	990	360	360	110	1,310	3,910	9,330
September	420	1,380	760	220	940	380	370	110	1,420	4,230	10,230
December	460	1,390	940	310	1,420	390	470	120	1,550	4,710	11,760
1966—March	460	1,190	680	240	960	430	480	120	1,320	4,770	10,650
June	410	1,180	680	260	980	480	570	120	1,590	5,210	11,480
September	470	1,120	940	290	1,380	560	600	130	1,570	5,890	12,950
December	560	1,450	1,230	260	1,700	610	720	160	1,750	6,640	15,080
1967—March	560	1,320	1,010	200	1,440	720	610	160	1,760	6,730	14,510
June	590	1,520	940	190	1,480	850	640	190	1,920	7,170	15,490
September	610	1,540	1,130	210	1,670	960	690	210	2,050	8,060	17,130
December	730	1,590	1,480	240	1,990	990	740	150	2,120	8,180	18,210
1968—March	790	1,630	1,910	230	1,880	1,150	780	140	2,430	9,140	20,080
June	870	1,710	1,640	280	1,740	1,240	750	160	2,360	10,750	21,500
September	950	1,960	1,680	370	1,880	1,340	750	180	2,500	11,340	22,950
December	1,060	2,190	2,600	450	2,480	1,450	860	190	2,500	12,580	26,360

TABLE 1 (continued)

Non-Resident Short-term Liabilities and Assets of Ten Countries' Commercial Banks in U.S. Dollars, 1963–8

B. Excluding Positions vis-à-vis the U.S.

2. Assets

Period Ending	Belgium	Canada	France	Germany	Italy	Japan	Netherlands	Sweden	Switzerland	U.K.	Total
1963—September	190	760	550	300	570	300	250	100	1,330	1,970	6,320
1964—March	220	620	540	290	450	340	230	90	1,530	1,740	6,050
September	230	890	530	190	460	510	190	120	1,710	2,010	6,840
December	260	1,210	660	160	600	550	300	140	1,610	2,460	7,950
1965—March	310	1,010	660	160	640	550	340	110	1,800	1,950	7,530
June	290	760	620	190	760	570	300	140	1,850	2,090	7,570
September	280	810	740	190	1,200	690	270	120	1,840	2,320	8,460
December	350	900	1,010	230	1,370	690	340	170	2,160	2,950	10,170
1966—March	420	840	910	290	1,110	680	280	130	2,070	2,660	9,390
June	360	830	1,050	310	1,140	720	350	140	1,850	3,150	9,900
September	430	800	1,150	470	1,670	780	350	170	1,830	3,280	10,930
December	560	930	1,270	260	1,870	790	470	240	2,300	3,830	12,520
1967—March	460	930	1,130	630	1,520	770	370	220	2,280	3,710	12,020
June	490	1,080	1,220	630	1,480	790	380	250	2,760	4,330	13,410
September	540	980	1,350	680	1,750	800	500	310	2,850	4,380	14,140
December	700	1,250	1,360	680	2,010	830	520	250	2,990	5,120	15,710
1968—March	740	1,360	1,760	950	1,930	850	640	250	3,090	5,420	16,990
June	1,010	1,370	1,900	520	1,990	970	650	320	3,550	5,830	18,110
September	1,020	1,470	1,930	860	2,270	1,060	690	310	3,520	6,360	19,490
December	1,060	1,800	2,320	960	2,910	1,240	840	330	3,540	7,720	22,720

Source: Bank for International Settlements, *Annual Report* (Basle: Bank for International Settlements, Annual).

APPENDIX E

The U.S. Voluntary Foreign Credit Restraint Programme

On 10 February 1965 against a background of rapidly expanding short- and long-term bank credit to foreigners, the U.S. administration instituted a voluntary programme to limit the expansion of foreign assets held by U.S. commercial banks and non-bank financial institutions. This programme commonly referred to as the Voluntary Guidelines Programme, has as its main element a call on all U.S. banks and financial non-banks to voluntarily limit their extension of credit to foreigners and their investment in foreign securities in accordance with a series of guidelines issued by the Federal Reserve System.

In the case of banks, the programme requested that they limit their credits to foreigners during 1965 so that they would not exceed 105 per cent of the amount outstanding as of 31 December 1964. In expanding their credits within this guideline the banks were to give priority to credits for U.S. exports and credits to underdeveloped countries. In addition, it was requested that funds owned by the banks and placed abroad in the form of U.S. dollar deposits outside the U.S. and in non-U.S. money market securities should not be expanded and that the banks should seek to reduce them in a reasonable and orderly manner.

These guidelines did not apply to the foreign branches of U.S. commercial banks as long as the funds used for credits to foreigners were derived from foreign sources—for example, through attracting Euro-dollar deposits from non-U.S. residents—and did not add to the dollar outflow from the U.S. Head-office advances to these branches, however, were covered and represented bank credit to non-residents for the purposes of this programme.

For 1966 the bank guidelines were revised to state that the expansion of foreign bank credits was not to exceed 109 per cent of the 31 December 1964 base figure. In addition, the expansion was not to exceed 106 per cent during the first quarter, 107 per cent during the second quarter, and 108 per cent during the third quarter. After including certain special considerations for banks operating with small end-1964 base figures—which would add about 1 per cent more to the total—the potential expansion of foreign credits allowed under the guidelines for 1966 was about 110 per cent of the 31 December 1964 level. During 1966 the banks, as before, were also asked not to place their own funds abroad for short-term investment purposes.

The bank guidelines for 1967 were essentially unchanged from the 1966 programme. The ceiling remained at 109 per cent of the 1964 base and the branches were requested not to use more than 20 per cent of their available leeway during any one quarter of the year. The initial guidelines for 1968, issued in November 1967, also retained the same ceiling and leeway requirements and, in addition, requested that the banks not increase loans to the developed countries of continental Western Europe above the amount outstanding on 31 October 1967.

After the devaluation of sterling in November 1967, the proposed 1968 programme was replaced by a series of more restrictive guidelines announced on 1 January 1968. The main feature of this revised programme was a reduction in the ceiling to 103 per cent of the 1964 base figure. In addition, the banks were asked not to make new term loans or renew maturing loans to the developed countries of continental Western Europe. Finally, the banks were to reduce their ceiling over the year by 40 per cent of the amount of short-term credits to countries of continental Western Europe outstanding on 31 December 1967 at the rate of 10 per cent each quarter. This was to be accomplished by reducing short-term credits to these countries by equivalent amounts. On 1 March 1968, Canada was exempted from all of the U.S. balance-of-payments guidelines and, as a result, assets held in Canada were excluded from the target ceilings.

For the U.S. non-bank financial institutions the guidelines requested that the holdings of liquid funds abroad be limited during 1965 to the 1964 year-end total and that the long-term objective be to gradually and orderly reduce such investments. On 21 June 1965, this guideline was revised to recommend that, if these holdings exceeded those as of the end of 1963 or 1964, then they should be reduced to the lesser of these totals—i.e. to the 1963 level for those who had increased their holdings during 1964 and to the 1964 level for those who had decreased their holdings during 1964.

Included under the term liquid holdings are the following types of securities (all maturing in one year or less):

(1) dollar and foreign currency deposits held in foreign banks and foreign branches of U.S. banks.

(2) short-term securities of foreign governments.

(3) foreign commercial paper, finance company credits, and bankers acceptances.

In addition, it was requested that U.S. financial non-banks limit their holdings of foreign securities having maturities of five years or less during 1965 to within 5 per cent of the end-1964 level. This ceiling was extended in June 1965 to cover loans and investments with maturities up to ten years. During 1965, however, there was no formal ceiling placed on the holding of foreign securities having maturities of greater than ten years by the financial non-banks.

For 1966, the guidelines for financial non-banks were revised to state that the investment of liquid funds abroad should be held to minimum practicable levels consistent with the operating needs of the institutions and should, in any case, not exceed the 30 September 1965 level. Secondly, investments and credits maturing in ten years or less should not exceed 10 per cent of the 31 December 1964 base figure; and, finally, total credits and investments in developed countries (other than Canada and Japan) would be subject to a ceiling of 105 per cent of the 30 September 1965 level.

In the 1967 programme for non-banks the guidelines were simplified by the establishment of a single ceiling for the 'covered' assets. These covered assets included liquid funds, loans and investments with maturities of ten years or less, and long-term and equity investments in developed countries other than Canada and Japan. For 1967 this ceiling was set at 105 per cent of the 30 September 1966 holdings. In addition, loans and investments to the developed countries of Western Europe were to be limited to the 30 September 1966 level. The initial 1968 programme established in late 1967 proposed a raising of the ceiling to 109 per cent of the 30 September 1966 base level.

On 1 January 1968, however, a more restrictive programme was announced. This reduced the ceiling to 95 per cent of the 31 December 1967 holdings. This was supplemented by requests to reduce liquid funds abroad to zero during 1968 (except for minimum working balances) and to not make any new investments—either debt or equity—in the developed countries of continental Western Europe. As in the case of the bank guidelines, Canada was given an exemption from the non-bank programme on 1 March 1968.

APPENDIX F

The U.S. Interest-Equalization Legislation

In order to reduce the large U.S. capital outflow on private account, the U.S. administration, on 18 July 1963, proposed the imposition of a temporary one-time tax on U.S. purchasers of foreign securities from foreigners at rates of up to 15 per cent on the purchase price of bonds, depending upon their maturity, and at a flat rate of 15 per cent on preferred and ordinary shares. This tax was to be applied to the purchase of both outstanding securities and new issues as of 19 July 1963. The primary purpose of this proposal was to raise the effective interest cost to foreigners on bonds sold to U.S. investors by about 1 per cent; and, thereby, discourage them from floating bond issues in the U.S. market.

This legislation, according to the original proposal, was not to be applied to long- or short-term bank loans granted to foreigners or to direct investment abroad by U.S. residents. In addition, the new issues of the less developed countries were to be exempt from the tax. On 21 July 1963, it was also agreed to exempt new Canadian bond issues on the understanding that Canada would refrain from building up foreign exchange reserves by means of borrowing in the United States.

The proposal, along with an amendment providing for the extension of the tax to long-term bank loans, if it was found that such loans were being used to circumvent the purpose of the legislation, was passed by the U.S. Congress in September of 1964. The tax was to be retroactive to 19 July 1963 and was to continue through 1965. In early 1965, the above amendment was acted upon and the legislation was extended as of 10 February 1965 to cover all bank and non-bank credits to foreigners with a maturity of one year or more. At the same time, it was also decided to continue the Interest-Equalization tax until the end of 1967. An amendment was enacted in July 1967 providing for an increase in the basic rate to $22\frac{1}{2}$ per cent and discretion to vary the rate between 15 per cent and $22\frac{1}{2}$ per cent. This legislation was retroactive to 26 January 1967 (from which date it was collected at the rate of $22\frac{1}{2}$ per cent) and was to continue until the summer of 1969. In August 1967, the basic rate was reduced to $18\frac{3}{4}$ per cent—thereby setting the additional cost of foreign borrowing in the U.S. at approximately $1\frac{1}{4}$ per cent.

APPENDIX G

Selected Three Month Euro-Currency, U.S., and U.K. Interest Rates, 1962-1967

F O R the purposes of this study we have selected the following three-month interest rates as being representative of short-term interest rates prevailing in the Euro-currency market, in the U.S., and in the U.K.: (1) The Euro-dollar rate; (2) the Euro-sterling rate; (3) the U.S. treasury bill rate; (4) the U.S. negotiable time certificate rate; (5) the U.K. treasury bill rate; (6) the U.K. local authority deposit rate. These rates, although they are not the only ones that could have been chosen, are the most representative and readily available rates in each of the markets. In addition, they are the rates most widely used in calculating covered and uncovered arbitrage margins between the three markets.

These rates, as presented in Table 1, are defined as follows:

(1) Euro-dollar rates are the middle closing rates paid on three-month U.S. dollar deposits in London. Prior to 1 October 1965 these rates were Thursday closing rates; while after this date they are Friday closing rates.

(2) Euro-sterling rates are the middle closing rates paid on three-month sterling deposits in Paris. Prior to October 1965 these rates were Thursday closing rates; while after this date they are Friday closing rates.

(3) U.S. treasury bill rates are the market offer rates on the latest ninety-one day treasury bills at 11 a.m. Friday in New York.

(4) U.S. negotiable time certificate rates are the rates paid on three-month negotiable time certificates in New York on the Wednesday before the Friday shown in Table 1. Prior to 18 May 1963 weekly data on these rates were not available.

(5) U.K. treasury bill rates are opening offer rates on the latest ninety-one day treasury bills in London prior to 11 a.m. on Friday. Rates in London for ninety-one day bills, which are calculated on a 365 day discount basis, have been adjusted to make them more comparable with U.S. treasury bill yields, which are computed on a 360 day discount basis.

(6) U.K. local authority rates are the mean of the spread of rates for local authority deposits placed for a minimum term of three months and thereafter at seven days' notice. Prior to July 1965 these rates were for the Monday after the Friday shown in Table 1; while after this date they are for the Friday shown.

TABLE 1

Selected Three Month Euro-Currency, U.S. and U.K. Interest Rates (Weekly), 1962–7

(Per Cent per Annum)

Week Ending (Friday)		U.S. Treasury Bill Rate	U.K. Treasury Bill Rate	Euro-Dollar Rate	Euro-Sterling Rate	U.K. Local Authority Rate	U.S. Time Certificate Rate
1963							
January	4	2·86	3·45	3·75	4·38	4·25	—
	11	2·86	3·36	3·63	4·19	4·25	—
	18	2·89	3·36	3·56	4·06	4·00	—
	25	2·91	3·36	3·38	4·00	4·13	—
February	1	2·91	3·32	3·38	4·44	4·25	—
	8	2·93	3·36	3·50	4·25	4·25	—
	15	2·90	3·29	3·50	4·25	4·25	—
	22	2·86	3·29	3·38	4·31	4·25	—
March	1	2·87	3·29	3·50	4·19	4·25	—
	8	2·86	3·26	3·50	4·19	4·25	—
	15	2·85	3·26	3·75	4·63	4·25	—
	22	2·88	3·67	3·69	5·25	4·50	—
	29	2·90	3·61	3·63	5·00	4·50	—
April	5	2·89	3·61	3·69	4·81	4·50	—
	12	2·88	3·54	3·69	4·81	4·50	—
	19	2·87	3·54	3·69	4·81	4·50	—
	26	2·87	3·61	3·69	4·50	4·50	—
May	3	2·87	3·61	3·69	4·50	4·50	—
	10	2·89	3·58	3·72	4·50	4·50	—
	17	2·88	3·51	3·81	4·50	4·38	3·12
	24	2·93	3·51	3·88	4·50	4·38	3·12
	31	2·97	3·56	3·81	4·50	4·38	3·50
June	7	2·97	3·54	3·75	4·50	4·38	3·20
	14	2·96	3·51	3·81	4·44	4·25	3·25
	21	2·96	3·58	3·78	4·25	4·25	3·25
	28	2·97	3·58	3·84	4·31	4·25	3·25
July	5	3·01	3·67	3·91	4·25	4·25	3·30
	12	3·19	3·67	3·94	4·38	4·25	3·37
	19	3·15	3·64	4·06	4·38	4·25	3·37
	26	3·18	3·64	4·00	4·38	4·25	3·37
August	2	3·21	3·64	3·94	4·31	4·25	3·37
	9	3·27	3·54	3·88	4·31	4·25	3·50
	16	3·31	3·58	3·94	4·19	4·13	3·50
	23	3·35	3·58	4·00	4·19	4·13	3·62
	30	3·38	3·58	4·00	4·13	4·13	3·62

TABLE 1 (continued)

Selected Three Month Euro-Currency, U.S. and U.K. Interest Rates (Weekly), 1962–7

Week Ending (Friday)	U.S. Treasury Bill Rate	U.K. Treasury Bill Rate	Euro-Dollar Rate	Euro-Sterling Rate	U.K. Local Authority Rate	U.S. Time Certificate Rate
1963						
September 6	3·32	3·58	4·19	4·19	4·00	3·50
13	3·34	3·58	4·09	4·06	4·00	3·62
20	3·88	3·62	4·06	4·06	4·25	3·55
27	3·34	3·54	4·13	4·38	4·13	3·55
October 4	3·42	3·48	4·19	4·31	4·13	3·75
11	3·42	3·48	4·06	4·31	4·13	3·75
18	3·47	3·61	4·13	4·25	4·13	3·75
25	3·43	3·61	4·13	4·31	4·13	3·75
November 1	3·46	3·63	4·13	4·38	4·13	3·75
8	3·53	3·61	4·13	4·31	4·13	3·75
15	3·52	3·61	4·13	4·38	4·25	3·80
22	3·48	3·61	4·13	4·31	4·25	3·80
29	3·47	3·61	4·19	4·38	4·25	3·80
December 6	3·49	3·64	4·44	4·63	4·38	3·80
13	3·49	3·61	4·63	4·75	4·50	3·80
20	3·51	3·61	4·56	4·63	4·50	3·80
27	3·50	3·61	4·56	4·38	4·50	3·80
1964						
January 3	3·51	3·61	4·06	4·25	4·38	3·87
10	3·52	3·61	3·94	4·19	4·25	3·85
17	3·52	3·61	4·03	4·25	4·25	3·87
24	3·49	3·61	4·06	4·25	4·25	3·80
31	3·48	3·61	4·96	4·25	4·38	3·75
February 7	3·49	3·64	4·00	4·31	4·38	3·75
14	3·50	3·64	4·00	4·44	4·38	3·80
21	3·51	3·64	4·00	4·44	4·38	3·85
28	2·56	4·16	4·06	4·88	5·13	3·75
March 6	3·52	4·16	4·31	4·88	5·00	3·85
13	3·53	4·16	4·25	4·75	5·13	3·80
20	3·52	4·16	4·19	4·88	5·13	3·80
27	3·52	4·16	4·31	4·75	5·13	3·85
April 3	3·50	4·16	4·25	4·88	5·13	3·85
10	3·44	4·16	4·13	4·94	4·88	3·85
17	3·45	4·16	4·19	4·88	4·88	3·80
24	3·43	4·16	4·13	4·94	5·00	3·80
May 1	3·43	4·16	4·19	4·94	5·00	3·75
8	3·47	4·16	4·19	4·88	5·00	3·75
15	3·45	4·25	4·19	4·75	5·00	3·75
22	3·45	4·25	4·19	4·94	5·00	3·75
29	3·46	4·25	4·19	5·06	5·00	3·80

TABLE 1 (continued)

*Selected Three Month Euro-Currency, U.S. and U.K. Interest Rates
(Weekly), 1962-7*

Week Ending (Friday)	U.S. Treasury Bill Rate	U.K. Treasury Bill Rate	Euro-Dollar Rate	Euro-Sterling Rate	U.K. Local Authority Rate	U.S. Time Certificate Rate
1964						
June 5	3·45	4·32	4·25	4·88	5·00	3·80
12	3·46	4·32	4·38	4·88	5·00	3·80
19	3·46	4·32	4·38	4·94	5·00	3·80
26	3·45	4·34	4·38	4·81	5·00	3·85
July 3	3·46	4·34	4·31	4·75	5·00	3·85
10	3·45	4·34	4·38	4·75	4·88	3·80
17	3·39	4·44	4·31	4·63	5·00	3·80
24	3·43	4·50	4·31	4·88	5·06	3·80
31	3·44	4·50	4·25	4·88	5·13	3·80
August 7	3·47	4·50	4·25	5·00	5·00	3·80
14	3·48	4·50	4·25	4·94	5·00	3·80
21	3·48	4·50	4·25	4·81	5·00	3·80
28	3·48	4·50	4·25	4·75	5·00	3·80
September 4	3·48	4·50	4·25	4·75	4·88	3·80
11	3·50	4·50	4·25	4·75	4·88	3·80
18	3·52	4·50	4·19	4·81	5·00	3·80
25	3·52	4·50	4·19	4·88	5·13	3·80
October 2	3·53	4·50	4·50	5·13	5·25	3·80
9	3·56	4·53	4·50	5·19	5·13	3·85
16	3·56	4·59	4·50	5·38	5·25	3·80
23	3·56	4·59	4·50	5·38	5·25	3·80
30	3·53	4·59	4·50	5·13	5·38	3·80
November 6	3·54	4·53	4·50	5·25	5·38	3·80
13	3·56	4·53	4·50	5·31	5·38	3·85
20	3·59	4·62	4·50	5·38	5·50	3·85
27	3·79	6·41	5·00	8·00	7·25	4·00
December 4	3·76	6·41	4·81	7·50	7·38	4·13
11	3·80	6·41	4·75	7·38	7·63	4·13
18	3·84	6·41	4·75	7·38	7·75	4·13
24	3·84	6·41	4·88	7·25	7·75	4·13
31	3·80	6·41	4·50	7·63	7·50	4·13
1965						
January 8	3·77	6·44	4·50	7·00	7·13	4·13
15	3·74	6·44	4·50	7·13	7·25	4·13
22	3·81	6·41	4·50	7·00	7·25	4·13
29	3·83	6·38	4·50	7·00	7·25	4·13
February 5	3·89	6·32	4·50	6·88	7·25	4·13
11	3·89	6·32	4·56	6·81	7·25	4·13
19	3·94	6·32	4·56	7·19	7·50	4·13
26	3·97	6·29	4·56	7·13	7·75	4·25

TABLE 1 (continued)

Selected Three Month Euro-Currency, U.S. and U.K. Interest Rates
(Weekly), 1962–7

Week Ending (Friday)		U.S. Treasury Bill Rate	U.K. Treasury Bill Rate	Euro-Dollar Rate	Euro-Sterling Rate	U.K. Local Authority Rate	U.S. Time Certificate Rate
1965							
March	5	3·93	6·26	4·75	7·13	7·88	4·25
	12	3·91	6·20	5·13	7·50	7·88	4·30
	19	3·90	6·35	4·88	7·38	7·63	4·30
	26	3·86	6·35	4·94	7·75	8·00	4·30
April	2	3·91	6·35	4·81	7·63	7·50	4·30
	9	3·90	6·32	4·81	7·69	7·50	4·25
	15	3·91	6·29	4·81	7·25	7·50	4·25
	23	3·92	6·26	4·78	7·13	7·25	4·30
	30	3·90	6·20	4·81	7·00	7·00	4·25
May	7	3·87	6·13	4·81	6·88	7·00	4·25
	14	3·88	6·13	4·88	6·63	6·75	4·30
	21	3·88	6·10	4·94	6·63	6·75	4·30
	28	3·85	6·20	5·19	7·38	6·75	4·30
June	4	3·82	5·49	5·06	7·13	6·38	4·30
	11	3·79	5·42	5·00	6·63	6·38	4·30
	18	3·77	5·42	4·94	6·88	6·38	4·30
	25	3·74	5·39	4·88	6·50	6·50	4·30
July	2	3·80	5·36	4·94	6·88	6·38	4·30
	9	3·84	5·42	4·88	6·75	6·38	4·30
	16	3·82	5·46	4·81	6·50	6·38	4·30
	23	3·79	5·46	4·63	6·50	6·50	4·25
	30	3·78	5·46	4·69	6·50	6·38	4·25
August	6	3·82	5·46	4·69	7·00	6·50	4·25
	13	3·81	5·36	4·63	6·88	6·63	4·25
	20	3·81	5·36	4·56	7·00	6·63	4·25
	27	3·83	5·39	4·50	6·81	6·63	4·25
September	3	3·84	5·36	4·44	6·88	6·63	4·25
	10	3·87	5·36	4·44	6·50	6·50	4·25
	17	3·86	5·36	4·50	6·38	6·38	4·25
	24	3·94	5·36	4·50	6·25	6·25	4·35
October	1	3·99	5·27	4·94	6·50	6·38	4·35
	8	3·98	5·24	5·13	6·38	6·19	4·45
	15	3·99	5·30	5·06	6·44	6·13	4·45
	22	4·01	5·30	5·00	6·25	6·13	4·45
	29	4·03	5·27	5·06	6·31	6·19	4·45
November	5	4·04	5·33	5·00	6·25	6·19	4·50
	12	4·05	5·33	5·03	6·38	6·19	4·50
	19	4·07	5·33	5·13	6·38	6·13	4·50
	26	4·09	5·24	5·19	6·25	6·19	4·50

TABLE 1 (continued)

Selected Three Month Euro-Currency, U.S. and U.K. Interest Rates (Weekly), 1962-7

Week Ending (Friday)	U.S. Treasury Bill Rate	U.K. Treasury Bill Rate	Euro-Dollar Rate	Euro-Sterling Rate	U.K. Local Authority Rate	U.S. Time Certificate Rate
1965 continued						
December 3	4·10	5·24	5·31	6·31	6·25	4·50
10	4·31	5·33	5·59	6·56	6·50	4·50
17	4·40	5·36	5·44	6·56	6·38	4·85
23	4·44	5·36	5·56	6·38	6·36	4·85
30	4·45	5·36	5·31	6·25	6·38	4·80
1966						
January 7	4·52	5·36	5·19	6·25	6·25	4·80
14	4·58	5·36	5·31	6·31	6·25	4·90
21	4·56	5·36	5·25	6·25	6·19	4·90
28	4·53	5·36	5·38	6·25	6·19	5·00
February 4	4·61	5·39	5·41	6·25	6·22	5·00
11	4·63	5·42	5·44	6·19	6·13	5·00
18	4·63	5·54	5·41	6·38	6·16	5·00
25	4·64	5·45	5·41	6·38	6·16	5·00
March 4	4·57	5·45	5·56	6·69	6·31	5·00
11	4·64	5·45	5·72	6·75	6·38	5·00
18	4·61	5·45	5·75	6·75	6·38	5·25
25	4·46	5·45	5·81	6·75	6·38	5·25
April 1	4·49	5·45	5·78	6·75	6·38	5·25
7	4·53	5·45	5·81	6·75	6·38	5·25
15	4·64	5·45	5·78	6·69	6·38	5·25
22	4·62	5·49	5·78	6·63	6·41	5·25
29	4·61	5·49	5·78	6·66	6·38	5·25
May 6	4·65	5·49	5·78	6·50	6·41	5·30
13	4·59	5·49	5·78	6·50	6·38	5·30
20	4·62	5·52	5·84	6·50	6·25	5·38
27	4·61	5·52	5·84	6·50	6·25	5·38
June 3	4·53	5·52	5·81	6·34	6·25	5·38
10	4·54	5·55	5·81	6·50	6·31	5·38
17	4·47	5·55	5·91	6·59	6·38	5·38
24	4·31	5·61	6·13	6·75	6·38	5·38
July 1	4·43	5·61	6·09	6·63	6·38	5·50
8	4·63	5·67	6·25	7·00	6·38	5·50
15	4·88	6·50	6·56	8·00	7·25	5·50
22	4·85	6·50	6·44	8·03	7·44	5·63
29	4·66	6·53	6·44	8·00	7·44	5·55
August 5	4·81	6·53	6·47	8·25	7·56	5·55
12	4·88	6·53	6·56	8·19	7·56	5·65
19	5·06	6·53	6·81	7·75	7·50	5·75
26	4·99	6·57	6·84	7·88	7·50	5·75

Tᴀʙʟᴇ 1 (continued)

Selected Three Month Euro-Currency, U.S. and U.K. Interest Rates
(Weekly), 1962–7

Week Ending (Friday)	U.S. Treasury Bill Rate	U.K. Treasury Bill Rate	Euro-Dollar Rate	Euro-Sterling Rate	U.K. Local Authority Rate	U.S. Time Certificate Rate
1966 continued						
September 2	5·04	6·60	6·81	7·94	7·50	5·75
9	5·16	6·60	6·72	7·81	7·50	5·85
16	5·42	6·60	6·72	7·50	7·58	5·85
23	5·47	6·60	6·66	7·50	7·44	5·85
30	5·30	6·60	7·06	7·94	7·50	5·80
October 7	5·34	6·52	7·03	7·94	7·38	5·85
14	5·45	6·44	7·00	7·88	7·38	5·85
21	5·31	6·47	7·06	7·56	7·38	6·00
28	5·21	6·35	7·06	7·78	7·38	5·63
November 4	5·29	6·38	7·06	7·50	7·38	5·75
11	5·38	6·38	6·88	7·75	7·34	5·75
18	5·32	6·57	7·03	7·66	7·25	5·75
25	5·25	6·60	7·19	7·69	7·25	5·75
December 2	5·13	6·57	7·19	7·75	7·28	5·65
9	5·14	6·53	7·00	7·69	7·34	5·65
16	4·88	6·47	6·84	7·50	7·28	5·65
23	4·77	6·47	6·75	7·38	7·28	5·65
30	4·79	6·35	6·56	7·38	7·28	5·65
1967						
January 6	4·74	6·29	6·31	6·97	7·00	5·70
13	4·77	6·20	5·94	6·69	6·88	5·70
20	4·68	6·10	5·81	6·44	6·69	5·70
27	4·58	5·95	5·69	6·44	6·53	5·40
February 3	4·44	5·79	5·56	6·41	6·50	5·40
10	4·50	5·83	5·56	6·44	6·44	5·40
17	4·58	5·89	5·56	6·25	6·31	5·15
24	4·59	5·89	5·69	6·38	6·31	5·15
March 3	4·35	5·83	5·63	6·50	6·31	5·15
10	4·33	5·73	5·63	6·44	6·38	5·15
17	4·21	5·55	5·44	6·13	6·13	5·15
23	4·11	5·49	5·44	6·28	6·22	5·15
31	4·09	5·44	5·38	6·25	6·25	5·15
April 7	3·88	5·44	5·13	5·88	6·16	5·15
14	3·86	5·30	4·94	5·88	5·88	4·30
21	3·75	5·28	4·86	5·88	5·75	4·30
28	3·68	5·30	4·69	5·69	5·88	4·30
May 5	3·65	5·12	4·84	5·63	5·75	4·50
12	3·63	5·09	5·00	5·75	5·56	4·50
19	3·52	5·09	5·06	5·75	5·50	4·38
26	3·45	5·13	5·06	5·69	5·56	4·38

TABLE 1 (continued)

Selected Three Month Euro-Currency, U.S. and U.K. Interest Rates (Weekly), 1962–7

Week Ending (Friday)	U.S. Treasury Bill Rate	U.K. Treasury Bill Rate	Euro-Dollar Rate	Euro-Sterling Rate	U.K. Local Authority Rate	U.S. Time Certificate Rate
1967 continued						
June 2	3·37	5·12	5·31	5·94	5·50	4·38
9	3·40	5·12	5·31	6·00	5·63	4·38
16	3·56	5·12	5·34	5·75	5·50	4·50
23	3·35	5·12	5·38	5·75	5·59	4·75
30	3·82	5·12	5·38	5·88	5·50	4·75
July 7	4·19	5·18	5·50	5·78	5·56	4·75
14	4·10	5·21	5·38	5·75	5·56	4·90
21	4·20	5·21	5·13	5·84	5·59	5·00
28	4·10	5·21	5·06	5·66	5·59	5·00
August 4	4·13	5·21	5·25	5·81	5·59	5·00
11	4·13	5·21	5·19	5·84	5·56	4·88
18	4·17	5·16	5·13	5·84	5·56	4·88
25	4·34	5·16	5·06	5·78	5·50	4·88
September 1	4·33	5·14	5·03	5·81	5·52	4·65
8	4·27	5·14	5·00	5·75	5·53	4·75
15	4·36	5·14	5·13	6·00	5·50	4·75
22	4·55	5·24	5·25	5·94	5·59	5·00
29	4·37	5·33	5·78	6·50	5·66	4·90
October 6	4·47	5·33	5·66	6·41	5·94	5·00
13	4·58	5·33	5·63	6·38	5·91	5·00
20	4·53	5·58	5·66	6·69	6·25	5·25
27	4·50	5·58	5·69	6·69	6·38	5·25
November 3	4·56	5·73	5·75	6·88	6·38	5·25
10	4·62	6·10	5·81	7·25	6·69	5·25
17	4·57	6·26	5·81	7·38	6·84	5·25
24	4·76	7·40	7·00	8·56	7·63	5·25
December 1	4·93	7·33	6·66	7·69	7·69	5·25
8	4·89	7·32	6·34	8·53	7·75	5·50
15	4·98	7·27	6·44	10·31	7·78	5·50
22	4·92	7·26	6·44	11·06	7·81	5·50
29	4·98	7·26	6·31	9·25	7·81	5·50

Sources: Samuel I. Katz, 'Yield Differentials in Treasury Bills, 1959–64', *Federal Reserve Bulletin* (Washington: Board of Governors of the Federal Reserve System, October 1964), 1255–7. *Federal Reserve Bulletin* (Washington: Board of Governors of the Federal Reserve System, Monthly). Bank of England, *Quarterly Bulletin* (London: Bank of England, Quarterly). *The Economist* (Weekly).

APPENDIX H

Covered and Uncovered Differentials between Selected Three Month Euro-currency, U.S. and U.K. Interest Rates, 1962-7

ARBITRAGE between short-term sterling and U.S. dollar securities can be conducted in three different ways: (1) between U.S. and U.K. securities; (2) between Euro-dollar and U.K. securities; and (3) between Euro-dollar and Euro-sterling securities. In order to study the three month covered and uncovered arbitrage margins involved in these three possibilities we have calculated three differentials: (1) between U.S. and U.K. treasury bill rates; (2) between Euro-dollar and U.K. local authority deposit rates; and (3) between Euro-dollar and Euro-sterling deposit rates. Although these differentials are not the only ones that could have been calculated they are the most representative of the arbitrage margins existing between the markets.

The uncovered differentials are calculated by subtracting U.S. treasury bill rates from U.K. treasury bill rates, Euro-dollar rates from U.K. local authority rates, and Euro-dollar rates from Euro-sterling rates—all of which can be found in Appendix G., Table 1. The covered differentials are then calculated by subtracting the forward sterling premium or discount from each of the uncovered differentials. In the case of either covered or uncovered differentials a positive differential is in favour of sterling securities while a negative differential is in favour of U.S. dollar securities. These differentials are presented in Table 1.

In Table 1 the forward sterling premium or discount is a rate per annum computed on the basis of the midpoint quotation (i.e. midpoint between bid and offer) for both spot and forward sterling in New York at noon on Friday prior to 27 December 1963 and at 11 a.m. on Friday thereafter.

TABLE 1

Calculation of Covered and Uncovered Differentials between Three Month Euro-Currency, U.S., and U.K. Interest Rates (Weekly), 1962-7

(Per Cent Per Annum)

Week Ending (Friday)	Uncovered Differentials				Covered Differentials		
	U.S.-U.K. Treasury Bill Rates	Euro-dollar-Euro-Sterling Rates	Euro-dollar-U.K. Local Authority Rates	Forward Sterling Premium (+) Discount (−)	U.S.-U.K. Treasury Bill Rates	Euro-dollar-Euro-Sterling Rates	Euro-dollar-U.K. Local Authority Rates
1963							
January 4	+ ·59	+ ·63	+ ·50	− ·45	+ ·14	+ ·18	+ ·05
11	+ ·50	+ ·56	+ ·62	− ·51	− ·01	+ ·05	+ ·11
18	+ ·47	+ ·50	+ ·44	− ·55	− ·08	− ·05	− ·11
25	+ ·45	+ ·62	+ ·75	− ·59	− ·14	+ ·03	+ ·16
February 1	+ ·41	+ 1·06	+ ·87	− ·74	− ·33	+ ·32	+ ·13
8	+ ·43	+ ·75	+ ·75	− ·69	− ·26	+ ·06	+ ·06
15	+ ·39	+ ·75	+ ·75	− ·67	− ·28	+ ·08	+ ·08
22	+ ·43	+ ·93	+ ·87	− ·75	− ·32	+ ·18	+ ·12
March 1	+ ·42	+ ·69	+ ·75	− ·77	− ·35	− ·08	− ·02
8	+ ·40	+ ·69	+ ·75	− ·83	− ·43	− ·14	− ·08
15	+ ·41	+ ·88	+ ·50	− 1·14	− ·73	− ·26	− ·64
22	+ ·79	+ 1·56	+ ·81	− 1·28	− ·49	+ ·28	− ·47
29	+ ·71	+ 1·37	+ ·87	− 1·33	− ·62	+ ·04	− ·46
April 5	+ ·72	+ 1·12	+ ·81	− 1·14	− ·42	− ·02	− ·33
12	+ ·66	+ 1·12	+ ·81	− 1·21	− ·55	− ·09	− ·40
19	+ ·67	+ 1·12	+ ·81	− 1·15	− ·48	− ·03	− ·34
26	+ ·74	+ ·81	+ ·81	− ·89	− ·15	− ·08	− ·08

TABLE 1 (continued)

Differentials between Three Month Euro-Currency, U.S., and U.K. Interest Rates (Weekly), 1962–7

Week Ending (Friday)	Uncovered Differentials			Forward Sterling Premium (+) Discount (−)	Covered Differentials		
	U.S.–U.K. Treasury Bill Rates	Euro-dollar–Euro-Sterling Rates	Euro-dollar–U.K. Local Authority Rates		U.S.–U.K. Treasury Bill Rates	Euro-dollar–Euro-Sterling Rates	Euro-dollar–U.K. Local Authority Rates
1963 continued							
May 3	+ ·74	+ ·81	+ ·81	− ·70	+ ·04	+ ·11	+ ·11
10	+ ·69	+ ·78	+ ·78	− ·73	− ·04	+ ·05	+ ·05
17	+ ·63	+ ·69	+ ·57	− ·71	− ·08	− ·02	− ·14
24	+ ·58	+ ·62	+ ·50	− ·75	− ·17	− ·13	− ·25
31	+ ·59	+ ·69	+ ·57	− ·65	− ·06	+ ·04	− ·08
June 7	+ ·57	+ ·75	+ ·63	− ·64	− ·07	+ ·11	− ·01
14	+ ·55	+ ·63	+ ·44	− ·62	− ·07	+ ·01	− ·18
21	+ ·62	+ ·47	+ ·47	− ·49	+ ·13	+ ·02	− ·02
28	+ ·61	+ ·47	+ ·41	− ·50	+ ·11	− ·03	− ·09
July 5	+ ·66	+ ·34	+ ·34	− ·46	+ ·20	− ·12	− ·12
12	+ ·48	+ ·44	+ ·31	− ·38	+ ·10	+ ·06	− ·07
19	+ ·49	+ ·32	+ ·19	− ·27	+ ·22	+ ·05	− ·08
26	+ ·46	+ ·38	+ ·25	− ·32	+ ·14	+ ·06	− ·07
August 2	+ ·43	+ ·37	+ ·31	− ·31	+ ·12	+ ·06	—
9	+ ·27	+ ·43	+ ·37	− ·33	− ·06	+ ·10	+ ·04
16	+ ·27	+ ·25	+ ·19	− ·20	+ ·07	+ ·05	− ·01
23	+ ·23	+ ·19	+ ·13	− ·15	+ ·08	+ ·04	− ·02
30	+ ·20	+ ·13	+ ·13	− ·12	+ ·08	+ ·01	+ ·01
September 6	+ ·26	—	− ·19	− ·02	+ ·24	− ·02	− ·21
13	+ ·24	− ·03	− ·09	− ·02	+ ·22	− ·05	− ·11
20	+ ·24	—	+ ·19	− ·05	+ ·19	− ·05	+ ·14
27	+ ·20	+ ·25	—	− ·15	+ ·05	+ ·10	− ·15

TABLE 1 (continued)

Differentials between Three Month Euro-Currency, U.S., and U.K. Interest Rates (Weekly), 1962–7

Week Ending (Friday)	Uncovered Differentials			Covered Differentials			
	U.S.–U.K. Treasury Bill Rates	Euro-dollar–Euro-Sterling Rates	Euro-dollar–U.K. Local Authority Rates	Forward Sterling Premium (+) Discount (−)	U.S.–U.K. Treasury Bill Rates	Euro-dollar–Euro-Sterling Rates	Euro-dollar–U.K. Local Authority Rates
1963 continued							
October 4	+ ·06	+ ·12	− ·06	− ·22	− ·16	− ·10	− ·28
11	+ ·06	+ ·25	+ ·07	− ·35	− ·29	− ·10	− ·28
18	+ ·14	+ ·12		− ·29	− ·15	− ·17	− ·29
25	+ ·18	+ ·18		− ·23	− ·05	− ·05	− ·23
November 1	+ ·17	+ ·25		− ·25	− ·08	−	− ·25
8	+ ·08	+ ·18	+ ·12	− ·21	− ·13	+ ·03	− ·21
15	+ ·09	+ ·25	+ ·12	− ·22	− ·13	+ ·03	− ·10
22	+ ·13	+ ·18	+ ·06	− ·17	− ·04	+ ·01	− ·05
29	+ ·14	+ ·19	+ ·06	− ·16	− ·02	+ ·03	− ·10
December 6	+ ·15	+ ·19	− ·06	− ·17	− ·02	+ ·02	− ·23
13	+ ·12	+ ·12	− ·13	− ·14	− ·02	− ·02	− ·27
20	+ ·10	+ ·07	− ·06	− ·13	− ·03	− ·06	− ·19
27	+ ·11	− ·18	− ·06	− ·16	− ·05	− ·34	− ·22
1964							
January 3	+ ·10	+ ·19	+ ·32	− ·24	− ·14	− ·05	+ ·08
10	+ ·09	+ ·25	+ ·31	− ·35	− ·26	− ·10	− ·04
17	+ ·09	+ ·22	+ ·22	− ·31	− ·22	− ·09	− ·09
24	+ ·12	+ ·19	+ ·19	− ·35	− ·23	− ·16	− ·16
31	+ ·13	+ ·19	+ ·32	− ·31	− ·18	− ·12	+ ·01

Table 1 (continued)

Differentials between Three Month Euro-Currency, U.S., and U.K. Interest Rates (Weekly), 1962–7

Week Ending (Friday)	Uncovered Differentials			Forward Sterling Premium (+) Discount (−)	Covered Differentials		
	U.S.–U.K. Treasury Bill Rates	Euro-dollar–Euro-Sterling Rates	Euro-dollar–U.K. Local Authority Rates		U.S.–U.K. Treasury Bill Rates	Euro-dollar–Euro-Sterling Rates	Euro-dollar–U.K. Local Authority Rates
1964 continued							
February 7	+·15	+·31	+·38	−·44	−·29	−·13	−·06
14	+·14	+·44	+·38	−·45	−·31	−·01	−·07
21	+·13	+·14	+·38	−·45	−·32	−·01	−·07
28	+·60	+·82	+1·07	−·69	−·09	+·13	+·38
March 6	+·64	+·57	+·69	−·66	−·02	−·09	+·03
13	+·63	+·59	+·88	−·65	−·02	−·15	+·23
20	+·64	+·69	+·92	−·71	−·07	−·02	+·21
27	+·64	+·44	+·82	−·71	−·07	−·27	+·11
April 3	+·66	+·63	+·88	−·77	−·11	−·14	+·11
10	+·72	+·81	+·75	−·76	−·04	+·05	−·01
17	+·71	+·69	+·69	−·76	−·05	−·07	−·07
24	+·73	+·81	+·87	−·76	−·03	+·05	−·09
May 1	+·73	+·75	+·81	−·76	−·03	−·01	+·05
8	+·69	+·69	+·81	−·76	−·07	−·07	+·09
15	+·80	+·56	+·81	−·77	−·03	−·21	+·04
22	+·80	+·75	+·81	−·79	+·01	−·04	+·02
29	+·79	+·87	+·81	−·76	+·03	+·11	+·05
June 5	+·87	+·63	+·75	−·66	+·21	−·03	+·09
12	+·86	+·50	+·62	−·60	+·26	−·10	+·02
19	+·86	+·56	+·62	−·57	+·29	−·02	+·05
26	+·89	+·43	+·62	−·49	+·40	−·06	+·13

TABLE 1 (continued)

Differentials between Three Month Euro-Currency, U.S., and U.K. Interest Rates (Weekly), 1962–7

Week Ending (Friday)	Uncovered Differentials				Covered Differentials		
	U.S.–U.K. Treasury Bill Rates	Euro-dollar–Euro-Sterling Rates	Euro-dollar–U.K. Local Authority Rates	Forward Sterling Premium (+) Discount (−)	U.S.–U.K. Treasury Bill Rates	Euro-dollar–Euro-Sterling Rates	Euro-dollar–U.K. Local Authority Rates
1964 continued							
July 3	+ ·88	+ ·44	+ ·69	− ·57	+ ·31	− ·13	+ ·12
10	+ ·89	+ ·37	+ ·50	− ·54	+ ·35	− ·17	− ·04
17	+1·05	+ ·32	+ ·69	− ·50	+ ·55	− ·18	+ ·19
24	+1·07	+ ·57	+ ·75	− ·73	+ ·34	− ·16	+ ·02
31	+1·06	+ ·63	+ ·88	− ·67	+ ·39	− ·04	+ ·21
August 7	+1·03	+ ·75	+ ·75	− ·72	+ ·31	+ ·03	− ·03
14	+1·02	+ ·69	+ ·75	− ·67	+ ·35	+ ·02	+ ·08
21	+1·02	+ ·56	+ ·75	− ·60	+ ·42	− ·04	+ ·15
28	+1·04	+ ·50	+ ·75	− ·64	+ ·40	− ·14	+ ·11
September 4	+1·02	+ ·50	+ ·63	− ·62	+ ·40	− ·12	+ ·01
11	+1·00	+ ·50	+ ·63	− ·66	+ ·34	− ·16	− ·03
18	+ ·98	+ ·62	+ ·81	− ·72	+ ·26	− ·10	+ ·09
25	+ ·98	+ ·69	+ ·94	− ·75	+ ·23	− ·06	+ ·19
October 2	+ ·97	+ ·63	+ ·75	− ·75	+ ·22	− ·12	—
9	+ ·97	+ ·69	+ ·63	− ·76	+ ·21	− ·07	− ·13
16	+1·03	+ ·88	+ ·75	− ·96	+ ·07	− ·08	− ·21
23	+1·03	+ ·88	+ ·75	− ·91	+ ·12	− ·03	+ ·16
30	+1·06	+ ·63	+ ·88	− ·82	+ ·24	− ·19	+ ·06
November 6	+ ·99	+ ·75	+ ·88	− ·91	+ ·08	− ·16	− ·03
13	+ ·97	+ ·81	+ ·88	− ·92	+ ·05	− ·11	− ·04
20	+1·03	+ ·88	+1·00	−1·01	+ ·02	− ·13	− ·01
27	+2·62	+3·00	+2·25	−2·65	− ·03	+ ·35	− ·40

TABLE 1 (continued)

Differentials between Three Month Euro-Currency, U.S., and U.K. Interest Rates (Weekly), 1962–7

Week Ending (Friday)	Uncovered Differentials				Covered Differentials		
	U.S.–U.K. Treasury Bill Rates	Euro-dollar–Euro-Sterling Rates	Euro-dollar–U.K. Local Authority Rates	Forward Sterling Premium (+) Discount (−)	U.S.–U.K. Treasury Bill Rates	Euro-dollar–Euro-Sterling Rates	Euro-dollar–U.K. Local Authority Rates
1964 continued							
December 4	+2·65	+2·69	+2·51	−2·54	+·11	+·15	−·04
11	+2·61	+2·63	+2·88	−2·68	−·07	−·05	+·20
18	+2·57	+2·63	+3·00	−2·62	−·05	+·01	+·38
24	+2·57	+2·37	+2·87	−2·69	−·12	−·32	+·18
31	+2·61	+3·13	+3·00	−2·72	−·11	+·41	+·28
1965 January 8	+2·67	+2·50	+2·63	−2·61	+·06	−·11	+·02
15	+2·70	+2·63	+2·75	−2·71	−·01	−·08	−·04
22	+2·60	+2·50	+2·75	−2·61	−·01	−·11	−·14
29	+2·55	+2·50	+2·75	−2·65	−·10	−·15	−·10
February 5	+2·43	+2·38	+2·75	−2·55	−·12	−·17	−·20
11	+2·43	+2·25	+2·69	−2·52	−·09	−·27	−·17
19	+2·38	+2·63	+2·94	−2·85	−·47	−·22	−·09
26	+2·32	+2·57	+3·19	−2·82	−·50	−·25	−·37
March 5	+2·33	+2·38	+3·13	−2·78	−·45	−·40	−·35
12	+2·29	+2·37	+2·75	−2·54	−·25	−·17	−·21
19	+2·45	+2·50	+2·75	−2·74	−·29	−·24	−·01
26	+2·49	+2·81	+3·06	−3·25	−·76	−·44	−·19
April 2	+2·44	+2·82	+2·69	−3·02	−·58	−·20	−·33
9	+2·42	+2·88	+2·69	−2·97	−·55	−·09	−·28
15	+2·38	+2·44	+2·69	−2·55	−·17	−·11	−·28
23	+2·34	+2·35	+2·47	−2·29	+·05	+·06	−·14
30	+2·30	+2·19	+2·19	−2·33	−·03	−·14	−·14

TABLE 1 (continued)

Differentials between Three Month Euro-Currency, U.S., and U.K. Interest Rates (Weekly), 1962-7

Week Ending (Friday)	Uncovered Differentials				Covered Differentials		
	U.S.–U.K. Treasury Bill Rates	Euro-dollar–Euro-Sterling Rates	Euro-dollar–U.K. Local Authority Rates	Forward Sterling Premium (+) Discount (−)	U.S.–U.K. Treasury Bill Rates	Euro-dollar–Euro-Sterling Rates	Euro-dollar–U.K. Local Authority Rates
1965 continued							
May 7	+2·26	+2·07	+2·19	−2·01	+·25	+·06	+·18
14	+2·25	+1·75	+1·87	−1·96	+·29	−·21	−·09
21	+2·22	+1·69	+1·81	−1·82	+·40	−·13	−·01
28	+2·35	+2·19	+1·56	−2·44	−·09	+·25	−·88
June 4	+1·67	+2·07	+1·32	−1·82	−·15	+·25	−·50
11	+1·63	+1·63	+1·38	−1·68	−·05	−·05	−·30
18	+1·65	+1·94	+1·44	−1·96	−·31	−·02	−·52
25	+1·65	+1·62	+1·62	−1·60	+·05	−·02	+·02
July 2	+1·56	+1·94	+1·44	−1·93	+·37	+·01	−·49
9	+1·58	+1·87	+1·50	−1·82	−·24	+·05	−·32
16	+1·64	+1·69	+1·57	−1·85	−·21	−·16	−·28
23	+1·67	+1·87	+1·87	−1·98	−·31	−·11	−·11
30	+1·68	+1·81	+1·69	−2·09	−·41	−·28	−·40
August 6	+1·64	+2·31	+1·81	−2·54	−·90	−·23	−·73
13	+1·55	+2·25	+2·00	−2·49	−·94	−·24	−·49
20	+1·55	+2·44	+2·07	−2·51	−·96	−·07	−·44
27	+1·56	+2·31	+2·13	−2·49	−·93	−·18	−·36
September 3	+1·52	+2·44	+2·19	−2·59	−1·07	−·15	−·40
10	+1·49	+2·06	+2·06	−2·09	−·60	−·03	−·03
17	+1·50	+1·88	+1·88	−1·88	−·38	—	—
24	+1·42	+1·75	+1·75	−1·73	−·31	+·02	+·02

TABLE 1 (continued)

Differentials between Three Month Euro-Currency, U.S., and U.K. Interest Rates (Weekly), 1962–7

Week Ending (Friday)	Uncovered Differentials			Covered Differentials			
	U.S.–U.K. Treasury Bill Rates	Euro-dollar–Euro-Sterling Rates	Euro-dollar–U.K. Local Authority Rates	Forward Sterling Premium (+) Discount (−)	U.S.–U.K. Treasury Bill Rates	Euro-dollar–Euro-Sterling Rates	Euro-dollar–U.K. Local Authority Rates
1965 continued							
October 1	+1·28	+1·56	+1·44	−1·38	−·10	+·18	+·06
8	+1·26	+1·25	+1·06	−1·35	−·09	−·10	−·29
15	+1·31	+1·38	+1·07	−1·27	+·04	+·11	−·20
22	+1·29	+1·25	+1·13	−1·23	+·06	+·02	−·10
29	+1·24	+1·25	+1·13	−1·29	−·05	−·04	−·16
November 5	+1·29	+1·25	+1·19	−1·33	−·04	−·08	−·14
12	+1·28	+1·35	+1·16	−1·32	−·04	+·03	−·16
19	+1·26	+1·25	+1·00	−1·26	—	+·01	−·16
26	+1·15	+1·06	+1·00	−1·10	+·05	−·04	−·26
December 3	+1·14	+1·00	+·94	−1·07	+·07	−·07	−·10
10	+1·02	+·97	+·91	−·97	+·05	—	−·13
17	+·96	+1·12	+·94	−1·02	−·06	+·10	−·06
23	+·92	+·82	+·82	−·88	+·04	−·06	−·08
30	+·91	+·94	+1·07	−1·03	−·12	−·09	+·04
1966 January 7	+·84	+1·06	+1·06	−1·03	−·19	+·03	+·03
14	+·78	+1·00	+·94	−1·03	−·25	−·03	−·09
21	+·80	+1·00	+·94	−·95	−·15	+·05	−·01
28	+·83	+·87	+·81	−·87	−·04	—	−·06

TABLE 1 (continued)

Differentials between Three Month Euro-Currency, U.S., and U.K. Interest Rates (Weekly), 1962-7

Week Ending (Friday)	Uncovered Differentials				Covered Differentials		
	U.S.–U.K. Treasury Bill Rates	Euro-dollar–Euro-Sterling Rates	Euro-dollar–U.K. Local Authority Rates	Forward Sterling Premium (+) Discount (−)	U.S.–U.K. Treasury Bill Rates	Euro-dollar–Euro-Sterling Rates	Euro-dollar–U.K. Local Authority Rates
1966 continued							
February 4	+·78	+·84	+·81	−·86	−·08	−·02	−·05
11	+·79	+·75	+·69	−·87	−·08	−·12	−·18
18	+·91	+·97	+·75	−·92	−·01	+·05	−·17
25	+·81	+·97	+·75	−·97	−·16	—	−·22
March 4	+·88	+1·13	+·75	−1·11	−·23	+·02	−·36
11	+·81	+1·03	+·66	−1·03	−·22	—	−·37
18	+·84	+1·00	+·63	−1·00	−·16	—	−·37
25	+·99	+·94	+·57	−·92	+·07	+·02	−·35
April 1	+·96	+·97	+·60	−·96	—	+·01	−·36
7	+·92	+·94	+·57	−·87	+·05	+·07	−·30
15	+·81	+·91	+·60	−·89	−·08	+·02	−·29
22	+·87	+·85	+·63	−·80	+·07	+·05	−·17
29	+·88	+·88	+·60	−·83	+·05	+·05	−·23
May 6	+·84	+·72	+·63	−·75	+·09	−·03	−·12
13	+·90	+·72	+·60	−·72	+·18	—	−·12
20	+·90	+·66	+·41	−·69	+·21	−·03	−·28
27	+·91	+·66	+·41	−·67	+·24	−·01	−·26
June 3	+·99	+·53	+·44	−·62	+·37	−·09	−·18
10	+1·01	+·69	+·50	−·79	+·22	−·10	−·29
17	+1·08	+·68	+·47	−·62	+·46	+·06	−·15
24	+1·30	+·62	+·25	−·61	+·69	+·01	−·36

TABLE 1 (continued)

Differentials between Three Month Euro-Currency, U.S., and U.K. Interest Rates (Weekly), 1962–7

Week Ending (Friday)	Uncovered Differentials			Forward Sterling Premium (+) Discount (−)	Covered Differentials		
	U.S.–U.K. Treasury Bill Rates	Euro-dollar– Euro-Sterling Rates	Euro-dollar– U.K. Local Authority Rates		U.S.–U.K. Treasury Bill Rates	Euro-dollar– Euro-Sterling Rates	Euro-dollar– U.K. Local Authority Rates
1966 continued							
July 1	+1·18	+·54	+·29	−·59	+·59	−·05	−·30
8	+1·04	+·75	+·13	−·72	+·32	+·03	−·59
15	+1·62	+1·44	+·69	−1·46	+·16	−·02	−·77
22	+1·65	+1·59	+1·00	−1·45	+·20	+·14	−·45
29	+1·87	+1·56	+1·00	−1·58	+·29	−·02	−·58
August 5	+1·72	+1·78	+1·09	−1·83	−·11	−·05	−·74
12	+1·65	+1·63	+1·00	−1·61	+·04	+·02	−·61
19	+1·47	+·94	+·69	−1·03	+·44	−·09	−·34
26	+1·58	+1·04	+·66	−1·05	+·53	−·01	−·39
September 2	+1·56	+1·13	+·69	−1·11	+·45	+·02	−·42
9	+1·44	+1·09	+·78	−·95	+·49	+·14	−·17
16	+1·18	+·88	+·66	−·85	+·33	+·03	−·19
23	+1·13	+·84	+·78	−·90	+·23	−·06	−·12
30	+1·30	+·88	+·44	−·94	+·36	−·06	−·50
October 7	+1·18	+·91	+·35	−·77	+·41	+·14	−·42
14	+·99	+·88	+·38	−·78	+·21	+·10	−·40
21	+1·16	+·50	+·32	−·52	+·64	−·02	−·20
28	+1·14	+·72	+·32	−·65	+·49	+·07	−·33
November 4	+1·09	+·44	+·32	−·60	+·49	−·16	−·28
11	+1·00	+·87	+·46	−·75	+·25	+·12	−·29
18	+1·25	+·63	+·22	−·66	+·59	−·03	−·44
25	+1·35	+·50	+·06	−·54	+·81	−·04	−·48

TABLE 1 (continued)

Differentials between Three Month Euro-Currency, U.S., and U.K. Interest Rates (Weekly), 1962–7

Week Ending (Friday)	Uncovered Differentials			Covered Differentials			
	U.S.–U.K. Treasury Bill Rates	Euro-dollar–Euro-Sterling Rates	Euro-dollar–U.K. Local Authority Rates	Forward Sterling Premium (+) Discount (−)	U.S.–U.K. Treasury Bill Rates	Euro-dollar–Euro-Sterling Rates	Euro-dollar–U.K. Local Authority Rates
1966 continued							
December 2	+1·44	+ ·56	+ ·09	− ·52	+ ·92	+ ·04	− ·43
9	+1·39	+ ·69	+ ·34	− ·73	+ ·66	− ·04	− ·39
16	+1·59	+ ·66	+ ·44	− ·59	+1·00	+ ·07	− ·15
23	+1·70	+ ·63	+ ·53	− ·67	+1·03	− ·04	− ·14
30	+1·56	+ ·82	+ ·72	− ·74	+ ·82	+ ·08	− ·02
1967							
January 6	+1·55	+ ·66	+ ·69	− ·55	+1·00	+ ·11	+ ·14
13	+1·43	+ ·75	+ ·94	− ·63	+ ·80	+ ·12	+ ·31
20	+1·42	+ ·63	+ ·88	− ·69	+ ·73	− ·03	+ ·19
27	+1·37	+ ·75	+ ·84	− ·74	+ ·63	+ ·01	+ ·10
February 3	+1·35	+ ·85	+ ·94	− ·75	+ ·60	+ ·10	+ ·19
10	+1·33	+ ·88	+ ·88	− ·81	+ ·52	+ ·07	+ ·07
17	+1·31	+ ·69	+ ·75	− ·75	+ ·56	− ·06	+ ·00
24	+1·30	+ ·69	+ ·62	− ·75	+ ·85	− ·06	− ·13
March 3	+1·48	+ ·87	+ ·68	− ·79	+ ·69	+ ·12	− ·11
10	+1·40	+ ·81	+ ·75	− ·80	+ ·60	− ·01	− ·05
17	+1·34	+ ·69	+ ·69	− ·70	+ ·64	− ·01	− ·01
24	+1·38	+ ·84	+ ·78	− ·85	+ ·53	− ·01	− ·07
31	+1·35	+ ·87	+ ·87	− ·82	+ ·53	+ ·05	+ ·05

TABLE 1 (continued)

Differentials between Three Month Euro-Currency, U.S., and U.K. Interest Rates (Weekly), 1962-7

Week Ending (Friday)	Uncovered Differentials				Covered Differentials		
	U.S.-U.K. Treasury Bill Rates	Euro-dollar-Euro-Sterling Rates	Euro-dollar-U.K. Local Authority Rates	Forward Sterling Premium (+) Discount (−)	U.S.-U.K. Treasury Bill Rates	Euro-dollar-Euro-Sterling Rates	Euro-dollar-U.K. Local Authority Rates
1967 continued							
April 7	+1·56	+·75	+1·03	−·89	+·67	−·14	+·14
14	+1·44	+·94	+·94	−·89	+·55	+·05	+·05
21	+1·53	+1·02	+·89	−·89	+·64	+·23	·00
28	+1·62	+1·00	+1·19	−·99	+·63	−·01	+·20
May 5	+1·47	+·79	+·91	−·81	+·66	−·02	+·10
12	+1·46	+·75	+·56	−·78	+·68	−·02	−·22
19	+1·57	+·69	+·44	−·70	+·87	−·01	−·26
26	+1·68	+·63	+·44	−·69	+·99	−·06	−·25
June 2	+1·75	+·63	+·19	−·70	+1·05	−·07	−·51
9	+1·72	+·69	+·32	−·45	+1·27	+·24	−·13
16	+1·56	+·41	+·16	−·48	+1·08	−·07	−·32
23	+1·77	+·37	+·21	−·39	+1·38	−·02	−·18
30	+1·30	+·50	+·12	−·43	+·87	+·07	−·31
July 7	+·99	+·28	+·06	−·29	+·70	−·01	−·23
14	+1·11	+·37	+·18	−·43	+·68	−·06	−·25
21	+1·01	+·71	+·46	−·67	+·34	+·04	−·21
28	+1·11	+·60	+·53	−·62	+·49	−·02	−·09
August 4	+1·08	+·56	+·34	−·57	+·51	−·01	−·23
11	+1·08	+·65	+·37	−·65	+·43	·00	−·28
18	+·99	+·71	+·43	−·69	+·30	+·02	−·26
25	+·82	+·72	+·44	−·75	+·07	−·03	−·31

TABLE 1 (continued)

Differentials between Three Month Euro-Currency, U.S., and U.K. Interest Rates (Weekly), 1962–7

Week Ending (Friday)	Uncovered Differentials			Covered Differentials			
	U.S.–U.K. Treasury Bill Rates	Euro-dollar–Euro-Sterling Rates	Euro-dollar–U.K. Local Authority Rates	Forward Sterling Premium (↑) Discount (−)	U.S.–U.K. Treasury Bill Rates	Euro-dollar–Euro-Sterling Rates	Euro-dollar–U.K. Local Authority Rates
1967 continued							
September 1	+ ·81	+ ·78	+ ·50	− ·80	+ ·01	− ·02	− ·30
8	+ ·87	+ ·75	+ ·53	− ·81	+ ·06	− ·06	− ·28
15	+ ·78	+ ·87	+ ·37	− ·80	+ ·02	+ ·07	− ·43
22	+ ·69	+ ·69	+ ·34	− ·69	·00	·00	− ·35
29	+ ·96	+ ·72	+ ·88	− ·68	+ ·28	+ ·04	+ ·20
October 6	+ ·86	+ ·75	+ ·28	− ·69	+ ·17	+ ·06	− ·41
13	+ ·75	+ ·75	+ ·28	− ·75	·00	·00	− ·47
20	+ 1·05	+ 1·03	+ ·59	− ·96	+ ·09	+ ·05	− ·37
27	+ 1·08	+ 1·00	+ ·69	− ·98	+ ·10	+ ·02	− ·29
November 3	+ 1·17	+ 1·13	+ ·63	− 1·11	+ ·06	+ ·02	− ·48
10	+ 1·48	+ 1·44	+ ·88	− 1·35	+ ·13	+ ·09	− ·47
17	+ 1·69	+ 1·57	+ 1·03	− 1·64	+ ·05	+ ·07	− ·61
24	+ 2·64	+ 1·56	+ ·63	− ·99	+ 1·65	+ ·57	− ·36
December 1	+ 2·40	+ 1·03	+ 1·03	− 1·17	+ 1·23	− ·14	− ·14
8	+ 2·43	+ 2·19	+ 1·41	− 2·83	− ·40	− ·64	− 1·42
15	+ 2·29	+ 3·87	+ 1·34	− 4·72	− 2·43	− ·85	− 3·38
22	+ 2·34	+ 4·62	+ 1·37	− 4·67	− 2·33	− ·05	− 3·30
29	+ 2·28	+ 2·94	+ 1·50	− 2·83	− ·55	+ ·11	− 1·33

Sources: Samuel I. Katz, 'Yield Differentials in Treasury Bills, 1959–64', *Federal Reserve Bulletin* (Washington: Board of Governors of the Federal Reserve System, October 1964), 1255–7. *Federal Reserve Bulletin* (Washington: Board of Governors of the Federal Reserve System, Monthly). Appendix G, Table 1.

16

BIBLIOGRAPHY

BOOKS

BLOCH, ERNEST, *Euro-Dollars: An Emerging International Money Market*, New York: New York University, 1966.

CHALMERS, ERIC, ed. *Readings in the Euro-Dollar*, London: W. P. Griffith & Sons, 1969.

EINZIG, PAUL, *The Euro-Dollar System*, London: Macmillan and Co. Ltd., 1964.

JOHNSON, NORRIS O., *Euro-Dollars in the New International Money Market*, New York: First National City Bank, 1964.

KLOPSTOCK, FRED H., *The Euro-Dollar Market: Some Unresolved Issues*, Princeton: Princeton University, 1968.

MORTENSON, G. CARROLL, *The Euro-Dollar Market*, Boston: Bankers Publishing Co., 1964.

REIERSON, ROY L., *The Euro-Dollar Market*, New York: Bankers Trust Company, 1964.

SWOBODA, ALEXANDER K., *The Euro-Dollar Market: An Interpretation*, Princeton: Princeton University, 1968.

ARTICLES

ALTMAN, OSCAR L., 'Foreign Markets for Dollars, Sterling and Other Currencies', *International Monetary Fund Staff Papers*, VIII (1961), 313–52.

—— 'Recent Developments in Foreign Markets for Dollars and Other Currencies', *International Monetary Fund Staff Papers*, X (1963), 48–96.

—— 'Euro-Dollars: Some Further Comments', *International Monetary Fund Staff Papers*, XII (1965), 1–16.

BANK OF ENGLAND, 'U.K. Banks' External Liabilities and Claims in Foreign Currencies', *Quarterly Bulletin*, IV (1964), 100–8.

BELL, G. L., 'Credit Creation Through Euro-Dollars', *The Banker*, CXIV (1964), 494–502.

CHRISTIE, HERBERT, 'Euro-Dollars and the Balance of Payments', *The Banker*, CXVII (1967), 34–45.

CLENDENNING, E. WAYNE, 'Euro-Dollars: The Problem of Control', *The Banker*, CXVIII (1968), 321–9.

EINZIG, PAUL, 'Dollar Deposits in London', *The Banker,* CX (1960), 23–7.

—— 'Statics and Dynamics of the Euro-Dollar Market', *Economic Journal,* LXXI (1961), 592–5.

—— 'Recent Changes in The Euro-Dollar System', *Journal of Finance,* XIX (1964), 443–51.

HENDERSHOTT, P. H., 'The Structure of International Interest Rates: The U.S. Treasury Bill Rate and the Euro-Dollar Deposit Rate', *Journal of Finance,* XXII (1967), 455–65.

HOLMES, ALAN R. and KLOPSTOCK, FRED H., 'The Market for Dollar Deposits in Europe', *Federal Reserve Bank of New York Monthly Review,* XLII (1960), 197–202.

KINDLEBERGER, C. P., 'The Euro-Dollar and the Internationaliza-tion of U.S. Monetary Policy', *Banca Nazionale del Lavoro Quarterly Review,* XXII (1969), 3–15.

KLOPSTOCK, FRED H., 'The International Money Market: Structure, Scope and Instruments', *Journal of Finance,* XX (1965), 182–208.

—— 'Euro-Dollars in the Liquidity and Reserve Management of United States Banks', *Federal Reserve Bank of New York Monthly Review,* L (1968), 130–8.

READING, BRIAN, 'Euro-Dollars—Tonic or Toxic?', *The Bankers' Magazine,* CCIV (1967), 233–7.

TETHER, C. GORDON, 'Dollars—Hard, Soft, and Euro', *The Banker,* CXI (1961), 395–404.

INDEX

Accepting houses, 28, 30, 104, 129, 188, 194.

Altman, O. L., 25, 35, 47–8, 53.

Arbitrage, interest, 14–5, 52; covered, 17, 58–9, 74–9; definition of, 93; effect on short-term capital flows, 96; impact of the Euro-dollar market, 107–8.

Balance - of - payments, statistical measurement, 154; impact of the Euro-dollar market in the U.S., 154–6; in countries other than the U.S., 156–8.

Bank for International Settlements, 31, 38–42, 44, 47–51, 54–7, 171–7, 197.

Bank of England, 10, 28–30, 122, 188, 194.

Bloomfield, A. I., 147.

Brehmer, E., 146, 149.

Capital-uncertainty, 69.

Cash-reserve ratio, 123.

Chalmers, E., 162.

Commercial banks, role in the Euro-dollar market, 12–6; as suppliers of Euro-dollars, 45–6; as users of Euro-dollars, 53.

Convenience yield, 69.

Coombs, C. A., 173.

Credit creation, effect of international capital flows, 121–8; impact of the Euro-dollar market in a country other than the U.S., 128–33; in the U.S., 133–5.

Demand for Euro-dollars, factors affecting, 62–7.

Dorrance, G. S., 146.

Eastern European countries, 22, 44, 52.

Effectiveness of national monetary policy, under fixed exchange rates, 136–42; impact of the Euro-dollar market, 142–4; alternative methods of increasing effectiveness, 144–50.

Einzig, P., 8, 10, 21.

Elasticity, of supply of short-term arbitrage funds, 74–5, 81, 83, 87, 98–102, 138–9, 182; of demand for short-term arbitrage funds, 74–5, 81, 83, 87, 140, 182; of supply of forward exchange, 74–6, 82; of demand for government securities by the non-bank public, 125–7, 141–2; of demand for non-government securities by the non-bank public, 125–7, 141–2; of supply of non-government securities, 125–7, 141–2.

Euro-currency markets, 1–3, 24, 106.

Euro-dollars, use as a money market instrument, 14; 19; suppliers of, 43–51; users of, 51–7.

Euro-dollar market, institutional and geographical framework, 5–8; organization and methods, 8–12; definition of, 9; origins, 21–4; historical development, 28–35; size, 35–42.

Euro-dollar rates, determination of, 79–82; interdependence with national interest rates, 82–91.

Euro-dollar transactions, definition of, 16; types, 16–20.

Euro-sterling rates, 114–7.

Exchange controls, 75, 90, 99, 104, 143, 145, 164.

Exchange Equalization Account, 122.

Exchange rates, impact of the Euro-dollar market, 151–4.

External claims and liabilities, of U.K. banks in U.S. dollars, 30–2, 194–6.

Federal Reserve System, 6, 170–7, 186, 202.

INDEX

INDEX   235